Sports and Labor
in the United States

Sports and Labor
in the United States

Michael Schiavone

Published by State University of New York Press, Albany

For information, contact State University of New York Press, Albany, NY
www.sunypress.edu

Production, Laurie D. Searl
Marketing, Michael Campochiaro

Library of Congress Cataloging-in-Publication Data

Schiavone, Michael.
  Sports and labor in the United States / Michael Schiavone.
     pages cm
  Includes bibliographical references and index.
  ISBN 978-1-4384-5681-2 (Hardcover : alk. paper)
  ISBN 978-1-4384-5683-6 (e-book)
  1. Professional sports—Economic aspects—United States. 2. Professional sports
contracts—United States. 3. Professional sports—Law and legislation—United
States. 4. Professional athletes—Labor unions—United States. 5. Collective
bargaining—Sports—United States. I. Title.

  GV716.S35 2015
  338.47796—dc23   2014029019

10 9 8 7 6 5 4 3 2 1

For Su Lan

Contents

Acknowledgments   ix

1. Greedy Millionaires Wanting More?   1

2. Labor Relations in Baseball: Labor War and Peace
   in the National Pastime   9

3. The National Football League: Victory through
   the Legal System   51

4. NBA: The Rise and Fall of the NBPA   89

5. Labor Struggles in the NHL: The Rise and Fall
   of the NHLPA   125

6. The Inevitability of Conflict?   159

Notes   169

Bibliography   195

Index   217

Acknowledgments

While my name is on the cover, many people have helped me along the way. I would particularly like to thank William Gould IV and Lee Lowenfish who read portions of an earlier version of the book. They offered invaluable suggestions and undoubtedly made the book you are reading better than it would have been otherwise. Likewise, the anonymous reviewers for SUNY Press offered important recommendations on how to improve the manuscript. I would also like to thank Andrew Zimbalist who offered sound advice on what I should focus on.

Michael Rinella, senior editor at SUNY Press, was incredibly helpful from the beginning and through every stage of the process. Every author should have an editor like him.

Finally, my wholehearted thanks to my beautiful wife Su Lan, for her patience and support, for providing the inspiration to write the book, and for her love that inspires me every day.

Greedy Millionaires Wanting More?

The Labor Movement and Sport

The United States labor movement is a dinosaur. It is on its last legs. These are just some of the common perceptions about organized labor in America. While it is certainly true that the labor movement is strug-gling, it is a long way from death, and that is a good thing for tens of millions of workers. Without the labor movement it is very doubtful that workers would have "[t]he eight-hour workday, five-day workweek, paid vacations, retirement and health-care benefits, safety regulations, bans on sweatshops or child labor, protections against employment discrimina-tion, and other workplace advances now taken for granted. . . . [These] were the result of struggles—invariably protected, often bloody, and sometimes even deadly—by workers and their unions."[1] Quite simply, unions have helped *all* workers lead a better life. Indeed, as I argued in *Unions in Crisis?*: "Union members receive better wages, health care and pensions compared to non-union members. Moreover, the decline in the average American's weekly wage corresponds with the decline in unionism. Unions are essential to the livelihood of the American people. . . . Without a strong union movement, ordinary Americans' quality of life will suffer."[2] However, one could easily be thinking to oneself, What does this have to do with professional athletes in the big four American sports?

After all, it is often assumed that professional athletes in baseball, basketball, football, and hockey are greedy millionaires always wanting more money and better working conditions. They are selfish individuals who have no idea how ordinary people live. When it comes to labor issues in sports, it involves millionaires in dispute with billionaires; each group as self-interested as the other. Apart from 1904, the World Series was played every year in times of war and depression. That was of course, until 1994 when the self-serving players destroyed the entire season. Multimillion-dollar contracts were not good enough for them. Likewise, the 2005 National Hockey League (NHL) season was cancelled and the Stanley Cup finals not played thanks to similar gluttonous beasts. After all, one can never have enough sports cars, Armani suits, and Rolexes. These are the common perceptions of athletes in the United States when they go out on strike. This is also true when owners lockout the players. Indeed, it is easy to blame the players. After all, they are lucky to play sports, so-called children's games, for a living; that is something so many wish and/or strive for, yet so few are able to do. The players are rich and famous, but that is not enough for them. Indeed, in just three years of the current decade there have been work stoppages in the NHL, National Basketball Association (NBA), and the National Football League (NFL). Only baseball has been spared the ever-increasing greed of the players; even then, the players have never had it so good. These individuals have ruined the sports we all love.

However, as is often the case, the truth is vastly different. There is a link between an ordinary worker and a professional athlete. As the doyen of sports broadcasting, Howard Cosell, argued: "Maybe you don't see a connection between those men and women who risked everything they had to ask for minimum wage, overtime, and safe working conditions, and football players, basketball players, and baseball players, especially given the rather substantial wages some of them receive. The connection is there, however, and it is as real as the Super Bowl, the NBA finals, and the World Series. And I'm telling you it's every bit as important, because what is at stake when professional athletes strike is a principle, and a protection for every working man and woman, a protection once fought for in the streets of our nation, with fists and guns, and lynching and mass arrests."[3] Even when it comes to money, certainly athletes in Major League Baseball (MLB), NBA, NFL, and NHL receive substantially more than the average American. However, a person working at a factory or an office may be employed for decades—although with the advent of neoliberal globalization such a luxury is often not afforded to an employee anywhere else in the world. An athlete's career may last only one, two, or five years, and a career-ending injury might happen at any moment. Generally, they have very little to fall back on. In the end, a sportsperson only has a limited time in the sun. Their struggles may be more high profile and involve a larger amount of money than the average worker's, but like any employee, baseball, basketball, football, and hockey players want, and often deserve, a larger slice of the economic pie and to have better working conditions. Quite simply, they want what we all want.

Likewise, when they have gone on strike the players generally did not do so to just fatten their wallets, but also for matters of principle. Despite the higher profile and greater sums of money involved, labor relations in MLB, NBA, NFL, and NHL are no different than labor relations in any other occupation. Even when it comes to money, as I note in the following chapter, owners were complaining about baseball players' salaries in the 1880s. It was a similar situation in basketball, football, and hockey. Throughout history, people have always claimed that players received too much money. Sports have become a multibillion-dollar industry; as the profits and net worth of teams have grown, so have player salaries. Just because the players receive higher salaries than in the past does not make the issues they face any less important. Considering how many people are fans and/or directly or indirectly employed by the respective sports, major labor unrest in MLB, NFL, NBA, and NHL that leads to a strike or lockout in any of the big four sports is something that affects millions of people around the world.

Traditional Unions versus Unions in Sports

While labor relations in MLB, NBA, NFL, and NHL may be no different than in any other occupation, it can be argued that player associations/unions in sports are different than traditional unions. Indeed, there are a number of differences. The most important is that while a traditional union deals with a single employer and sets a certain wage for its members, sports unions deal with multiple employers and do not negotiate a set wage (outside of the minimum), only the bargaining parameters. Likewise, while there may be some differences in income and skill level among members of a traditional union, these are magnified significantly in a sports union. The difference in income between, for example, a starting pitcher and a journeyman reliever struggling to stay in the majors can amount to millions of dollars per year. Such differences are true in each of the big four sports.

In addition, a person might belong to a traditional union for a number of years, if not decades, during which the membership is relatively stable. However, a number of rookies join sports unions every year, so that, combined with retirements and players being fired, the turnover in sports unions is immense. A further difference is that, unlike in many industries across the United States, sports owners cannot threaten players that their jobs can be outsourced overseas. As we shall see, however, team owners have used other means to try to convince players to agree to concessions.

Finally, as Robert C. Berry and William B. Gould note, "A union exists for the representation of all workers in its organization. This premise seems simple, but in sports it is complex. A player who views himself or herself as special likely will feel loyalties to his or her perceived best interests or to the persons or entities that can best satisfy these interests, such as an agent, other counselors, or even the club owners. These loyalties may supplant this player's allegiance to the union, thereby impeding the union from fulfilling its representative function."[4] However, despite these differences, there are important similarities between the two types of union.

First, traditional unions attempt to secure wage increases for their members; they want their members to have a growing share in the revenues of a company. Likewise, sport unions want their members to secure higher wages. Of course, as the following chapters will highlight, in recent years they have generally not been successful.

Second, traditional unions have been successful in narrowing wage inequality. In contrast, through achieving free agency for their members sports unions have inadvertently increased wage inequality. On the surface this does seem a difference between the two types of unions. However, free agency has helped all players and led to them receiving vastly higher salaries. For example, when the NFL implemented "Plan B" which granted free agency to players not rated as among the best thirty-seven players on a team, the players saw a massive increase in salary. Their wages increased by 61 percent when they switched teams. Free agency is beneficial to star and non-star players. Thus, even though a key aspect of a sports union's platform seemed to lead to increased wage inequality, in fact it helped everyone. In addition, there have been instances where sports unions have tried to narrow the inequality in compensation between stars and journeymen; for example, the National Basketball Players Association pushed for this in the 1998 collective bargaining agreement (see the NBA chapter for details). Helping all workers is a key aspect of both traditional unions and sports unions.

Third, there is a similarity between the two types of unions regarding nonwage collective bargaining issues. Both traditional unions and sports unions give their members a collective voice and have negotiated grievance procedures in collective bargaining agreements, to protect workers from "arbitrary, capricious, or discriminatory discipline meted out by managers" in the workplace or penalties imposed by owners and league officials in the sporting realm.

Seniority is also an important consideration in the values held by both traditional unions and sports unions. In traditional unions, protection of workers according to their seniority is important as it usually ensures job security in the event of layoffs, by assuring that the last person hired is the first person fired. For sports unions, seniority is important because it is often the case that players with X number of years of service are eligible for full pensions, and that players with more service time receive a higher level of pay compared to those with less. Moreover, as we shall see, players with X number of years of service are eligible for free agency. For both traditional and sports unions, seniority is a cornerstone.

Finally, both traditional unions and sports unions have accepted two-tier wage structures. Some traditional unions have accepted companies giving new employees a lower level of salary compared to current employees. In some sports unions, rookies are subjected to a salary cap well below established players' pay.[5]

There is one more similarity; this being crucial. The majority of traditional unions across America have been fighting a rearguard action against concession bargaining. "Concession bargaining" refers to the practice whereby a union is forced by an employer to accept lower wages, pensions, and benefits as well as worse working conditions. Employers demand concessions irrespective of whether the company is making or losing money. In many ways, concession bargaining has become the new norm, occurring in almost every industry. As labor academics Rick Fantasia and Kim Voss argue, "From the makers of agricultural implements, aluminum, automobiles, buildings, glass, newspapers, oil, processed meats, rubber, steel, to airlines, mine owners, supermarket chains, trucking companies, to local and regional governments and school districts, came demands for wage cuts, wage and pension freezes, reduction or elimination of automatic cost-of-living adjustments, and the establishment of permanently lower pay scales for newly hired workers."[6]

In the NBA, NFL, and NHL the respective unions have engaged in concession bargaining for a number of years. Only the Major League Baseball Players Association has managed to generally, though not always, resist concessions. Sports unions, like many traditional unions, are trying to hang onto hard fought gains. Their off-the-field battles mirror the collective bargaining struggles waged by traditional unions in the United States.

The following chapters highlight many instances where owners have argued that they could not afford to pay players more and/or have demanded concessions because their teams were losing money. On the surface, this seems like a reasonable argument. After all, no business owner likes losing money. However, it is crucial to remember that owning a sporting side is usually not the same as owning any other business. In the overwhelming number of cases, the team is not the owner's primary source of income; he (or she) has acquired it more for prestige than as a money-making operation. Nonetheless, businesspeople want to receive a good return on their investment. In this regard, by owning a sports team a person benefits economically in a number of ways. First, unlike in any other business, tax laws allow that once a person buys a team they can deduct whatever player contracts they have inherited, at present as well as into the future. As Lance Taubin notes, "If Donald Trump bought the Miami Heat tomorrow, he would deduct LeBron James' entire six-year $110 million contract that Micky Arison (the current owner) awarded James in 2010 under [tax section] 197, while also deducting the $17–22 million per year for the four remaining years on his contract under [section] 162. This is incredibly favorable for Trump, as he already deducted James' entire $100 million contract under [section] 197 and can also deduct the remaining $80 or so million over the next four years, merely under a different provision of the code-section [tax section] 162." In other words, it is a double deduction.

Second, an owner can use his/her team as a tax shelter for their other business(es). If a team is losing money, an owner can allocate the loss, a loss being "revenue minus costs minus amortization," to any of their other businesses; "The practical effect significantly reduces owners' tax liability, which is as valuable (arguably more valuable) than if the IRS simply handed the owners millions of dollars every year." Moreover, "if Donald Trump bought the Yankees for $1.5 billion, he could deduct about $100 million per year for 15 years on profits not only from the Yankees but from his other companies that made a profit."

An owner can also conceal profits by lending money to the team. In return, the owner receives interest; interest that is considered a cost on the team's profit and loss statement. Finally, under accounting rules and regulations it is relatively "easy" to use legal creative techniques to make it seem as the team is worse off financially than is the case. For example, current Toronto Blue Jays president Paul Beeston stated, "Under generally accepted accounting principles, I can turn a $4 million profit into a $2 million loss and I can get every national accounting firm to agree with me." Taubin correctly argues that roster depreciation allowance and "non-monetized benefits help to explain why most of the owners, who are allegedly operating at a loss, refuse to sell their teams. If the NBA were a typical profit-maximization business, as the NBA claims, any rational owner who consistently brings in losses would jump at the chance to sell their business for what is sure to be a healthy premium." This rarely happens in the NBA or MLB, NFL, or NHL because owning a sporting team is quite often the same as owning a proverbial gold mine.[7] In contrast, if a player has a contract that pays him $1 million per year, he receives $1 million, minus taxes, management fees, etc. This is something to consider the next time an owner cites financial hardship, claiming that his/her team is losing millions of dollars, and that as a result players need to agree to concessions.

Structure of the Book

The book will look at labor struggles in baseball, basketball, football, and hockey. The underlying theme throughout is that solidarity is essential. As Sara Ahmed eloquently states, "Solidarity does not assume that our struggles are the same struggles, or that our pain is the same pain, or that our hope is for the same future. Solidarity involves commitment, and work, as well as the recognition that even if we do not have the same feelings, or the same lives, or the same bodies, we do live on common ground."[8] For the players, whether a star or a journeyman, the current common ground is one in which the owners in recent years have been trying to claw back the gains made by the players in previous eras. The owners want the players to engage in concession bargaining irrespective of whether their teams are economically successful, as is the case in the NFL, or not, as in a minority of cases in the NBA and NHL. Where the players have been united, no matter what sport and decade, they have been able to achieve substantially more compared to when they have shown a lack of unity. Another theme, especially when it comes to free agency, is that while at times there has been a lack of distinct success in collective bargaining, the players have been a lot more successful through the court system in achieving their goals.

Chapter 2 looks at labor struggles in baseball. For decades, baseball players did not earn their just rewards. This changed with the formation of the Major League Baseball Players Association (MLBPA), specifically under the leadership of Marvin Miller. The MLBPA under Miller was militant and the players were united. This led to the players' gaining a fair share of the economic pie, something that continues to the present day.

Chapter 3 analyzes labor struggles in the NFL. In contrast to their brethren in baseball, football players have often lacked solidarity and this has cost them at the negotiating table, but in a promising development the players displayed unity during the 2011 lockout. While often struggling during collective bargaining, via the court system the players have achieved economic success through obtaining free agency. The biggest issue facing NFL players today is that of concussions. Unfortunately, despite some changes by the NFL not enough is being done.

Chapter 4 looks at the athleticism and individualism of the NBA. While the individualism has, depending on one's taste, made the game more exciting, it also manifests itself off the court, which has hurt the players in collective bargaining, as they have displayed a lack of unity that first manifested itself in 1995.

Chapter 5 looks at the "rough and tumble" of the NHL. For decades, NHL players achieved very modest gains under the company union approach of Alan Eagleson. Following Eagleson's resignation, NHL players achieved significant gains under more militant leadership. This, however, led to a significant backlash from the owners and NHL Commissioner Gary Bettman who implemented a series of lockouts. This has resulted in the National Hockey League Player Association engaging in concession bargaining that has economically impacted the players.

Finally, chapter 6 provides an overview of what has been discussed before and what the future may hold.

Labor Relations in Baseball

Labor War and Peace in the National Pastime

> The truth is that from the beginning of baseball's professional
> era . . . players were always keenly interested in such unheroic
> matters as salaries and working conditions.
>
> —William B. Gould, *Bargaining with Baseball*

Baseball has captured the imaginations of many generations. People
remember their first ballgame and when they fell in love with the game.
I fell in love with baseball watching Game 1 of the 1988 World Series;
Kirk Gibson's walk-off home run is still as vivid in my mind now as
it was when I saw it on television in Australia twenty-five years ago.
Moreover, many baseball fans clearly remember the statistics of their
favorite players. Indeed, in no other sport around the world are statistics
so cherished, debated, and argued over. This was true even before the
rise of "moneyball" and sabermetrics. People know that Barry Bonds hit
762 home runs, Hank Aaron hit 755, and Babe Ruth hit 714. Likewise,
most fans know that Pete Rose had 4,256 hits, while Carl Ripken Jr.
played in 2,632 consecutive games. However, for the players, the statistic
they know is the small chance, maybe one in seventy, that a person who
signs a professional contract will make it to "The Show," and the even
smaller chance of having a long career.

Another set of numbers the majority of baseball fans might not
care to remember is that there have been six strikes and three lockouts
in Major League Baseball (MLB) history. However, apart from a one-day
strike in 1912 by players from the Detroit Tigers, there was labor "peace"
until 1972. Of course, even with the absence of strikes and lockouts

during this period, relations between players and management were far from harmonious. From 1972 until 1995 there was constant conflict between the players and the owners, with numerous strikes and lockouts. However, unlike in the NBA, NFL, and NHL, since 1995 there has been relative labor harmony.

The decades of labor conflict were due in part to the Major League Baseball Players Association (MLBPA) gaining strength in the 1960s, beginning with the appointment of Marvin Miller as the union's executive director. It was also due in part to the owners trying to regain their lost strength. Following the appointment of Miller, the MLBPA became the strongest union/player association in American professional sports. It was this strength that allowed it to gain just rewards for the players after decades of exploitation. While the strength of the association led to industrial conflict, it is because of this strength that there ended up being labor peace.

The Rise and Fall of Various Baseball Players Associations

For a long time baseball players were exploited by owners, despite owners' constantly arguing that they were in financial hardship. This was true even as far back as 1881, when Chicago White Stockings owner Albert Spalding derided the amount players were earning, saying, "Salaries must come down or bankruptcy stares every team in the face."[1] In view of Spalding's rhetoric and the threat it implied, it was not surprising that the players would attempt to form a collective voice and improve their standing. Eighteen eighty-five witnessed the first players' association in baseball and the first in professional sports. The National Brotherhood of Baseball Players was founded by a number of players, but it was John Montgomery Ward who was the driving force. In addition to being an exceptional player, Ward was also a lawyer. The Brotherhood's aims were to eliminate the reserve clause and increase salaries from a maximum amount of $2,000.

The reserve clause tied a player to a club from his first contract. Contracts were generally only for one year, which provided no long-term security to the players, and the only way a player could play for a different club was if his current team sold the player to another team. In later years, the reserve clause was amended so that, although his contract still tied a player to the team, it was only for an additional year, on the same terms as the existing contract. Ward argued that the reserve clause meant that players were property; something to be owned and bought and sold by a few wealthy individuals. He stated, "Like a fugitive-slave law, the reserve-rule denies him a harbor or a livelihood, and carries him back, bound and shackled, to the club from which he attempted to escape."[2] Rather than believe the owners would continually agree to the demands of the players, the Brotherhood formed its own league, the Players League.

The Players League had a modicum of success in its only year of existence. By one estimate, it outdrew the National League in total attendance. However, it encountered intense competition from the National League and the American Association. The National League owners were willing to do almost everything in their power to undermine the Players League. This included Spalding offering Michael "King" Kelly the player-manager of the Boston Reds a $10,000 bribe to abandon the Players League and rejoin the National League. The money losses incurred by the Players League forced its financial backers to withdraw support. This led to the Players League folding on November 22, 1890, and a number of players, including Ward, returning to the National League or the American Association. In the 1880s, largely due to the formation of the Brotherhood, player salaries increased by approximately 30 percent. However, the owners also benefited as their profits increased as much as 300 percent. By the end of the 1890s, the maximum salary was $2,500, but it had stagnated at that level for the last decade. Only star players received more, but their salaries were not entered into a club's official documents.[3]

Nineteen hundred witnessed the next attempt to form a strong players' association; the Players Protective Association. The association sought higher wages and better working conditions for the players. Like the majority of the labor movement at that time, it was not that successful. Among its "achievements" were agreeing to the National League's demands that it expel any of its members who signed with an American League club. However, players largely ignored the Protective Association in determining whether to join an American League club, and it ceased to exist in 1903, with the owners still having virtually unchecked power. In his autobiography, Ty Cobb explained the power the owners had over the players in regard to the reserve clause. He stated, "Now an option contract was issued by the AL and NL by which the player reserved his own services to his team for the following season, and paid for the reservation out of his salary. By signing, the player tacitly agreed to put himself on option . . . and so rendered the courts unable to act. As smooth as goose grease was this agreement, and few players understood the number of rights they signed away."[4] For the next ten years the players had no collective group to voice their concerns. Nonetheless, this did not mean that the players did not try to overcome the owners' power. Indeed, in 1912 the first strike in professional baseball occurred, and it was due to Ty Cobb.

After Cobb attacked a fan in response to constant verbal abuse at a game in New York, American League president Ban Johnson suspended Cobb for ten games. While it is fair to say that Cobb was not a popular player, his Detroit Tigers teammates conducted a wildcat strike and refused to play against the Philadelphia A's on May 18, a Saturday. The Tigers quickly rounded up replacement players, who proceeded to lose 24–2. There was no game scheduled on Sunday, and Johnson canceled Monday's game. He also fined the striking players $100 each and vowed to ban them from baseball if the strike continued. Not surprisingly given this demand, the players backed down. This was in part because Cobb also wanted his teammates to go back to work. In response, Johnson reduced the players' fines to $50 each and promised that so-called special policeman would be employed to maintain order at ballparks.[5] While it is arguable whether the strike was a success, what is beyond dispute is that it had the effect of forging solidarity. This led to the formation of the Fraternity of Professional Baseball Players of America, in 1912.

As had its predecessors, the Fraternity demanded better wages and working conditions for its members. However, it was a very cautious organization and tried to distance itself from the "radicalism" of the Brotherhood of Professional Baseball Players. It viewed itself as an association rather than a union, and simply asked that "every reasonable obligation of the player's contract is lived up to by both contracting parties." Aiding the Fraternity was the formation of the Federal League. More than 240 players jumped from the American and National Leagues to the Federal League despite the threat of being blacklisted. In an attempt to prevent even more players from joining the Federal League, the National Commission, baseball's governing body, recognized the Fraternity in 1914, agreeing to provide players' home and away uniforms and grant unconditional releases to ten-year veterans who requested them, and promising not to discriminate against any Fraternity members. These concessions, however, were more in response to the threat of the Federal League than the strength of the Fraternity. Membership in the Fraternity increased to 1,100, with the players paying annual dues of $18, but a large percentage of those who joined were minor league players. While the Federal League only lasted two years, the threat of established players jumping to it led to gains in the average player salary, which almost doubled to $7,300. However, following the failure of the Federal League, which limited the options for players, and an unwise threat in 1917 to implement a strike in support of minor leaguers, which was not supported by the majority of major leaguers, the National Commission no longer recognized the Fraternity. American entry into World War I doomed this latest attempt to establish a collective voice for the players and the Fraternity soon ceased to exist. Nonetheless, one of the most important lessons learned by future baseball players' associations was not to include minor leaguers in its ranks, as there was little natural solidarity between major league and minor league players.[6]

The failure of the Fraternity was the last major attempt at solidarity among baseball players until the mid-1940s. The Association of Professional Ballplayers did form in 1924, but it was only a charitable group. In 1918, players from the Boston Red Sox and Chicago Cubs refused to play game 5 of the World Series until the leagues guaranteed the Series' winners $1,500 per player and the losers $1,000. The game was delayed for one hour until the owners agreed to the players' demands and promised no retaliation against the players. However, following the World Series the victorious Red Sox players only received just over $1,000 each, while the Cubs players received approximately $670 apiece. In addition, the players were fined and the Red Sox players did not receive any mementoes to commemorate their victory.[7] As there was no union or player association to support the players, there was little they could do in response.

In 1922, a court ruling was issued that had a major effect on players for the next fifty-plus years; namely, the Supreme Court ruled that the Sherman Antitrust Act did not apply to baseball. The Sherman Act prohibits "every contract, combination . . . or conspiracy, in restraint of trade or commerce among the several States." The crucial requirement is that the anticompetitive practices must occur in more than one state. As Stuart Banner notes in *Baseball Trust*, the Court held that baseball was not interstate commerce but a largely local activity that only had minor interstate impact. Its ruling stated, "The business is giving exhibitions of baseball, which are purely state affairs." While it is often assumed that the ruling allowed baseball an antitrust exemption, this was not the case. Baseball's antitrust exemption actually was not enunciated until the 1953 Supreme Court case *Toolson v. New York*

Yankees. In 1922, the judges simply ruled that baseball was not interstate commerce. The amount spent by the American and National Leagues on court cases over the years demonstrates the importance to the owners of the Sherman Act's not applying to baseball. Between 1914 and 1922, it is estimated, the two leagues spent approximately 5 percent of their income battling antitrust accusations.[8] Thus, in the 1920s, 1930s, and into the 1940s, players had no collective voice, were the "property" of their clubs, and were subjected to artificially curtailed wages. This was in contrast to "normal" employees in the United States as a wave of unionization spread across many industries, resulting in better wages and working conditions. Considering the situation, it was almost inevitable that in baseball another attempt for a collective voice would emerge.

Before this happened, another event occurred that was beneficial to some players, namely, the formation of the Mexican League. The Mexican League was a blessing to African American players, as it often engaged in bidding wars with the Negro Leagues; this, combined with the shortage of players during World War II, led to higher salaries for all players. For example, in 1942 Satchel Paige was allegedly the second-highest paid baseball player in America, while Buck Leonard saw his salary double for the 1942 season. African American players received, on average, an official $400–$500 a month, although many salaries were augmented by unofficial payments by owners.

Beginning in 1946, the Mexican League attempted to raid players from MLB. Twenty-three major leaguers jumped to the Mexican League, with others using interest from the Mexicans to get large increases from their MLB clubs. Eventually, approximately 20 percent of Mexican League rosters were compromised of American talent. However, the allure of the Mexican League did not last. MLB commissioner Happy Chandler imposed a five-year ban on any major league players who joined the Mexican League, and three-year bans for non–major league players. This, combined with the Mexican League's enduring financial difficulties, stopped the flow of talent going south of the border. By 1947, only a few former major league players were still with Mexican League teams; there were none in 1948.

Despite the decline of the rival league, MLB owners refused to lift the sanctions. This led one player, Danny Gardella, to sue MLB on antitrust grounds. Gardella, a fringe New York Giants player, joined the rival league in 1946. However, the collapse of the league led to him to seek reemployment in America. He was unable to do so due to the ban imposed by Chandler. In 1947, Gardella sued MLB and the Giants, seeking $300,000 in damages. The action was initially unsuccessful, as a federal court judge dismissed the lawsuit, citing the 1922 ruling that baseball was not interstate commerce and as such not subject to antitrust laws. However, Gardella appealed the decision, and in February 1949, in a 2-1 ruling, the federal appeals court ordered a full retrial. Fearful that the new trial could result in baseball being bound by the Sherman Act, in June 1949 Chandler rescinded the ban on players who had joined the Mexican League. MLB also offered to settle out of court with Gardella. Faced with the prospect of another costly trial that he was not guaranteed to win, Gardella eventually accepted MLB's offer of $60,000 in damages and a position with the St Louis Cardinals. Gardella joined the Cardinals for the 1950 season and had one at bat before being demoted to the minors. He later regretted his decision: "They gave me $60,000, but my lawyer got 31 of it. . . . I was interested in carrying through with the suit, but you sell for money because it's real. One has to eat. A principle is invisible no matter how precious it is to you. I feel I sold a principle down the river. I feel the way many of us do when we sell out."[9] The chance to bind baseball to the Sherman Act, which would have benefited all players, was gone. However, at the same time that the Mexican League was attempting to raid players, another attempt at player solidarity was occurring in America.

In 1945 and 1946, Robert Murphy, a lawyer from Boston, secretly sought support for forming a baseball union. Baseball attendance was at record levels, but player salaries had stagnated. Murphy's efforts came to fruition when the American Baseball Guild was founded, on April 17, 1946. Among the Guild's demands were a minimum salary of $7,500, an arbitration system for contract disputes, compensation of up to 50 percent of the price if a player were sold to another team, the elimination of the reserve clause and its replacement bylong-term contracts in which the financial terms were renewable every year, and benefits related to spring training, insurance, and pensions. Another demand was that player contracts no longer be one-sided.[10] Quite simply, the Guild wanted to overhaul the system so that it was more equitable for the players.

Murphy decided that Pittsburgh, a strong union city, would be the perfect place to kick-start the Guild into life. A large majority of Pittsburgh Pirates players wanted the Guild to represent them in collective bargaining. They were willing to strike in June if the Pirates' management did not agree to this. Murphy set a deadline of June 5 for the Pirates to accept the Guild as representing the players. However, on the afternoon of June 5 Pirates management claimed they needed more time to study the request. This angered the players, and they wanted to strike immediately. However, following a meeting with Pirates management, Murphy agreed to delay a strike vote by forty-eight hours. He later admitted that this was a major mistake, for it allowed both management and the National League enough time to metaphorically "work over" the players and employ replacement players in the event a strike went ahead. While a majority of players did vote to strike, by a vote of twenty to sixteen, this was less than the two-thirds needed under strike and election procedures established by the Pennsylvania Labor Relations Board.

The aftermath of the failure in Pittsburgh led to Boston Braves players deciding not to strike. Nonetheless, the owners were worried that the Guild could be successful, which in turn would threaten their profits and control of the game. This led them to hold a number of meetings with player representatives from various clubs. Following the meetings, in late July a series of recommendations was announced: a $5,500 minimum salary, spring training per diem of $25 a week, which was informally called Murphy Money, and a pension to be funded by the owners with the players also contributing. The pension would be available to all players over fifty who played at least five years in the major leagues. The minimum amount the pension paid was set at $50 per year. Player contributions were $45.45 for the first year, $90.90 the next, up to $454.75 in the tenth year. This resulted in a total player contribution of $2,500. Of course, the average length of a major league player's career was less than five years, and fewer than 10 percent had careers that lasted ten or more years. Yet this did not seem to concern the players. These recommendations pacified the players, and the death knell for the Guild was sounded in August 1946. Pittsburgh players voted fifteen to three, with more than twelve abstaining, against certifying the Guild as their collective bargaining agent. Once the threat from the Guild vanished, the owners and leagues demonstrated that what they could give, they could take away. The minimum salary was reduced to $5,000. As Murphy so eloquently and prophetically stated at the time, "The new generation of intelligent, nonsubservient players [would] recognize that their greatest weapon is the strike, and will not hesitate to employ it." Quite simply, "The players have been offered an apple, but they could have had an orchard."[11]

The failure of the Guild led to another long period in which the players had no collective voice. Nevertheless, this did not mean that some players did not consider striking. In this instance, the issue was Jackie Robinson. As is well known, Jackie Robinson was the first African American to play in the major leagues, in 1947 with the Brooklyn Dodgers. Unfortunately, the prospect of African Americans as teammates and opponents was not palatable to a number of players, whether due to outright racism or fear of losing their places to more talented players who just happened to have a different skin color. A number of Dodgers players, led by player representative Dixie Walker, signed a petition demanding that no African Americans play for the team. In addition, Walker allegedly attempted to organize a wildcat strike across the National League on Opening Day, to begin when Robinson stepped onto the field. Walker also asked to be traded from the Dodgers. (This might have occurred if fellow Dodger Pete Reiser was not constantly injured.) The strike failed to materialize when Dodger management came down hard on its dissenting players. At the end of the season, Walker stated that Robinson was a fine teammate and a gentleman.

St. Louis Cardinals players are also alleged to have planned a sit-down strike for May 6, when Robinson and the Dodgers came to town for the first time. Whether in fact they did plan to strike has never been determined, but the threat of lifetime bans ensured that any players would not publicly protest against Jackie Robinson via strike action. National League president Ford Frick wrote to the Cardinals, stating, "If you do strike, you will be suspended from the League. You will find that you will be outcasts. I do not care if half the league strikes. Those who do will encounter quick retribution." Eventually, more African Americans joined Jackie Robinson in the majors and racial integration became the norm rather than the exception, although it was not until the 1970s that non-superstar African Americans entered the big leagues in any great numbers. More recently, however, the overall number of African Americans in the major leagues has declined greatly, in what is a sad turn of events.[12]

The next attempt at achieving a collective voice and collective action was more successful and evolved into an extremely profitable endeavor, namely, the formation of the Major League Baseball Players Association in 1954.

The Birth of the MLBPA

The genesis of the Major League Baseball Players Association was inspired by an unfortunate event. Ernie Bonham, who had played in the majors for ten years, died in 1949. He was only thirty-six years old.

As Lee Lowenfish notes in *The Imperfect Diamond*, the amount of money in the pension fund was inadequate to pay his widow. This in turn led to the baseball commissioner deliberately selling the broadcast rights to the World Series and the All-Star Game at below their market value. Since the money from these contracts funded the players' pensions, they were understandably unhappy both with the shortfall and the discounted sale of the broadcast rights, and requested a detailed analysis of the pension. However, by 1953 the commissioner still had not provided them with one. This led player representatives Allie Reynolds and Ralph Kiner to ask to speak at the annual owners' meeting. Kiner, basically the only star player on the Pittsburgh Pirates, admitted that he became the team representative "almost by default, since I was the only guy who had the stature to stand up to the owners. . . . There was a general feeling that they would ship you out if you were disruptive . . . and even though I didn't have much education, at least I had enough not to be intimidated by owners."

Not only the owners but some former players as well opposed the formation of a players' association. Indeed, Reynolds tried to distance his and Kiner's efforts from unionism, stating that "I have nothing against unions in industry. But if I had any suspicion that we in baseball were moving towards a union, I would not have anything to do with the enterprise." Nonetheless, Reynolds and Kiner sought a rise in the minimum wage, an analysis of the pension system, and permission for players who earned less than $10,000 to play winter ball in Latin America. The owners did not look favorably on the players' requests. In response, the players hired a lawyer, Jonas Norman Lewis, to act as liaison between them and the owners. The move was greeted with hostility by the owners, who stated that they did not want so-called outsiders becoming involved in baseball labor relations.

During this period, the Supreme Court, in *Toolson v. New York Yankees*, upheld the major leagues' monopoly, stating unequivocally that baseball enjoyed antitrust exemption. This meant that the reserve clause applied to each and every player's contract. The decision reaffirmed the owners belief that they could control the game as they pleased. Although they invited player representatives to the owners' meeting in December 1953 in Atlanta, players' liaison Jonas Norman Lewis was not invited. This upset the players. Kiner stated that it "was un-American, not [to] be allowed to have your lawyer there. [We] were competitive by nature and were angry . . . but we were in over our heads. After all, we were ballplayers not businessmen."

Whether the owners truly would have been hostile to Lewis is arguable, in view of the fact that his law firm had previously represented New York Giants management and he was the coauthor of a 1945 article in the *New York Law Journal* that characterized a player's salary of $5,000 as enviable. Nonetheless, in response to their representative's exclusion, the players' representatives held their own meeting in Atlanta in December 1953, at which they formed the Major League Baseball Players Association (MLBPA), with its charter finalized in the spring of 1954. However, following the formation of the American Federation of Labor-Congress of Industrial Organizations (AFL-CIO), it refused to allow the MLBPA to join. The federation's leadership believed that the players were not cohesive and would never be able to engage in the collective action that was a necessary part of being an AFL-CIO member.[13] While the AFL-CIO was not entirely incorrect in its assessment during the initial years of the MLBPA, in time its pronouncement proved hollow, as the MLBPA became not just the strongest association/union in sports, but one of the strongest in the United States.

Due to the hostility encountered by the MLBPA and Lewis, the first gains made by the union were no more than modest in nature, and grudgingly yielded. For instance, after negotiating a contract with Gillette in 1956 for the broadcast rights to the World Series and All-Star Game for a price of $3.25 million per year, the owners increased the players' pension fund, yielding 60 percent of the broadcast revenues as well as 60 percent of the revenue from the All-Star Game. However, rather than cut into the owners' share of the latter, between 1959 and 1962 MLB held a second All-Star Game, to cover the pension fund contribution. Minimum salary was increased to $6,000, and the players received life, hospital, and disability insurance. Considering these gains, one might think that the players would have been at least somewhat pleased by the performance of Lewis. Further, in 1958 the minimum salary was increased again, to $7,000. However, a more "radical" proposal by Lewis that would have guaranteed players 20 percent of the teams' revenues and 25 percent of national television revenue infuriated the owners. Rather than stand united, the players withered in the face of owner hostility, claiming that they had not been consulted about the more radical agenda. (Failing to consult with the rank and file is not a good strategy for a union at any time, let alone in the first few years of its existence.) Confronted by the rumor that Lewis wanted to strike in support of minor league players, union members decided to seek a new representative. It must be noted that the lack of a good relationship between the players and Lewis was, at the very least, partly Lewis's fault as he did not make an effort to get to know the players. In contrast, once he became the leader of the MLBPA, Marvin Miller was the exact opposite, and this had a large bearing on the support he received. In 1959, Judge Robert C. Cannon became the MLBPA's legal counsel.[14]

Quite simply, Cannon was the wrong choice for the MLBPA. From the start, he tried to appease the owners. He expressed the view that "if the Association, in the future, proceeds cautiously and carefully many more deserving benefits will accrue to the player." Under Cannon's watch, he sought harmony between management and labor, claiming that he did not want to "jeopardize the fine relationship existing between the players and the club owners." He was "satisfied that the Commissioner and the Presidents of the respective leagues sit as quasi judicial officers and it is presumed that they will accord fair treatment to both the player and the club owner,"[15] which must have surprised the players. Minimum salary remained the same, Cannon allowed the owners to withdraw money from the pension fund, to which they had over-contributed in the previous year, and he voiced no objections when the owners made changes to the strike zone and pitching mound in 1963 and increased the schedule from 154 games to 162, without consulting with the players. Although Cannon made the rather absurd claim that the players "have it so good we don't know what to ask for next," the reality was quite different. Former player Steve Boros clearly summed up the situation: "Players had no leverage. . . . They were taken advantage of, but nothing to do. There were lots of horror stories, distrust, and anger, but we had no weapons."[16] This state of affairs led the players to seek someone who could revitalize the MLBPA. It led them to Marvin Miller.

The MLBPA under Miller

Before accepting the position of Executive Director of the Major League Baseball Players Association, Marvin Miller had been an official of the United Steelworkers, whose ideology could be summed up with the traditional union phrase: us versus them. Miller was happy to work with baseball owners and officials, but at his core he believed that employers would never willingly give good wages and working conditions to employees. Thus, in baseball and in society as a whole, employees such as the players would have to be united and fight for their fair share of gains.

This ideology served the players well. However, almost bizarrely, despite Cannon's performance as the players' legal counsel he came very close to becoming the executive director of the union. It was only because he made a series of last-minute demands that the player representatives turned to Miller, whom they had initially rejected.

Campaigning for the directorship, Miller made an effort to gather support by meeting with the players in various cities during spring training. His efforts not only sowed the seed of solidarity which would serve the players well, but resulted in a resounding endorsement of his candidacy from the majority of teams, as the players voted 489–136 to elect him to head the MLBPA. The "no" votes came overwhelmingly from a few teams, such as the San Francisco Giants, who voted 27–0 against. As a long-time Dodgers fan, he found it amusing that the Giants players responded negatively to him initially.[17]

The election of Miller was greeted by a wave of negativity from the media. At the time, sporting journalists almost always sided (and in many cases still do) with management in any labor dispute. Indeed, they were basically the mouthpieces for owners. The thought that the MLBPA would now be led by a former powerful union official had them worried. *Atlanta Journal* sports editor Furman Bisher wrote that "professional baseball players are going to have to decide if they are common laborers or professional men." He went on to claim that "I cannot see the major league baseball player demeaning himself to the status of a unionized laborer." Likewise, the owners were far from happy that Miller had been elected. They had agreed to pay the director's salary under the assumption that Cannon would fill the position, thereby in effect making him their employee, but with Miller now in charge, they wavered on their commitment. That was fine with Miller, who proposed that instead the players voluntarily pay yearly union dues of $344 apiece. The owners, assuming that a large number of players would choose not to contribute, agreed to the proposal. To their surprise, the overwhelming majority of players paid their dues, and for the first time the MLBPA was on the path to sound financial footing.[18]

Under Miller's leadership, the MLBPA enjoyed early successes. The association signed a licensing agreement with Coca-Cola for $60,000 in 1966, granting the company rights to use players' pictures in its advertising. The deal paved the way to a much larger payday for the players in 1968. For years, the card manufacturer Topps had signed contracts with individual players by which, in return for a fee, the company could sell a card bearing the likeness of the player. After a series of negotiations, during which Miller told players to abstain from signing further contracts with Topps, the company agreed to a new deal whereby players received royalties on the cards sold. This led to a significant increase in revenue for the players. As Miller noted, "Topps agreed to double the payment from $125 to $250 per member, and more importantly, pay 8 percent on sales up to $4 million a year and 10 percent on sales above that figure." In the first year of the new contract, the amount earned by the players was $320,000. The money was welcomed by a number of players, especially considering that between 1947 and 1967 the minimum wage in the major leagues only increased by $1,000. Moreover, the average salary of a major leaguer was only $19,000, the median being $17,000, with 40 percent of players earning $12,000 or lower.[19] However, as beneficial as the card agreement was to the players in 1968, the first Basic Agreement negotiated by Miller and the MLBPA was much more important.

The first Basic Agreement represented only a moderate windfall for the players, but it set the stage for what was to come. In addition to the implementation of uniform contracts, under the terms of the agreement the minimum salary increased from $7,000 to $10,000, spring training money increased to $40 per day, in-season meal money increased $3, to $15 a day, players would fly first class, and a formal grievance procedure was established. The grievance procedure was controlled by the commissioner, but this was soon to change. Miller and the MLBPA achieved further success over pension reform in 1969. Under the new terms, owners increased their contribution to the players' pension fund to $6.5 million per year, players were now eligible to join the fund after four years of service rather than the previous five, and the changes were was applied retroactively back to 1947.

The successes continued with the second Basic Agreement, in 1970. The minimum salary increased to $12,000, with a further rise to $15,000 in 1972. Moreover, following on from the first Basic Agreement, the players achieved the right for grievance procedures (arbitration) not controlled by the commissioner.[20] This was to be most beneficial aspect of the agreement for all players, as it played a role in the downfall of the reserve clause.

The Reserve Clause and Free Agency

Following the signing of the first Basic Agreement, the MLBPA and Miller began to focus on the reserve clause, as they believed that in addition to preventing players joining whatever team they wanted, it artificially reduced wages. The association's first major challenge to the clause was brought on behalf of Curt Flood. Flood, a star outfielder with the St. Louis Cardinals, was informed by the team via a phone call in late 1969 that he had been traded to the Philadelphia Phillies. After discussing the issue with the MLBPA, he decided to challenge the reserve clause. He wrote to baseball commissioner Bowie Kuhn, stating:

> After twelve years in the Major Leagues, I do not feel I am a piece of property to be bought and sold irrespective of my wishes. I believe that any system which produces that result violates my basic rights as a citizen and is inconsistent with the laws of the United States and of the sovereign States.
>
> It is my desire to play baseball in 1970, and I am capable of playing. I have received a contract offer from the Philadelphia Club, but I believe I have the right to consider offers from other clubs before making any decisions. I, therefore, request that you make known to all Major League Clubs my feelings in this matter, and advise them of my availability for the 1970 season.
>
> Sincerely Yours, Curt Flood.

In response, Kuhn wrote, "I certainly agree with you that you, as a human being, are not a piece of property to be bought and sold. . . . [However,] I cannot see its applicability to the situation at hand." Whether he really did not see the applicability or was just trying to protect baseball is open to debate. Following Kuhn's reply, Flood and the MLBPA challenged baseball's antitrust exemption and, as such, the reserve clause in court. In an interview, Flood categorized himself as a "well-paid slave." Flood lost the initial court case, but in presenting their defense baseball's lawyers inadvertently laid the groundwork for the elimination of the reserve clause by claiming that the issue between Flood and MLB was "only a labor dispute over a mandatory collective bargaining issue." In other words, the union should be able to challenge the reserve clause in negotiations with baseball's ownership.

Flood and the MLBPA appealed the court's decision, and on June 18, 1972, the Supreme Court, in a decision that perplexed the majority of observers (there were opinion polls stating that the public agreed with Flood by a margin of eight to one), ruled against him, five to three.

The Court acknowledged that the 1922 decision that baseball was not subject to the Sherman Act had been wrongly decided, but insisted that their decision was based on adherence to principle, and that it was up to Congress, not the courts, to overturn baseball's antitrust exemption. Despite the decision in his favor, Commissioner Kuhn realized that protection for the reserve clause as it was, was coming to an end. He stated that the "players and the clubs are in the best decision to determine for themselves what the form of the reserve clause should be." As for Flood, after sitting out the 1970 season, he signed a contract with the Washington Senators in 1971. However, the layoff and his age led to deterioration of his skills, and he lasted less than one month before retiring from the game. He was also subjected to hate mail by so-called baseball fans who accused him of trying to destroy baseball. At one stage, he was receiving four or five death threats a day.[21] Unfortunately, Curt Flood himself did not benefit from the elimination of the reserve clause. Nonetheless, it was his principled stand that made the general public aware of the injustice the clause represented, and it inspired the MLBPA to continue to focus its efforts on making sure that players were not simply "well-paid slaves."

Ironically enough, it was a blunder by an owner that created baseball's second free agent, Jim "Catfish" Hunter, in 1974. Technically, Ken Harrelson had become baseball's first true free agent in 1967, when he was placed on irrevocable waivers by Kansas City Athletics owner Charles O. Finley after Harrelson called him a "menace to baseball." This in effect made Harrelson a free agent, with the right to negotiate with whatever team he wanted, which he exercised by signing with the Boston Red Sox.

Catfish Hunter's free agency was achieved as follows: Under the terms of his contract with the Oakland Athletics, in 1974 he was to receive one-half of his $100,000 salary in the form of an annuity from an insurance company, paid for by the ball club. However, A's owner Charles O. Finley, realizing that the annuity would not be declarable by the club as a tax-deductible expense until several years later, refused to pay for it, which turned out to be a notoriously foolish decision. Marvin Miller later recalled, "If there is a violation of the contract, the player has the right to send notice to the club, calling attention to the violation. Hunter did that. The club has 10 days to correct the violation. If the club does that, that's the end of it. The Oakland club did not correct the violation." In response, the MLBPA claimed that the A's had breached Hunter's contract and that as a result he was a free agent.

While it was clear that the A's had breached Hunter's contract, what was uncertain was what it entitled him to. In previous years, the commissioner would have dictated the outcome, which would have certainly meant that Hunter would not be declared a free agent. However, as noted above, in the 1970 collective bargaining agreement the owners and the MLBPA had agreed to the adoption of a grievance procedure that did not include the commissioner. Instead, a three-person panel comprised of Miller, John Gaherin, representing the owners, and Peter Seitz, as an independent arbitrator, would decide the matter. Not surprisingly, Miller sought free agency for Hunter, while Gaherin opposed it. Seitz concluded that because the breach of the contract was so significant, the contract was no longer valid and Hunter was a free agent. This led to Hunter's signing a five-year contract with the New York Yankees in 1975 worth almost $3.5 million, an indication of the stifling effect of the reserve clause on player salaries.[22] However, while Hunter became a free agent his situation was not applicable to other players as he had achieved free agency only because the A's had breached his contract.

One of the immediate benefits of the Hunter decision was that owners started guaranteeing player contracts. For the first time, players knew that when they signed a contract for x number of years and dollars they would receive all the money the contract promised. Furthermore, the downfall of the reserve clause drawing near.

In 1975, Marvin Miller instructed the players to honor the last year of their contracts, but without signing new ones, that is, to play for one year under the reserve clause. Nearly twenty players almost played out their option year, including star players such as Ted Simmons and Al Downing, but by the end of the season, only Andy Messersmith and Dave McNally had not signed new contracts. This led the MLBPA to file a grievance seeking free agency on their behalf. The resolve of McNally to put the greater good above his own interests was demonstrated, as he effectively retired rather than accept a contract from the Montreal Expos that included a $25,000 signing bonus. Likewise, the Dodgers were willing to offer Messersmith a no-trade clause. This is what Messersmith initially wanted, but the Dodgers constantly refused, which led him to seek free agency. Both players went to arbitration, where it was left up to Seitz to break the deadlock between Miller and Gaherin once again.

Seitz delayed his decision as long as possible to encourage the owners and the MLBPA to work out a compromise, but while Miller and the MLBPA were willing to negotiate, the owners were not. In a landmark decision, on December 23, 1975, Seitz ruled in favor of the players, rendering the reserve clause invalid. All baseball players now had the right to become free agents. In a vindictive action, the owners fired Seitz almost immediately. Seitz stated, "I shall go to eternal rest wondering why the Leagues gave a negative response to my suggestion to seize the opportunity to bargain for a less rigid reserve system in advance of the date when I should have to wield the surgical knife of arbitration." The owners had decided to play hardball rather than make concessions, and it had resulted in failure. The ruling did not mean the end of baseball, as some had feared, but it was the end of the era in baseball when players were exploited without recourse, and although MLB appealed the ruling, the courts upheld Seitz's decision.

The era of the unrestricted reserve clause had come to an end. In the 1976 collective bargaining agreement, the MLBPA and the owners agreed that the reserve clause would apply to a player during his first six years with a club. After six years, the player automatically became a free agent. As we shall see below, this led to a dramatic escalation in salaries. While McNally remained retired, Messersmith signed a three-year contract with the Atlanta Braves worth $1 million. In his final year with the Dodgers, Messersmith earned $90,000. However, as in the case of Curt Flood, so-called fans were hostile to Messersmith and McNally. Messersmith later noted that "I came out as the dirty dog. I always had a good energy rapport with most of the fans. After that incident, the energy was 95, 100 percent negative. That was a real hard thing for me. I just wasn't ready for it."

Despite Seitz's ruling, baseball's antitrust exemption still largely holds sway. In 1998, Congress passed the Curt Flood Act, which states that baseball is covered under antitrust laws only in regard to the "employment of major league players." Baseball is not bound by antitrust law in regard to "matters relating to broadcasting, to the minor leagues, to the relationship among teams, to the location and ownership of franchises, and to the employment of umpires." The Curt Flood Act is important to major league players because, as Stuart Banner argues, "baseball's antitrust exemption meant that free agency in baseball depended entirely on the existence of a collective bargaining agreement providing for it, and . . . that they [the players] could not necessarily count on bargaining to succeed."

As former National Labor Relations Board chairman William Gould IV notes, the Curt Flood Act came about thanks to the impact of *Brown v. Pro Football* (see NFL chapter for details on the court case). The *Brown* ruling lessened the impact of antitrust laws. Players could only take their respective leagues to court on antitrust grounds and hope to be successful if their union were defunct, decertified, or recognition of it had been withdrawn. With the favorable ruling, baseball owners lobbied Congress for the act. They were willing to give up some of their antitrust exemption, namely in regard to the employment of major league players, for the remaining antitrust exemption to be intact. They were successful insofar as the act does not totally overturn baseball's antitrust exemption.[23] Thus, at the time of publication (2015) the antitrust exemption is still largely in place and there are no signs that it will be overturned in the foreseeable future.

An Era of Strikes and Lockouts under Miller's Leadership

As noted above, the Detroit Tigers conducted a one-day strike in support of Ty Cobb in 1912. The strike was not successful. Following that time, there were sixty years of labor "peace." However, with the burgeoning strength of the MLBPA it was almost inevitable that baseball would begin a series of industrial conflicts. After having almost unfettered power for a number of years, the owners would continually attempt to regain some of their lost power. For the most part, just as in their attempts to prevent free agency, they would be unsuccessful.

The first work stoppage of the Miller era occurred in 1972 and was largely over player pensions. The MLBPA wanted a 17 percent increase in the owners' contribution to the pension fund, to $6.5 million, which was in line with inflation since the 1968 Basic Agreement. In addition, the MLBPA wanted an increase in health care premiums to cover inflation. Miller believed that the negotiations would go smoothly as the players were not asking for too much, just enough to cover the rise in inflation. However, he was mistaken. The owners decided to take a hardline approach initially. The owners offered only an increase of $372,000 for three years. The attitude of the owners was clearly summed up by St. Louis Cardinals owner Gussie Busch. He stated, "We're not going to give them another goddamn cent. If they want to strike—let'em." The owners thought that Miller was pushing the players to strike. However, Miller was the one urging caution. He told the players, "You only get once chance at your first strike, and if you do not win that one you have lost the union." Indeed, Miller thought that the players would not strike. He was mistaken. In a near-unanimous decision, by a margin of

663–10 the players gave the MLBPA strike authorization. Miller was still uncertain, however, as two days before the strike deadline he proposed that the parties accept binding arbitration from a neutral observer. Furthermore, Miller thought that the MLBPA would have to back down from the proposed strike. Quite simply, he underestimated the players resolve and willingness to strike. The MLBPA board matched the players resolve and voted 47–0, with one abstention, to begin the strike. The Dodgers player representative was later removed from the post by his teammates for abstaining. On April 1, 1972, the first baseball strike since 1912 began.[24]

The baseball press, with a few exceptions, generally reacted with outrage against the players and Miller. One journalist stated that "Marvin Miller has struck out. He would do the game of baseball a great favor if he disappeared, got lost, or found the nearest hole and jumped into it." Unfortunately for the press, the players were united behind Miller. As the player representative for the Texas Rangers Don Mincher, stated at the time, "I don't think anyone really wants a strike. . . . But we've made no progress in our demands for a 17 per cent cost of living increase in our pension fund payments. And that's what it's all about." As the players would not be paid during the strike, Miller removed himself from the MLBPA's payroll in solidarity with the players. Such simple gestures can be crucial in industrial struggles, and it was appreciated by the players. While for the most part the players were united, the same was not true for the owners. Less than one week after the start of the strike MLB's negotiator offered to increase the amount the owners contributed by $400,000. In addition, three teams allowed the players to work out at the club's facilities. The break in ranks led to a quick resolution and the owners and players announced the end of the strike and a new agreement on April 13. The strike would have been over sooner if the owners, after agreeing to the players' demands, did not insist games being made up with the players receiving no pay. This was not palatable to the players, and the owners decided not to push the issue. The owners agreed to increase their contributions to the pension plan by $500,000 and to increase health care premiums. The strike cost the owners $5.2 million in revenue, while the players lost $600,000 in salary. Eighty-six games were lost, and arguably the biggest losers were the Boston Red Sox. Due to the lost games, some teams played 156 games, while others, including Boston, only played 153. At the end of the season, Boston trailed Detroit by a half-game in the AL East. The strike, arguably, cost Boston the pennant.[25]

The success of the strike for the players continued with the signing of the latest Basic Agreement just before the start of the 1973 season. However, before the contract was agreed upon, the Player Relations Committee (PRC), which had been created in 1967 to handle negotiations with the MLBPA on behalf of the owners, ordered the teams to lock the players out and not let them report to spring training unless an agreement was reached. However, not all clubs agreed to do this and while the lockout technically lasted twelve days, it had no impact on the players, teams, fans, or in forcing the MLBPA to modify its demands. As such, this lockout is barely remembered today. In late February, a new deal was reached. The pension plan was strengthened and the minimum salary was increased to $15,000 and by 1975 it would increase to $16,000. In addition, spring training money rose to $57 a week, while money for food on the road during the season increased to $19 a day. Also, players not eligible for free agency were allowed to have their salaries decided by an arbitrator. This allowed players to have an independent arbitrator determine their salary if they could not agree to a deal with their club. Salary arbitration came about because MLB told the court in the Flood case that any differences between the leagues and the players could be settled through collective bargaining; privately, some MLB officials believed that if they granted the players salary arbitration the MLBPA would be less likely to seek free agency for players.

The issue of salary arbitration would occur frequently in future collective bargaining negotiations. Initially, the owners were only willing to allow salary arbitration in alternate years, but Miller refused to back down and eventually the owners agreed to Miller's proposal that salary arbitration occur every year. While the owners feared that salary arbitration would lead to a bonanza for the players, the reality was that most cases were settled before coming to arbitration. When a player went to arbitration there was an even split between whether the owner or player was successful, with the overall result being a less than 15 percent increase in any team's payroll on all arbitration cases.[26] Nonetheless, even if the player "lost" his arbitration case this usually meant that he still obtained a healthy wage rise. With the demise of the unqualified reserve clause and the potential escalation of player salaries, at the end of the 1975 season the stage was set for the next major industrial dispute in baseball; the 1976 lockout.

The major question confronting the owners and the players at the end of the 1975 season was what the future would bring, given the potential for free agency for players. The owners decided to take preemptive action and terminate the 1973 Basic Agreement. They proposed that free agency be granted to a ten-year veteran (nine years' service time, plus the option year) only if the club was not willing to pay the player more than $30,000 a year, with only eight teams allowed to offer a contract to a free agent. In response, the MLBA told its unsigned members not to agree to new contracts but to play out their option year so that they could become free agents at the end of the 1976 season. This covered approximately 350 players. However, Miller did not want hundreds of free agents on the market as he believed that this would drive wages down, and he was further concerned that under baseball's labor exemption there was nothing to prevent the owners colluding against the players. Miller's concern was later vindicated as collusion did occur in the mid-1980s (see below for details).

Unable to reach a compromise, the 1976 spring training began with a lockout in place. Impeding compromise was the fact that Commissioner Kuhn was totally against free agency. He stated it was "nothing more than one of those myths Miller spent so much time inventing." Interestingly, Miller noted, "A significant number of baseball writers and commentators took the occasion to reveal that they didn't know the difference between a strike and a lockout . . . by roundly condemning the players and their Association for striking!" Helping solidarity was that a number of players attended the negotiations, which were held in Florida at Miller's suggestion, one of the locations for spring training, making it easy for players to attend. After seventeen days, during which neither the owners nor the MLBPA was willing to give ground, the owners, led by Dodgers owner Walter O'Malley, called off the lockout on March 17 and spring training got underway. Miller was pleased that the lockout was over, but noted that it was increasing solidarity. He stated, "People might not know it, but the lockout was making players angrier and angrier, not weaker as the owners had hoped."[27]

Although the lockout ended, an agreement was yet to be reached. Eventually, after months of negotiations, on July 12 a new agreement was signed. As noted above, the reserve clause would apply to a player in his first six years with a club. After six years, the player became a free agent. In addition, the minimum salary increased to $19,000 for the 1976 and 1977 seasons, with another rise to $21,000 for the 1978 and 1979 seasons. Moreover, the owners' contribution to the players' pension fund increased by almost $2 million. In response to Miller's fears that the owners would collude against the players, the agreement included a clause preventing both the owners and the MLBPA from interfering in the free agent process. The owners had demanded the clause, as they feared that the MLBPA and/or player agents would collude and drive up salaries.

The onset of free agency led to a dramatic increase in player salaries. Good, but not great, players began receiving multiyear contracts; as Robert Burk notes, in *Much More than a Game*, "In 1977, the first year of widespread free agency, the average big league salary jumped nearly 50 percent to $76,066. Even when adjusted for inflation, real wages registered a 39 percent rise and went up another 31 percent the next season. By 1979 the mean major league salary stood at $113,558, more than double the pay since the inauguration of free agency." In addition to raising salaries, free agency gave players greater job security as teams began signing players to multiyear contracts to a much greater extent than in the past. In 1980, approximately 40 percent of players had multiyear contracts. Before 1975, there had been none; Catfish Hunter was the first.[28] Thus, Kuhn's belief that free agency was a myth had been mistaken. Free agency led to a significant increase in salary for all players and gave them job security. However, all too often success leads to resentment, and even though the owners were the ones giving out multiyear contracts, they were not happy with the escalating salaries and the MLBPA's continuing success.

The negotiations for the next basic agreement began in ominous circumstances, with MLB announcing that a $500,000 fine would be levied on any owner who publicly spoke about the 1980 negotiations. The owners were attempting to show a united front to the public, even if they were not as united in private. They wanted to eliminate salary arbitration for players with less than six years' experience and to replace it with a maximum salary of $153,000, a figure below what many players were already earning. In addition, the owners wanted compensation for any player lost to free agency, to consist of another active major league player, rather than draft pick, as previously was the case. It was thought that the likelihood that a free agent would change teams would diminish if the new team had to give up another major league player in return. Miller and the MLBPA rejected the proposals. Once again the players were united. As St. Louis Cardinal Ted Simmons stated, the "key word about Marvin [Miller] is that he is essential. . . . Without him, strong and intelligent as he is, we might not have that bright light that serves us as a beacon." Unity was demonstrated in the strike authorization vote, which was 967–1 (the one dissenting vote made on religious grounds) in favor of striking. The players were not asking for anything; they just did not want to give up their hard-earned gains.[29]

On April 1, 1980, the players formally struck, cancelling spring training games. The MLBPA stated that the season would still begin as scheduled—which it did—but that they would strike again on May 23 if the owners refused to back down from their demands. Once again, the baseball press was generally against the players. For example, Jim Murray wrote that the players "were lucky baseball is around to keep them in minks and Rolls [Royces]. . . . They should be grateful for the spadework done by generations of promoters, reporters, announcers, technicians, contractors and so forth who made it all possible. They're grateful to a man who had nothing to do with it, Marvin Miller, the only labor leader in history to represent a company of millionaires." He further stated that players' "skills were not transferable to anything that mattered. Some guys make more money than they can count to." After a series of meetings, the two sides reached an agreement on May 22.

The agreement largely came about because some owners were surprised that their players were about to go on strike; they had thought the players were bluffing. Management had totally underestimated the resolve of the players. This led to an agreement being arranged quickly. The minimum salary increased by $5,000, to $35,000 by 1984, and the owners' pension contribution would rise to $15.5 million per year. Moreover, while players previously had to be in the majors for four years to receive a pension, now as soon as they played one game they were eligible. Finally, players were able to gain salary arbitration after two years rather than the previous three. Thus, the players gained better wages, even though they'd struck just to protect what they had. However, quite ominously, on the issue of free agency no decision was made. Instead, a four-person committee was appointed to look at the issue. If no agreement was reached, the owners could implement a severe curtailing of free agency, but the players could inform the owners by March 1, 1981, that they planned to strike on or before June 1. The owners and commissioner tried to portray the agreement as a victory, which had the effect of making their relationship with Miller and the MLBPA even more hostile.[30] In other words, labor conflict was averted, but not solved. It was almost inevitable that things would erupt the following year.

The 1981 stoppage was over the issue of free agency compensation. As noted above, the owners wanted compensation for losing a free agent player to another team. MLBPA argued that any form of compensation would diminish the point of free agency. This time, the owners were well prepared for any "stoppage of play." They had purchased strike insurance from Lloyds of London to the tune of $50 million and they also had a

$15 million strike fund from their own contributions. The players also had a strike fund, and, crucially, they also were united. On February 17, 1981, the PRC's Ray Grebey announced at a press conference that the owners would impose a curtailment of free agency, as the committee charged to look at the issue could not come to an agreement. That the committee could not come to an agreement was not a surprise even though non-hawkish baseball GMs such as Frank Cashen and Harry Dalton were part of it.

The players wanted free agency and did not want it watered down in any form. On February 24, they authorized a strike, to begin on May 29 if no agreement could be reached. Management was caught out thinking that the players would simply accept a loss of their gains, as Grebey was shocked that the players were prepared to strike over free agency. However, due to the issues being brought before the courts, the actual strike was delayed until June 8. The players displayed good solidarity; cracks did form, but they were swiftly healed over. Chicago White Sox player representative Greg Pryor argued, "This strike is not designed to benefit players who have signed multi-million-dollar, multi-year contracts. . . . They have already received the benefits of their free agency. . . . Instead, the strike is for the benefit of all those present and future players who may become free agents."[31]

The unity of the players was not shared by the owners, but they did everything in their power to display a united front. New York Yankees owner George Steinbrenner stated, "Marvin [Miller] always waits for three or four owners to bolt. It won't happen this time." Indeed, Grebey fined Milwaukee Brewers general manager Harry Dalton $50,000 after he urged a compromise be reached. The press criticized the owners adopting such an approach. Moreover, somewhat surprisingly given the past hostility, more media than before supported the players. Most famously, *Sports Illustrated* ran a cover article during the strike entitled: "Strike! The Walkout the Owners Provoked." Interfering with any compromise was the bitterly antagonistic relationship between Miller, on the one side and owners' representative Grebey and Commissioner Kuhn, on the other. It is alleged that the strike was prolonged by the dislike they shared for each other. Indeed, Miller and Grebey refused to be photographed together once a settlement was reached. Moreover, as Burk notes, Kuhn "accused the players of becoming 'prisoners' of Miller's ego and knee-jerk hatred of management." Likewise, Miller labeled Kuhn "an idiot with delusions of independence." The owners strike insurance began after 153 games were cancelled. They would receive $100,000 for each canceled game up to a maximum of five hundred games. For some teams, such as the Los Angeles Dodgers, this was well below what they would earn for a home date, but others, like the Minnesota Twins, actually made money during the strike. The Dodgers lost almost $7.6 million in revenue from ticket sales and concessions alone during the strike. The owners' insurance policy was due to expire on August 8; by coincidence or not, a compromise was reached on July 29, with the All-Star Game the first game played after the strike's end, on August 9.

The 1981 strike was the longest in major league history; unfortunately, that record would soon be surpassed. The strike lasted for fifty days, with 713 games being abandoned. Even with the strike insurance, the estimated loss for the owners was $72 million, with the players losing approximately $28 million. The strike was not a success for either side. Clubs could no longer be directly compensated for the loss of free agents. However, they could retain players for six years and be compensated with other players from the amateur draft. Moreover, one-third of the teams would contribute players to a pool from which a team that lost players to free agency could choose, and the team that signed the free agent relinquished an amateur draft pick to the free agent's former club. While at the time the amateur draft was not that significant, now it serves as the entry point into the major leagues for more than 50 percent of active players.

Overall, that the players had held firm could be considered a victory in itself. Due to the unequal finances of employers and employees, in a strike situation it is generally the employees whose resolve is weakened due to economic necessity. Nonetheless, after the strike some owners thought that continued conflict with the players was pointless. Chicago White Sox owner Jerry Reinsdorf stated, "I don't think there was any point, from the owners' standpoint, to this strike. . . . This is an instance where the majority [of owners] doesn't know what's good for it." Of course, by 1994 Reinsdorf's position had changed, and he was one of the driving forces of the owners' no-compromise stance of 1994–95.

The final word on the 1981 strike should go to Marvin Miller:

The 1981 strike was the most principled I've ever been associated with. Through the entire ordeal, the players remained united and strong. In 1981 scores of players had nothing to gain personally from the strike, but there were veterans on every team who remembered how it used to be and the role of union solidarity in changing things. . . . I'll say it again:

It was the most principled strike I've ever been associated with; it was the Association's finest hour.[32]

The 1981 strike was to be Miller's last major stand as leader of the MLBPA. He resigned from his position in 1982, although he returned to serve as interim leader from November to December 1983. During his tenure as executive director of the MLBPA, the average player salary increased from $19,000 per year to $326,000, and (limited) free agency became the rule. Other MLBPA leaders built on his legacy, but it was Marvin Miller who turned the association into a powerhouse.

More of the Same: Strikes, Lockouts, and Collusion

There was a belief that Miller was the cause of labor disharmony in baseball and once he was gone things would return to "normal." Also, some players thought that after the successful 1981 strike the owners would not want another conflict. Players' negotiating committee member Doug DeCinces of the Baltimore Orioles stated that "I very seriously doubt that the owners will try to challenge the players again."[33] However, industrial conflict was always in the cards as long as the owners were unhappy with the gains the players had made in the Miller era and the players did not want to give up what they'd fought so hard to achieve. As such, it was only a matter of time before there was further labor disharmony.

Indeed, there was a minor work stoppage in 1985. The MLBPA under new executive director Donald Fehr wanted an increase in player salaries, especially since baseball's new television deal quadrupled the value of the previous one. The new six-year contract was worth $1.125 billion. Despite the dramatic increase in television revenue, the owners were claiming that they were hurting. While some reports supported the owners' claims, a report commissioned by the association disputed the owners' claims of financial hardship. Initially, the owners wanted a salary cap, but this idea did not last, as new commissioner Peter Ueberroth opposed it. Before the strike, owners increased their contribution to the players' pension by $33 million for the period 1985–1998 and $39 million in 1989. This was more than double the previous contribution, but it was less than the one-third share of television and radio revenues that was the norm agreed to by the owners in previous pension agreements. The two sides failed to reach agreement on other issues as well, and the players walked out during the middle of the season. However, the work stoppage was to be short-lived. The strike only lasted two days and led to the loss of twenty-five games, which were eventually replayed.

The strike was so short largely because Ueberroth did not want a work stoppage under his reign as commissioner. At the start of the strike he ordered the head of the Players' Relations Committee to finalize a deal with the MLBPA within twenty-four hours. Moreover, Ueberroth announced that a deal had been reached between MLB and the Players Association before it was approved by the owners. Under the new five-year collective bargaining agreement, minimum salary increased from $40,000 to $60,000, with cost of living adjustment for the subsequent years of the contract.

The players did grant some concessions. One was in regard to salary arbitration, which the owners had hoped would reduce salaries, though it had proven not to be the case. Under the 1985 agreement, a player needed to have had three years' experience before he could go for arbitration; previously, a player had needed only two years' worth. This was a reversal of what was achieved in the 1980 collective bargaining agreement.

In contrast to earlier strikes and lockouts, this time there was a lack of player solidarity. For example, Don Mattingly said at the time, "If I don't go to arbitration next year, so what? I'll probably go the next year." Miller, who was hired as a consultant by the MLBPA during the 1985 negotiations, noticed the change of attitude of some star players. In his autobiography he wrote, "The grumblings of high-profile players like Reggie Jackson, Bob Boone, and Mike Schmidt highlighted the shift in attitudes since the strike in 1981. These players, no doubt, had 'paid their dues,' but they also benefited beyond their wildest expectations, and their bellyaching didn't seem to take into account that there were stars before them . . . who had made similar sacrifices without ever having reaped anywhere near the same rewards."[34] In this regard, it was not greedy millionaires wanting more, but players being happy with what they had and not necessarily thinking about the future. Instead, it was the owners who wanted more. Even though they achieved some concessions from the players, they were not satisfied. This led them to illegally collude in manipulating the free agent market in an effort to drive wages down.

At the end of the 1985 season there were sixty-two free agents, of whom only 5 signed with new clubs; in comparison, the previous year twenty-six out of forty-six free agents had changed teams. While there was some interest expressed in the players, it was noticeably less than normal, and led to the MLBPA filing a grievance under Paragraph H, article XVII of the collective bargaining agreement. The paragraph states: "The utilization or non-utilization of rights under this Article XVII is an individual matter to be solely determined by each Player and each Club for his or its own benefit. Players shall not act in concert with other Players and Clubs shall not act in concert with other Clubs." As noted above, the owners wanted this clause included in the 1976 agreement following the lockout as they were fearful that the MLBPA and/ or player agents would collude to drive wages up. The association had agreed to include it only as long as teams were under the same restraint.

The architect of the collusion strategy was Commissioner Ueberroth. He harassed the owners at a series of meetings on the importance of financial prudence and questioned why they kept overspending on average players. In 1986 the collusion continued, when twenty-nine out of thirty-three players remained with their old clubs, with the majority of them only able to achieve one-year contracts. Likewise, despite the following year's free agents being a stronger crop, most were forced to sign with their current clubs at amounts less than they deserved. The 1987 free agents' salaries decreased 16 percent, and three-quarters were forced to accept one-year deals. It was not just free agents hurting; because they were earning less it meant that the average player earned less; the average salary of a player with two years' service time in the major leagues declined by 38 percent.

The collusion among the owners not only artificially lowered wages, it also provided less job security for the players. In effect, collusion was the reserve clause with a "different face." However, unlike the reserve clause, collusion was fated not to last for decades. In three separate rulings, the MLBPA was successful in proving that the teams had colluded against the players.

During the first collusion case the owners fired the arbitrator, Thomas Roberts, while the hearings were in progress. While there are grounds for both MLB and the MLBPA to fire an arbitrator and it has happened in the past, on this occasion the owners did so as a stalling tactic. The tactic was "successful" inasmuch as it had the effect of delaying the first grievance decision. Even though the MLBPA filed the grievance in February 1986, a decision was not reached until September 1987. During this period the MLBPA demanded a ruling on the legality of the owners firing Roberts. The association's contention was upheld in court, and Roberts was reinstated. The dispute over Roberts allowed the owners to collude further against the players as it delayed a decision being reached. However, it also had the effect of increasing the damages against the owners.

After the third collusion case was decided against the owners in 1990, the overall settlement for the three cases cost them more than $280 million. Nonetheless, this figure was minuscule compared to the television package secured by Ueberroth in 1988. CBS paid the league $1.1 billion and in return it won the rights to broadcast the World Series, the All-Star Game, and twelve regular season games from 1990 to 1993. Likewise, ESPN agreed to show 175 regular season games for $100 million per year for four years.[35] Despite these increases in revenue, after the 1985 agreement was in place the owners decided to reduce the size of their teams' rosters—and payrolls—by decreasing them from twenty-five to twenty-four players. Although the MLBPA filed a grievance, the decision was upheld in arbitration. Thus, as in previous years, the next round of labor disharmony between the players and the owners was only a matter of time.

Nearing the end of the 1985 collective bargaining agreement, in 1990 the owners locked out the players during spring training for thirty-two days. Both owners and players were ripe for an industrial dispute. The owners had a strike fund of $170 million and had agreed to a line of credit with a bank for an additional $130 million. Likewise, the players' strike fund was worth approximately $80 million and the MLBPA told the players to insist on a clause in their contracts that they would still be paid if there were a lockout or strike. Among other demands, the owners wanted players to only receive 48 percent of revenue and for there to be a salary cap.

Though negotiations were moving slowly, a compromise seemed possible, but rather than start spring training on time, the owners imposed a lockout on February 16. MLBPA Executive Director Donald Fehr noted, "The day before they gave us the proposal, they announced the lockout date and apparently they're stuck to it. But they're not doing it for any reason related to the negotiations or the industry." Moreover, after almost agreeing to a contract the owners introduced new demands. They asked for the elimination of maximum salary cuts for players with three to six years in the major leagues, and demanded that the players and MLBPA not be allowed to use "free agency and multiyear contract comparisons in salary arbitration cases." However, demonstrating a lack of unity on the MLB side, the next day baseball commissioner Fay Vincent alerted the MLBPA that these new demands were no longer in effect. Instead, he proposed an increase in the minimum salary to

$85,000 and a pension increase of approximately $44.8 million per year. Like Ueberroth in the 1985 strike, Vincent did not want a prolonged work stoppage under his reign as commissioner. Just before the start of televised spring training games, an agreement was reached. The agreement was basically similar to the previous one.

However, owners agreed to contribute an extra $16 million a year to the pension fund, to increase the minimum salary by $40,000, to $100,000, with a cost of living adjustment for future years of the contract, and to permit major league rosters to revert back to twenty-five players. Once again, there was to be no salary cap. The agreement also granted salary arbitration to approximately twelve players per team with between two and three years' experience, comprising roughly the best 17 percent of that team's personnel, which was a slight recovery of what the MLBPA had conceded in the 1985 collective bargaining agreement. This gain, although not as large as the players had wanted, was important for the association because players with less service time often mentioned the "lost year" before a player could gain arbitration. For a sports union/association, arguably one of the most important responsibilities is keeping newest members happy, since they will be the stars in the future, with the ability to influence future players' attitudes toward the union/association. Additionally, in an attempt to prevent any future collusion, the agreement tripled the damages to be assessed for any future occurrences by the owners.

The lockout had the effect of delaying the regular season and the postseason by a week.[36] Overall, the new contract was a victory for the MLBPA and the players. As is often the case, however, success came at a price. The price that the players paid was that the owners were sick of losing. They wanted to win at any cost. This set the stage for the 1994–95 strike, which eventually led the World Series not being played for only the second time in its history.

In 1992, the owners forced Commissioner Vincent to resign because they were unhappy with his performance, in part his handling of the 1990 lockout. The owners were not pleased that he had an amicable relationship with the MLBPA. He was replaced by one of their own, Milwaukee Brewers owner Bud Selig. While in the past the players believed that the commissioner favored the owners over themselves, Selig's appointment left little doubt in the matter. The role of commissioner would be more in tune with the owners' desires.

The 1994 season started without a collective bargaining agreement in place. Players' salaries were the main stumbling block. While national television revenue had increased 1,742 percent between 1971 and 1990, player salaries had increased by a similar amount, 1,741 percent. Thus, while the owners were receiving more money, they were spending almost all of it. The 1990 collective bargaining agreement had no effect in lowering player salaries. In fact, from 1990 to 1993 the average player's salary increased 86 percent, from $597,000 to $1.109 million. The players received approximately 55 percent of the revenues of major league baseball.

Of course, it was not the players' fault that the owners kept offering them more money; how many people would turn down an increase in their salary if it was offered? As William Gould states, "One cannot begrudge baseball's millionaires in their attempts to become billionaires like the owners. Indeed, by the standards of other entertainers, or the obscene income provided to American CEOs present and past, such demands are quite modest and reasonable and, on balance, their performance more praiseworthy than the latter group."

Even though MLB was arguing that economic conditions required the players to accept concessions, new San Francisco Giants owner Robert Lurie went out and signed Barry Bonds to a then-record six-year $43 million contract. However, the owners blamed the players and, determined to play hardball, announced their decision to opt out of the collective bargaining agreement a year before it was set to expire in December 1992. However, the decision was far from unanimous. The vote was 15–13.

Despite opting out of the previous collective bargaining agreement early and the belief that there would be a lockout in the coming season, the owners did not offer a proposal to the MLBPA in 1993. The reason they did not do so was that the owners could not come to any agreement among themselves concerning the nature or specifics of such a proposal. Indeed, they did not offer any proposal to the association until June 14, 1994, well after the 1994 season was underway and the previous collective bargaining agreement had expired. The owners wanted a seven-year contract, with the players receiving a maximum of 50 percent of revenues, and the elimination of salary arbitration. In return, players with four to six years' experience could become free agents, a decrease from six years under the current collective bargaining agreement. Moreover, the owners wanted a salary cap.

On July 18, the MLBPA rejected the proposal. The association estimated that accepting the proposal would lead to a reduction of player salaries of at least $1.5 billion over the life of the contract. Quite simply, the association had no choice but to reject the proposal. During the negotiations, the owners withheld $7.8 million that they were required to pay into the players' pension and benefit plans. Although the pension agreement had expired, MLB payments to it customarily came from revenues from the All-Star Game. As the game had already been played, the players felt the owners should have honored the customary arrangement. Their failure to do so inflamed the situation. Indeed, the players wanted to immediately go out on strike. However, the MLBPA urged restraint. Nonetheless, on July 28, the MLBPA authorized a strike, to begin on August 12 if a settlement could not be reached. Further threatening potential compromise was that Fehr and Players Relations Committee chairman Richard Ravitch had an acrimonious relationship. All things considered, it was no surprise that an agreement could not be negotiated before the deadline.

The timing of the strike was significant, as it was late in the season. Thus, the players would have already received the majority of their salaries, whereas the teams receive 75 percent of their revenue during the postseason. The situation favored the players, as they could strike longer without getting into financial difficulties. Moreover, the MLBPA strike fund amounted to approximately $33 million. Hampering any potential compromise was that 75 percent of the owners had to agree to a new contract and the owners were split into three groups. Paul Staudohar notes that "groups were largely based on market size, with the hawkish advocates of radical change from small market teams. . . . On the other end of the spectrum were owners with teams in large markets and some owners from smaller market teams that had recently built new stadiums and were doing well financially. . . . The remaining teams were somewhere in between, looking for moderate change, but susceptible to arm-twisting from either the hawks or doves." Thus, the owners were divided, wanting change, but the requirement that 75 percent had to agree to any new contract made it difficult for a swift resolution. After failing to come to an agreement, Commissioner Selig cancelled the season on September 14, to the dismay of the public.

The strike continued into the new year. Player solidarity was strong during the strike. One meeting summed up this solidarity. The MLBPA invited Curt Flood to speak to the players. When he walked into the room, the players gave him a standing ovation. It was from the struggles of the earlier generations of players that the current players reaped the benefits, which was something the group of players present at the meeting realized. By having Flood speak at a meeting, this notion was reinforced. In addition, the players understood that they had to struggle just to get to The Show. Houston Astros pitcher Pete Harnisch eloquently explained the situation: "The players understand that we've come this far from some really bad days, and we don't want to take steps back. People are amazed at how united we've been. That's because we've had strong leadership, and because most of the players, no matter how much they're making now, have struggled in the minor leagues as I did."

The owners were equally determined to remain united. During the strike, Cincinnati Reds owner Marge Schott stated, "We have lost twenty of these labor conflicts in a row. . . . It's about time we won one." In January, the owners were no longer demanding a salary cap, but a luxury tax instead. Moreover, they unilaterally eliminated salary arbitration, the anti-collusion clause in the previous agreement, and, crucially, the owners and the MLB office were willing to play the 1995 season with replacement players. This was how spring training began, though the replacement players were not top prospects.

The Baltimore Orioles broke ranks immediately, refusing to use replacement players. This was partly due to the team's wanting Cal Ripken Jr. to break Lou Gehrig's major league record for consecutive games played in 1995. The merchandising opportunities presented by that event were undoubtedly somewhere in their minds. Likewise, coaches on some other teams, including the Detroit Tigers and Toronto Blue Jays, refused to work with replacement players. Moreover, the Ontario Labor Board announced that the Blue Jays could not use replacement players as it would be a violation of Ontario law. The MLBPA argued that it would not call off the strike if replacement players were used during the regular season. The situation never came to this; a resolution was near.

On March 26, 1995, the National Labor Relations Board handed down its decision on a request filed by the MLBPA for a ruling against the owners that would enforce the mandatory bargaining rule and condemn the owners' unilateral action in imposing their position prior to the impasse between the two sides. By a vote of three to two, the NLRB agreed with the players and demanded a quick judicial opinion. The strike ended on March 31 when federal judge Sonia Sotomayor issued a preliminary injunction against the owners. She noted that at the end of a contract, "the parties must not alter mandatory subjects until a new agreement is reached or a good-faith impasse is reached." She further stated, "Opening Day is one of the most beautiful days on the baseball calendar and it should not be disturbed because one side has failed to fulfill its duties under the collective bargaining mandates of this country."

The owners lost the court case because, while they reopened nego-tiations in December 1992, they did not offer a proposal for negotiation until June 1994, and the proposal they offered then contained major changes. Moreover, because the owners made very few changes to their initial proposal there was a stalemate in the negotiations.

Judge Sotomayor's ruling ended the strike; the players called it off immediately and stated they would go back to work under the terms of the old contract, while the owners did not impose a lockout. The replacement players were quickly fired, although nineteen of them would eventually play in the major leagues. The aftermath of the strike wit-nessed a 20 percent decline in attendance in 1995, and there was still no agreement in place. Eventually, a contract was signed in November 1996, two years and three months after the strike had begun. Minimum salary increased by $41,000, to $150,000, but there were no changes made to salary arbitration and free agency.

One change that was adopted was that a luxury tax was agreed to, and revenue sharing was adopted. In regard to the luxury tax, as Zimbalist notes, "beginning in 1997 the teams with the top five payrolls paid a tax of 35 percent on the amount which their payroll was above the midpoint between the payroll of the fifth- and sixth-highest payroll teams. The 1998 tax was 35 percent on the top five payrolls on the amount they were above 1.078 times the 1997 threshold. The 1999 tax was 34 percent on the top five payrolls on the amount they were above 1.071 times the 1998 threshold." However, there was no luxury tax imposed for the 2000 and 2001 seasons, as revenue sharing was phased in. By the 2001 season, there was a 20 percent tax on every team's net local revenues. Seventy-five percent of the amount yielded was then divided equally between all clubs, with the remaining 25 percent being distributed on a proportional basis to teams whose revenue was below the league average. This led to the transfer of approximately $168 mil-lion from the top half revenue teams to the bottom half.[37]

Considering that the owners' initial proposal would have cost the players $1.5 billion over the term of the contract, even though the strike cost the players $300 million their decision to walk out made economic sense. Of course, it made particular sense to future players and players whose best years in the big leagues were ahead of them. On the other hand, the players who were never to play another major league game, or who had their prime earning years curtailed by the strike might have preferred that there had been no strike and the MLBPA had accepted the owners' demands. One crucial lesson from the 1994–95 strike was that no matter the resolve of the players, if the owners want to play hardball it is very difficult for a union to succeed. The victory for the players was that they did not capitulate to the owners' demands and paved the way for future generations of players to be fairly rewarded.

Another lesson learned from both sides is that no one in professional sports benefits from a long-term industrial dispute. The 1994–95 strike was the last work stoppage in baseball until at least 2016, when the current agreement expires. In this regard, the owners, the players, and the league are on a long winning streak. While there has been major industrial conflict in the NBA, NFL, and NHL, baseball has entered a period of relative labor harmony Player salaries have continued to climb every year and baseball has witnessed strong growth after a period of turmoil.

The negotiations for the next collective bargaining agreement, however, in 2002, came down to the wire. While there were informal discussions, Commissioner Selig and the owners did not engage in formal meetings with the MLBPA until well after the previous collective bargaining agreement had expired, in November 2001. The reason for the lack of a formal proposal from the owners was most likely due to disunity among them. Moreover, in October 2001 Selig announced that two teams would be eliminated before the start of the 2002 season. This would have led to the loss of eighty MLBPA members, as well as prospectively leading to a decline in wages due to an increase in competition for roster positions. While the elimination of teams did not eventuate, this, combined with the absence of negotiations and the presence of what the players viewed as hardball demands by Selig and the owners (such as teams being able to fire players whose wages were deemed too high after salary arbitration), increased the likelihood of a work stoppage. Following fruitless talks, on August 12, 2002, the MLBPA set a deadline of August 30 for a deal, or the players would go out on strike. This deadline had the effect of speeding up negotiations, and just before August 30 an agreement was reached on a four-year contract, the first time in thirty years that a deal had been finalized without a work stoppage. As Fehr stated at the time, "All streaks come to an end, and this is one that was overdue to come to an end." In the end, neither MLB nor the players had wanted another work stoppage so soon after the 1994–95 strike.

Under the terms of the agreement, minimum salary increased to $300,000 for the 2003 and 2004 seasons with cost of living adjustments for 2005 and 2006. In regard to revenue sharing, the final position was a lot closer to the owners' initial demands than the players'. Under the revised revenue sharing, as Staudohar notes, "all teams will contribute 34 percent of their local revenues to a fund that will be divided equally among teams. In addition, a central fund component was established by a formula that provides another $72.2 million, taken annually from richer teams and distributed to poorer teams. The component will be 60 percent funded in 2003, 80 percent in 2004, and 100 percent in 2005–06." As for the luxury tax, it was less draconian than in the 1996 collective bargaining agreement. However, that it was included was somewhat a victory for MLB, as there had been no luxury tax for the 2000 and 2001 seasons. Also, Fehr did not want a large luxury tax if there was going to be increased revenue sharing, and the tax was phased out as revenue sharing phased in under the previous agreement.

Fehr and the association eventually agreed to both revenue sharing and a luxury tax, but the luxury tax threshold and rate were a lot closer to the MLBPA's position than the owners'. The luxury threshold was $117 million in 2003, increasing to $136.5 million in 2006. The tax level for teams above the threshold was 17.5 percent, increasing to 30 percent for two-time repeat offenders, and 40 percent for consecutive three-time repeat offenders.[38] The 2002 collective bargaining agreement was one of compromise that benefited both the players and the owners and ensured labor peace for the next four years, which allowed baseball to rebuild after the 1994–95 strike. There was a similar outcome in the 2006 collective bargaining agreement.

The 2002 agreement proved fruitful for the players. By the end of the contract average player salaries had increased to $2.8 million. Moreover, unlike the negotiations for the 2002 agreement, which was only settled at the eleventh hour, and unlike all previous baseball collective bargaining sessions, the 2006 contract was arrived at nearly two months before the deadline and with no hint of industrial conflict. Commissioner Selig noted that "[t]his is the golden era in every way. . . . The economics of our sport have improved dramatically, and that's good. The last agreement produced stunning growth and revenue. I believe that five years from now people will be stunned at how well we grew the sport. This agreement encourages that, and I'm very confident that it will produce the same results that we're all concerned about and that I certainly am—not only economic growth, but parity." Likewise, Fehr claimed, "What was really different this time was that the approach to bargaining, while it had its difficult moments, was very workmanlike, very pragmatic, very day-by-day. . . . There was a shared desire to see if we could resolve this well ahead of time and if we could get it done by about the time of the World Series, before the free agency declaration period began." He further noted, "I'd been waiting for most of that time [since he became head in 1985] to see if we could ever get to the place where we reached an agreement prior to expiration. . . . And while I always understood intellectually it was possible and that was the goal, I'm not really sure I believed that it could happen." As for the contract itself, it was pretty much more of the same. Minimum salary increased to $380,000 for the 2007 season, $390,000 in 2008, $400,000 in 2009 and 2010, and $400,000 in 2011, with a cost of living adjustment included. In regard to the luxury tax, the tax rates for a first breach was 22.5 percent, 30 percent for a second and 40 percent for a three-time repeat offender, while the threshold increased to $148 million in 2007, $155 million in 2008, $162 million in 2009, $170 million in 2010, and $178 million in 2011. However, there was a change in regard to revenue sharing. Under the old system, as Zimbalist points out, "[h]igh-revenue teams actually experienced lower marginal tax rates than the low-revenue teams." As a result, high-revenue teams "had a lower disincentive to improve the talent base of their rosters and, thereby, to generate more revenue." Thus, there was not a lowering of payroll disparity, and large inequality between the teams remained. Under the new system, the tax rate was reduced to 31 percent, down 3 percent, for all teams and the "marginal tax rates in the system are now basically flat rather than regressive." This has resulted in more balanced competition, as "the different measurements of competitive balance have shown some improvement."[39] Quite simply, the agreement was a good contract for the players, owners, and Major League Baseball.

The same was true for the 2011 collective bargaining agreement. Under the terms of the new five-year agreement, minimum salary increased to $480,000 in 2012, $500,000 in 2014, and $500,000, plus cost of living adjustments for 2015 and 2016. The luxury tax threshold increased to $189 million in 2014, 2015, and 2016. However, the tax rate decreased to 17.5 percent for first-time offenders, but rises to 50 percent for teams that exceed the threshold four or more times consecutively. In a win for the association and players, the number of players with two to three years' service time in the major leagues eligible for salary arbitration increased 5 percent, to 22 percent beginning with the 2013 season. Commissioner Selig stated that "[l]abor peace has proven essential to the best interests of baseball and its millions of fans." Likewise, MLBPA head Michael Weiner claimed, "It's a good day for baseball and a good day for collective bargaining." It is surprising that neither Selig nor Weiner said it was a good day for the world.

Hyperbole aside, with the new five-year agreement, there is a guarantee of labor peace in baseball until at least 2016, which will mark twenty-one years without either a lockout or strike. This record is the envy of professional basketball, football, and ice hockey. As for player pensions, the bane of so many previous industrial conflicts, players are eligible to receive a partial pension after only one day in the majors. The amount players receive rises to at least $100,000 after ten years' service time, with most ten-year veterans receiving $195,000 annually. Furthermore, pre-1980 players are now eligible to receive $10,000 for at least two years as long as they played one game in the majors. This issue will be discussed further during the 2016 collective bargaining negotiations. The money for the pre-1980s players' pension was funded largely from the luxury tax.

There were also major changes to revenue sharing. Beginning in 2016, the teams in the fifteen largest markets will no longer receive any money from revenue sharing; teams cannot use revenue sharing income to pay off debt; and teams eligible to receive revenue sharing income must have a major league payroll 25 percent above the amount they obtain.

Finally, there were further changes to the free agency rules that favor the players. As ESPN reporter Jayson Stark notes, "For years, if a free agent was good enough to get 'Type A' or 'Type B' stamped on his back, his old team almost always got a draft pick or two if he signed with somebody else. . . . [However,] starting next winter, the old system will cease to exist. No more Type A's. No more Type B's. And theoretically, the only players who will deliver any kind of compensation to their old teams are a handful of 'elite' players who are so good that their former teams won't mind tendering them a 'qualifying offer.' That qualifying offer would be a one-year guaranteed contract that computes to the average salary of the 125 highest-paid players in baseball." For the 2014 season the qualifying offer was $14 million; this increased to $15.3 million for the 2015 season. Furthermore, if a player gets traded midseason there is no compensation.[40] The owners once argued that free agency would ruin baseball, now even compensation for losing a free agent is largely disappearing.

Baseball has gone from the sport with the most labor conflict to the one that has the most harmonious relationship, a state of affairs few could have imagined back in the dark days of early 1995. While the luxury tax has slightly curbed the rise in player salaries in some years, it has had little effect overall. In 2012, the average player salary stood at $3.44 million. By way of comparison, in 1989 the average player salary was just under $513,000 and in 1996, the first year of the luxury tax, it was $1.18 million. Thus, in regard to salaries the players are doing well. Likewise, the teams are generally doing well. Operating income for the teams fell 9 percent in 2012 to an average of $13.1 million, but only six of the thirty clubs showed an operating loss. Moreover, according to *Forbes* the average worth of the clubs is $744 million; an increase of 23 percent since 2011 and the highest level since they first started tracking team worth back in 1998. Demonstrating the desire to own a baseball team, the Los Angeles Dodgers were sold in 2012 for more than $2 billion and have an estimated worth of $1.6 billion, second only to the Yankees, whose net worth is $2.3 billion. Fueling the rise of net worth of the teams is that television rights fees have increased dramatically and many teams have or are looking at starting their own networks. Moreover, in 2011 MLB signed a new eight-year national broadcasting deal worth $12.4 billion. The most recent figures show the trend of team worth rising with operating income falling. Operating income for the teams fell 26 percent in 2013, a decline of $13.1 million from 2012. However, as *Forbes* notes, "that is nothing to be alarmed about. Remember: the name of the game is to upload as much revenue as possible to the team's holding company and download as much expenses as possible from the parent company to the team." The average worth of clubs is now $811 million, a 9 percent increase from 2012. The Yankees are now worth $2.5 billion, the Dodgers worth $2 billion, and all but three teams (the New York Mets, Miami Marlins, and Houston Astros) are worth more than they were in the previous year.[41]

The biggest issue that baseball has to confront is that of performance-enhancing drugs. For all the handwringing condemnation and moral outcry, in this regard baseball is no different to any other sport. Indeed, the testing program in baseball is one of the toughest in the world. Arguably, there are fewer drugs in baseball now then there were in the 1960s and 1970s, when amphetamines were freely available and recreational drug use was not tested, let alone performance-enhancing drugs.[42] As the recent Biogenesis scandal demonstrates, both MLB and the MLBPA are doing what they can to eradicate drugs in the sport. However, when millions of dollars and ego are involved there will always be players that try to gain an edge. Nonetheless, the performance-enhancing drugs are the biggest issue facing baseball says something about the state of the game. Baseball is healthy, the players are being adequately rewarded, and there is labor peace. Quite simply, it is a good state of affairs for everyone concerned.

The National Football League

Victory through the Legal System

Sunday and Monday Night Football have become an institution, with Thursday also fast becoming a football night. Likewise, many fans now spend Thanksgiving watching football. Under the auspices of the National Football League (NFL), professional football has risen from humble beginnings to rank as America's number one sport. The NFL has captured the imagination of the public and has become an economic powerhouse. Super Bowls have been among the most-watched shows in American television history and Super Bowl parties are a staple not only in the United States but around the world. Indeed, the 2012 Super Bowl was the most-watched television show ever in America. This popularity is reflected in the NFL's television contracts. For the 2011–12 season, the NFL was paid $3.7 billion for the rights to broadcast its games. For the 2012–13 season, this rose to an incredible $4.1 billion. The NFL is, quite simply, an economic juggernaut.

Moreover, no other sport represents a combination of such precise intricacies of individual skills, game strategy, and brute violence. As the sport has grown, many players have become multimillionaires. This is money well earned. Money aside, the life of an NFL player is not one to be envied. The violence of the game results in lasting physical and/or psychological problems for the majority of players. In view of the trauma to which the players subject their bodies simply to make a team, it is not surprising that they should seek fair wages and working conditions. However, unlike their attempts to make it to the NFL, their attempts at collective action have generally been unsuccessful. There have been six lockouts and strikes in the history of the NFL. The first occurred in 1968, the second in 1970, the third in 1974, the fourth in 1982, the fifth in 1987, and the sixth in 2011. Unlike their brethren in the Major League

Baseball Players Association, NFL players have generally displayed a lack of solidarity and a lack of planning. In industrial struggles, a lack of solidarity and an unclear path of action almost always lead to defeat. This has been the case for the players and their collective voice, the National Football League Players' Association (NFLPA). Nonetheless, while the players' strikes have not always been fruitful, they have been more successful fighting the owners and the NFL through the court system.

This chapter will look at players' struggles with management before the formation of the NFLPA, as well as after its birth and during subsequent industrial battles. Strikes and lockouts in NFL history will be covered in detail, as well as court cases that have led to player gains. As noted above, the physical toll on NFL players is immense, and the chapter will also provide an overview of the costs of playing this violent game that entertains hundreds of millions of people in America and around the world. Further, while the physical price is steep, the psychological aftereffects caused by concussions are increasingly becoming a problem that must be confronted.

The life of an NFL player might seem glamorous, but the lives of many retired players are marked by physical and mental hardship. Although many players have become multimillionaires, they pay an increasingly steep price for their riches. Hopefully, the settlement of the 2011 lockout, during which the players remained largely united, signaled the beginning of a future in which players' health will be less seriously jeopardized by playing what is, after all, only a game, albeit one that brings joy (and heartbreak) to so many people. If not, not only will their economic rewards be less than it should be, players' physical and mental health will continue to be marked by pain and suffering.

The Birth of the NFL

While the NFL is now an economic powerhouse, it had humble beginnings. The American Professional Football Association began in Ohio in 1920 with primarily Midwestern teams. It was not a success, and folded after one season, only to be resurrected the following year. In 1922, it was renamed the National Football League. As Michael E. Lomax notes, "There was no franchise in New York until 1925. The NFL was very unstable in this early period. Thirty-six different franchises played in the league between 1921 and 1932, with as many as 22 in 1926 alone.

Franchises were cheap and unprofitable because the professional game was not popular nor respected."

In its early years, the league included small cities such as Pottsville, Pennsylvania, with a population of 22,000. However, by 1934 small town teams had all but vanished. Green Bay, Wisconsin, was the town with the smallest population that had an NFL team. That team, the Packers, managed to survive and eventually flourish, and is the oldest NFL team operating under its original name in its original location. While various other leagues sprang up before 1960, none was in a position to challenge the dominance of the NFL. The All-America Football Conference (AAFC) survived the longest, from 1946–49. When it folded, franchises representing Cleveland, Baltimore, and San Francisco joined the NFL.[1]

Early labor relations were characterized by the players' belief that the owners would willingly provide them with good wages and working conditions. This did not prove to be the case. Although the Supreme Court had ruled that the Sherman Antitrust Act did not apply to baseball because it was not interstate commerce, the same was not true for the NFL.[2] One might assume that this would have led to early industrial conflict, but this did not happen. The NFL acted as though, just like baseball, the Sherman Act did not apply to it and, like baseball, the NFL implemented a reserve-type clause that tied a player to a club in perpetuity. This was not an unofficial policy; the NFL's first constitution set this out.

The reserve-type clause was eventually eliminated in the 1940s due to competition from the All-America Football Conference, although the NFL threatened players with five-year bans if they signed with an AAFC team. Also, instead of imposing the reserve clause, NFL teams signed players to contracts that included an option year. Thus, if a team wanted to keep a player for an additional year they just invoked the option in the player's contract. While in theory after the option year a player should have been a free agent eligible to play for whatever team he chose, in reality the owners regarded the option year as self-perpetuating, triggering another option year as soon as the first one expired. In other words, there was no difference between this and a reserve clause. A player was tied to a team so long as the team wanted the player.

In addition to denying the players free agency, starting in 1936 the NFL had implemented a draft for college players who wished to join the league. In theory, the draft was designed to ensure that the NFL stayed competitive, as teams chose players depending on where they had finished at the end of the previous season; the team finishing last chose first, second-to-last team second, and so on. The principal effect of the draft, though, was that it tied a college player to the team that drafted him, thereby preventing star college players from attempting to engage teams in bidding wars for their services, as had occurred in 1934 in the case of the great University of Minnesota fullback Stan Kostka.[3]

The draft artificially depressed players' wages and, combined with the reserve clause/option year, tied a player to a team, which restricted his ability to negotiate for higher pay. Prior to the formation of the National Football League Players Association, the players had no collective voice. Lomax argues, "Football owners, like baseball's barons, looked upon labour as a commodity to be bought and sold in the market and exploited to the fullest. They often employed stern measures to bend players into pliant submission. Many such measures were essential to place the game on a firm business footing, and some no doubt benefited players as well. Nevertheless, the players had no voice. The owners had full autonomy, but competition from rival leagues would challenge their control and at least improve some players' economic well being."[4] Any improvements in wages or working conditions were due to the owners not wanting players to switch to a rival league. The players themselves seemed to be unwilling to seek a collective voice through a players' association or union. This state of affairs continued until the 1950s, at which point the National Football League Players Association was born and the Supreme Court ruled that the NFL was subject to federal antitrust laws.

The NFLPA and Radovich versus the NFL

I didn't like to have a man tell me I could play for one club and nobody else.

—Bill Radovich

In the late 1930s and early 1940s, Bill Radovich was a star player for the Detroit Lions. In 1942 he left the Lions to join the Navy during World War II before returning to play with Detroit in 1945. However, at the end of the season he asked to be traded to the Los Angeles Rams, so that he could live closer to his father. Detroit refused to trade him. Radovich noted that Detroit's owner "said I'd either play in Detroit or I wouldn't play anywhere. . . . He also told me if I tried to play in the new league, he would put me on a blacklist for five years."[5] As a result, Radovich quit the Lions and joined the Los Angeles Dons, of the All-America Football Conference, remaining with the team until 1948. In response, the NFL blacklisted Radovich. Near the end of his playing career he was offered a position as player/coach with the San Francisco Clippers, in the Pacific Coast Professional Football league, which had an affiliation with the NFL. As part of the affiliation, teams in the Pacific Coast League were forbidden from hiring players on the NFL blacklist. The Clippers withdrew their offer to Radovich. Instead, he took employment as a waiter and, eventually, finished his playing career in Canada.

In 1949, on the advice of a lawyer he met at the restaurant where he was working, Radovich took the NFL to court seeking restitution on the grounds of antitrust violations. Although he tried to settle, the NFL refused. It looked like the correct decision when first the trial court and then the court of appeals dismissed the lawsuit, ruling that the NFL was exempt from antitrust laws. However, the Supreme Court decided to look at the case.[6] Before the Court issued a ruling, in 1957, another event occurred that had a big impact on current and future players alike: the formation of the National Football League Players Association, in 1956.

Like the NFL itself, the NFLPA sprang from humble beginnings. NFL players needed collective representation. They did not have a minimum salary, pension, or health insurance. Not surprisingly, the NFL teams were profitable. In 1956, the twelve teams earned $1,159,747 in profit before taxes.

Players from the Cleveland Browns and Green Bay Packers wanted the teams to provide basic things such as clean uniforms and salaries for injured players. To help them achieve their demands the Browns players sought the assistance of attorney and former player Creighton Miller in forming a players association. Miller and the Browns players contacted players across the NFL to join the new association, and by the end of the year enough players had signed authorizations to make the organization official. In November 1956, Miller was elected leader of the newly formed NFLPA. Among the union's initial requests was a minimum salary of $5,000, laundry money, a reduced training season, equipment provided by the teams rather than the players themselves, continued salaries for injured players, and, crucially, recognition from the league as the players' bargaining unit.

The League had lasted thirty-five years without having to deal with a players' association, so it is not surprising that the NFL was dismissive of the NFLPA. Miller noted that, in January 1957, "[w]e made arrangements with the Commissioner to go to Philadelphia during the owners' meeting. . . . [NFL Commissioner] Bert (Bell) put us up at the Racquet Club and the owners were meeting at some hotel. We got there maybe on a Sunday night and [player representatives] Kyle Rote had to leave on Wednesday and Norm Van Brocklin left about Friday. I was still there Saturday, and we never did get a chance to meet with the owners and we never got a response from any of the proposals at that time."[7] However, an informal poll of the owners by The New York Times saw six owners in favor of recognizing the NFLPA, one opposed, and four not opposed but noncommittal. Before long, a Supreme Court ruling would result in the NFL's becoming more hospitable to the players' demands.

In February 1957 the Supreme Court ruled six to three in favor of Radovich, thereby placing the NFL within the scope of the Sherman Act; the NFL was subject to antitrust laws. The league attempted to get Congress to give football an antitrust exemption, but its attempts failed. To this day, of the major sports in America, only baseball has an antitrust exemption, albeit limited to all aspects of its operations apart from the employment of major league players. It was, and still is, an odd state of affairs. The difference between baseball and football that hurt football's attempt to achieve exemption is that, although both the NFL and MLB employ reserve-type clauses, in baseball the employees—the players—were initially free agents and could choose the team they wanted to sign their first contract with, whereas because of the NFL draft, college players had no choice which team they would play for.

After eight years of litigation, Bill Radovich was successful. At the time, he stated that the Court's ruling "vindicates my feeling that a player shouldn't be treated like a piece of furniture." Quite simply, he made history. As he correctly stated decades later, "The suit is part of N.F.L. history, whether it's good or not. . . . It's the first time that any professional sport was ever taken to court and beaten. What I did opened doors." However, he opened doors for others, not himself. The Supreme Court did not award him any damages, though he did receive a settlement from the NFL. Not surprisingly, he was persona non grata at the NFL. Yet he was willing to pay the price, even though it did bother him. He stated in 1994, "That's the price you pay for standing up for what you believe. . . . You're an outcast and an outsider."[8]

The Supreme Court ruling was beneficial to the NFLPA and the players. Following the decision, the NFLPA threatened to take the owners to court, demanding $4.2 million in restitution for damages caused by antitrust violations. This led the NFL to agree to the NFLPA's initial demands of a minimum salary of $5,000, a $50 payment for every preseason or exhibition game, medical insurance, and continued salaries for injured players. Moreover, the NFL officially recognized the NFLPA as the collective bargaining agent for the players. However, by mid-1958 some players had not received any extra money for participating in preseason games, the injury protection clause was not operational, and a pension and benefits plan was not being taken seriously by management. In response, once again the NFLPA threatened to sue the NFL for antitrust violations. This led to the owners finally agreeing to the NFLPA's demands.

The NFLPA was in a position to greatly improve player welfare because the owners were afraid of an antitrust lawsuit. However, the association was too timid and too weak to take the league to court. There was a lack of solidarity among the rank and file. Many star players did not want the NFLPA to be a union, but preferred that it operate as a grievance committee. These players were already earning good money and could look forward to careers in coaching, management, and/or the media. Things such as a minimum salary increase, medical insurance, and a pension did not really interest them. It didn't add to their solidarity that team player representatives had to have three or four years' service in the NFL. This led to a revolving door of representatives.

At the same time, the NFLPA's leadership did not push hard for major changes. For example, Miller and the NFLPA did not try to eliminate the option year clause, so despite the Supreme Court's ruling, it remained in place, as did the college draft. Moreover, in 1959 the NFL announced a pension plan for the players, to be funded primarily from a television agreement that was to be finalized in 1961. The pension plan itself wouldn't begin until 1963. Strangely, the NFLPA acceded, accepting in 1959 a pension plan that would be funded by a television agreement that was to be negotiated in two years' time, in which players would not be eligible to participate until they had played a game in 1963.[9] It was a sorry state of affairs, yet the NFLPA seemed pleased with its achievement.

The AFL, the Rozelle Rule, and Industrial Conflict in the 1960s

Lamar Hunt and Kenneth S. Adams formed the American Football League (AFL) in August 1959. They wanted their own NFL team, but when they could not purchase an existing team they decided to form a new league. The AFL had teams in eight cities, including Dallas. In response, the NFL created its own franchise in the city in 1960—the Dallas Cowboys—as well as a new franchise—the Vikings—in Minnesota. By the start of 1961, there were fourteen NFL teams. The AFL was beneficial to the players as not only opened up more job opportunities but NFL rosters were increased from thirty-five to forty players. Furthermore, college players could enlist AFL teams to engage in a bidding war with their NFL counterparts for their services.

At the same time, football was becoming a valuable television commodity. For the 1962–63 season, the NFL's television contract with CBS was worth $4.65 million. This increased to $28.2 million for 1964–65 and $75.2 million for 1966–69. In addition, NFL attendance increased by two million between 1960 and 1964. As for the AFL, it signed its own five-year deal with NBC worth $42 million over the course of the contract. There was no shortage of money for football team owners and their respective leagues. However, the same was not true for the players. In 1962–63 the average player salary in the NFL was $20,000. This increased to $21,000 in 1964–65 and $22,000 in 1966–69. Thus, by the end of the 1960s, while the annual television income per team increased by $1.27 million, player salaries increased by only $2,000.[10] The limited salary growth was in large part due to the Rozelle Rule.

In 1962, San Francisco 49er R. C. Owens successfully played out his option year and then did the almost unheard of: he signed for another NFL team, the Baltimore Colts. If such a practice were permitted to proceed unhindered, players would be looking at a form of free agency and the prospect of dramatically increased salaries. For owners and teams, this would mean uncertainty and lower profits. As a result, NFL commissioner Pete Rozelle implemented a new rule to prevent players switching teams. Known informally as the Rozelle Rule, it authorized the commissioner to award compensation, in the form of players, draft picks, and/or money, to the player's previous team. Because the commissioner could unilaterally decide on the nature and amount of the compensation once a player had switched teams, there would always be doubt about what the compensation would be and how harsh. For example, when San Francisco 49er Dave Parks played out his option year in 1967 and signed with the New Orleans Saints, Rozelle awarded the 49ers the Saints' first round draft picks in 1968 and 1969. The Rozelle Rule was in existence between 1963 and 1976, and in this time while 174 players played out their option year, only thirty-four signed with a different team for the following year. The Rozelle Rule had the effect of artificially reducing player wages and inflating team profits.[11]

In addition to labor struggles in the NFL, there was also unrest in the AFL. The AFL All-Star Game was due to be played in New Orleans in 1965. Arriving at the airport, many African American players were unable to find transportation to their hotel as cab drivers refused to take them. Running back Sid Blanks noted, "I couldn't get any transportation to the hotel. . . . I finally got a skycap to tell me, 'You need to get the right cab because you're colored.' I said, 'What do you mean?' He said, 'They won't pick you up.' I asked why not, and he said, 'It's a little different here. If you're colored, you can't ride in just any cab.'" Restaurants and nightclubs refused some players admittance. Defensive end Earl Faison remembered, "We walked past four or five different clubs (and were refused entry). . . . One guy shouted, 'You so and so, get off the street. John F. Kennedy is not playing here tonight.'" Almost all of the African American players were subjected to racist abuse while walking down Bourbon Street. Moreover, Faison claimed, "A guy pulls out a gun and says, 'You are not coming in here. You n——s are not coming in here.'" This situation was not palatable and, following a vote, the black players refused to play in the All-Star Game as long as it was held in New Orleans. They were supported by some of their white teammates who also refused to participate. The following day, AFL commissioner Joe Foss announced that the game would be moved to Houston.[12] Such action demonstrated that change could happen if the players were united and willing to take militant action.

In the NFL, the NFLPA began to take a more aggressive stance, particularly with regard to the pension plan. It was reported in the press that because the NFL received more money than expected for the television rights to its championship game, the overall pension pool had increased from $50,000 in 1960 to $450,000 in 1963. At that level, a five-year veteran would receive approximately $5,244 a year starting at age sixty-five, a ten-year veteran $7,872, and a player with fifteen years' service $9,852. Players also received paid medical and life insurance worth between $10,000 and $20,000. By 1964, due to increased television revenue, all players received a $20,000 life insurance policy and an accidental death policy that was also worth $20,000, while an additional 110 players, coaches, trainers, and equipment personnel would be eligible for a pension once they reached sixty-five. Moreover, thanks to NFLPA agitation, players received $100 for each preseason game, which was double the previous amount.

Rozelle, however, admitted that regardless of the figures cited in the press reports, he was uncertain what amount the players would receive once they turned sixty-five, and that the numbers mentioned by the media were mere speculation. Understandably, this led to unease between the NFL and the NFLPA, which was exacerbated when Rozelle, without informing the NFLPA, decided that $300,000 earmarked for the pension from the 1964 championship game went instead to the owners.

The NFLPA's bargaining power was weakened considerably when, in 1966, the NFL and the AFL announced their decision to merge. Under the terms of the merger, all of the AFL teams would be accepted into the NFL, with another two franchises joining the newly enlarged league in 1968. The merger was not beneficial to a number of veteran and star players who, before it was announced, had planned to jump leagues, expecting to reap lucrative contracts with new teams. Under the terms of the merger, the contracts the players had signed upon switching leagues were suspended, which led to increased hostility between them and the owners.

While the veterans were angry at the NFL, some were also hostile to different attempts to form a union of professional athletes. For instance, players from the Detroit Lions and Cleveland Browns expressed interest in forming an independent union with the advice and assistance of the International Brotherhood of Teamsters. Clearly, such an action undermined the NFLPA by encouraging a lack of belief that the association could adequately represent the players. In 1968, a compromise was reached whereby, having rejected partnership with the Teamsters, the NFLPA technically remained an association rather than a union, although it registered as a union with the National Labor Relations Board (NLRB) and was a de facto union.

The owners had stated that they would formally recognize the NFLPA if the players turned down the advances of the Teamsters, but as soon as the players did so the owners reneged on their promise.[13] This further exacerbated the relationship between the players and the owners. It was only a matter of time before resentment grew to open conflict, in the form of the first lockout and strike in NFL history, marking the beginning of a sustained period of labor unrest in the league.

The first lockout and strike in NFL history took place in 1968 and was relatively minor. One of the major problems for the NFLPA was that although the AFL and the NFL had merged, the two leagues' players' associations had not. The NFLPA represented only sixteen out of the twenty-six teams. As a result, the NFL was able to pit one players' association against the other. In 1968, the NFLPA sought a better pension plan and increased wages for the players. It asked that minimum salaries of $15,000 be paid to rookies and $20,000 to veteran players, that players receive $500 for exhibition games, and that at age forty-five retired players start receiving their pensions. The NFLPA also wanted the owners to contribute $2.6 million a year into the pension fund, while the owners offered $1.25 million. The players were willing to strike over the issues, and a strike authorization vote was successful, but before they could walk out the owners locked them out by delaying the start of preseason training in July, although a day later they allowed rookies and free agents to train at the teams' facilities. The lockout only lasted one week. When it ended, the players went on strike. The strike was brief too, and neither lockout nor strike caused the loss of any games. While *The New York Times* claimed it was the first strike by professional sportspeople in seventy-eight years, in reality it was the first strike since the work stoppage by the Detroit Tigers in 1912.

Eventually, an agreement was reached. The most notable thing about the contract was that it was the first collective bargaining agreement in football. However, the agreement was a disappointment to the players, yielding results well short of their demands. Minimum salary was set at only $9,000 for rookies and $10,000 for veterans; exhibition pay remained the same, as did the age players started receiving their pension, while the owners contributed $1.5 million per year for two years to the pension fund. Hampering the NFLPA's efforts was that the players on AFL teams accepted the owners' offer without alerting the NFLPA. This left the NFLPA little room to bargain. Moreover, at times there was a lack of communication between the NFLPA and its members. This can and often does undermine solidarity, especially if the players have to rely on the media to get information about how talks are progressing. Once a settlement was reached, NFLPA president John Gordy stated, "It's about time the players sat down as players and the owners sat down as owners and reached a final agreement. Let's get down to the business of playing football."

While the agreement was a disappointment to the players, as they had to settle for less than their original demands, the *New York Times* expressed the belief that the players had achieved "remarkable gains."[14] Like baseball writers, football writers generally sided with the owners and considered any minor gains for the players to be remarkable and, while hoping that there would be no more strikes, conveniently forgot that the owners had initially locked out the players. The writers were to be disappointed, as the next lockout and strike were only two years away.

1970s: A Decade of Industrial Disputes

What some of these guys should do is work for a living.

—Unnamed fan in 1970

In 1970, the NFLPA and the AFL Players Association merged and, following tense negotiations, Baltimore Colts player John Mackey was elected president of the expanded NFLPA. Moreover, after filling a petition with the NLRB, the NFLPA became a certified union. Despite these positive developments, the NFLPA had a miniscule staff, was in debt, and could not adequately communicate with its members. As a result, it was not a surprise that the NFLPA could also not bargain effectively with the owners. Nevertheless, there was another conflict between labor and management in 1970. The players were unhappy that the NFL would not negotiate with them in good faith. Considering the state of the NFLPA, this should not have come as a shock. The owners briefly locked out the players during the offseason by delaying the start of training camps. Not understanding that the difference between a lockout and strike is based on who decides whether employees will show up for work, some media noted that by delaying the start of the training camps Rozelle had averted the start of a possible strike. At the same time, Rozelle claimed he had imposed a lockout in part because he did not want to weaken player unity. His reasoning was that if there were no lockout the players would have gone out on strike and if they did so some players would have attempted to undermine the strike. Whatever the case, the owners soon changed tactics and announced that camps were open to all veterans, to which the NFLPA countered by going out on strike.

Despite some media claims that the conflict was bitter and amounted to the "biggest labor rebellion in pro sports history," and that the players' demands were "too extreme," in reality, like the first strike and lockout in NFL history, the disruption caused by the second strike was relatively minor, and it only lasted two days. It didn't help the NFLPA's cause that several players broke ranks and showed up at training camps, once again demonstrating their lack of solidarity. Two days after they walked out, the players capitulated in the face of the owners' threat to cancel the season. Eventually, a new four-year collective bargaining agreement was signed.

Under the new CBA, the minimum salary was increased to $12,500 for rookies and $13,000 for veterans, and the pension and health care plans were improved to the tune of an additional $19.1 million. However, of this, owners' contributions to the pension fund only increased by $18.14 million. The owners had initially offered $16 million, while the union was seeking $26 million. On a more positive note, players were allowed to retain agents to represent them in salary negotiations.

Following the lockout and strike, the owners retaliated against the NFLPA's leadership. Many NFLPA player representatives were released by their teams, and John Mackey was traded from the Colts to the San Diego Chargers, and was basically forced to retire. The hardline approach was summed up by Chicago Bears owner George Halas. He stated, "I never ran away from a fight in my life. The power of the commissioner is undiminished. The fight for principle was upheld." Of course, the NFLPA was fighting for a different principle, one by which players are not exploited for the benefit of a select few wealthy individuals. Despite the setbacks, the NFLPA was in a defiant mood. Mackey claimed, "They gave us what they wanted to give us, made us smile and say 'thank you.' But from that day forward, we decided to build a legitimate union. All efforts since then have been designed to develop our strength. Now we have the strength to take them on." This newfound determination led the NFLPA to hire Ed Garvey as its inaugural executive director in 1971, and an education campaign was launched to inform the players of the union's goals.[15] Considering the previous absence of communication, this was a step in the right direction.

With the NFLPA taking a more antagonistic approach and the owners refusing to give in to the players' demands, it is not surprising that once again the labor "harmony" did not last long. Following the expiration of the 1970 collective bargaining agreement, another strike occurred. This time, the NFLPA prepared in advance. It amassed a strike fund of more than $200,000, eight staff, and of the slogan "No freedom, no football." The players wanted, among other things, total free agency, seeking the elimination of the Rozelle Rule and the option clause in player contracts, as well as impartial arbitration of all disputes and the elimination of the draft. If the media thought the association's demands had been too extreme in 1970, in 1974 they were on another level. The owners, however, refused to negotiate with the NFLPA. Bears owner Halas argued that football players were not "just like other people. . . . Other people are not given college scholarships that in turn enables them to get football jobs that pay approximately $40,000 annually in salary and benefits for six months of work." Of course, so-called other people have careers that generally last longer than football players', with a lot less risk that an accident can end their ability to participate in their chosen profession in an instant. The owners' hardline approach and their refusal to negotiate led to the players going out on strike on July 1, 1974.

The strike was not a success. Believing that they could win in the courts, the owners refused to agree to any of the players' demands. Moreover, once again player solidarity was badly lacking. Despite the efforts of the association, rookies and free agents reported to training camps, and by June 21, 108 veteran players had crossed the picket lines. By July 29 the number was up to 248, and eventually more than three hundred veteran players, approximately 25 percent of the membership of the NFLPA, had broken ranks including thirty-four out of forty-eight veteran players for the Miami Dolphins.

Some players spoke out in the media against the strike. For example, New York Jet Steve Tannen stated, "Ed Garvey is overmatched in this one." The overwhelming lack of solidarity doomed the strike from the beginning, and kept the players from getting their message across to the public. Once again, the media generally sided with the owners and as a result most of the public was against the players. One writer wrote that the players "can always try their hand in another business, but even under present limitations most of the players are enjoying enough fame, fortune and financial security to compensate them for the restrictions under which they work." The lack of solidarity and the owners' refusal to bargain led the association to suspend the strike on August 10, before totally abandoning it on August 28. Despite ending the strike, the warring parties could not settle on a new collective bargaining agreement; nor would they until 1977.

The NFLPA was badly hurt by the strike. Demonstrating the lack of faith the players had in the union, in 1975 fewer than 50 percent of them paid their dues. However, while the NFLPA had been soundly defeated at the negotiating table in 1974, it was to be a lot more successful fighting the NFL in the courts. As Garvey stated, "The strike had collapsed and we lost. . . . It was time for plan B."[16]

Plan B was already underway. Its aim was to win in the courts; specifically, over antitrust violations. In 1972, Mackey and thirty-five other players had filed suit in the Minnesota District Court claiming that the Rozelle Rule violated the Sherman Act. The court held that the Rozelle Rule was unlawful on two counts and constituted an unreasonable restraint of trade, and while some restrictions on free agency might be allowed, the Rozelle Rule had come about because of the weakness of the NFLPA and the league's refusal to bargain in good faith. The NFL appealed the decision and in 1977 the Eighth Circuit Court of Appeals upheld it; the Rozelle Rule was in violation of the Sherman Act. The appeals court stated that the rule "significantly deters clubs from negotiating with and signing free agents; that it acts as a substantial deterrent to players playing out their options and becoming free agents; that it significantly decreases players' bargaining power in contract negotiations; that players are thus denied the right to sell their services in a free and open market; that as a result, the salaries paid by each club are lower than if competitive bidding were allowed to prevail; and that absent the Rozelle Rule, there would be increased movement in interstate commerce of players from one club to another."

Plan B, NFLPA's alternative plan, had worked out exceedingly well. The NFL agreed to pay $15.8 million in damages to NFL players who had been under contract in the early 1970s. As evidence that the owners had acted in restraint of trade, while the Rozelle Rule had been in place, of 176 players eligible to switch teams after their option year expired, only thirty-four had signed with a new team. Of these thirty-four, in twenty-seven cases the two teams involved had worked out the compensation details, four had been decided by the commissioner, and in three cases there had been no compensation.[17]

Following the ruling by the appeals court, the players should have enjoyed, at the very least, something resembling true free agency. This was not to be the case. In the five-year collective bargaining agreement reached in 1977, the NFLPA was successful in gaining increased benefits as well as impartial arbitration of non-injury grievances, but on the crucial issue of free agency, for which the players held all the cards, the association mishandled the situation. Instead of allowing free agency, new rules were put into place under which veteran players could negotiate the elimination of the option clause from their contracts, but if they waived that right they received at least a 10 percent salary increase for their final year under contract. If a player received a qualifying offer from another team, his current team had the right to match the offer, but if the team failed to do so and the player switched teams, the team he left was compensated with high draft choices whose number and position were based on the player's salary. While in theory the new rules might have resulted in more players changing teams and hence achieving higher salaries, this was not the case. During the course of the five-year agreement, although six hundred players' contracts expired, fewer than fifty received offers from other teams and only one solitary player moved. Quite simply, the players had not achieved free agency and the issue had been totally bungled by the NFLPA. The one positive outcome for the players was that their salaries were increasing. In 1977, the average player salary was $55,288; by 1980 it was $78,657, and it increased another 14.5 percent, to $90,102, the following year. At the same time, the NFL was benefiting from increased television money. Its 1978–1981 broadcast deal was worth $646 million, or an annual income per team of $5.8 million.

Of course, not everyone benefited. It was by players such as John Mackey that the road to free agency had been paved. He wrote in 1992, "My name has long been associated with the cause of free agency in the N.F.L. . . . What most people don't know is that my commitment stemmed mostly from one incident in the N.F.L. in which I was handed a piece of paper, a contract, and was told to sign it. Of course I didn't, and from that moment of youthful pique evolved the fight by N.F.L. players to choose for whom they work." In later life, Mackey suffered from dementia, which most likely was caused by playing football. In 2006, the NFL and the NFLPA, following a plea for help from Mackey's wife, created the 88 Plan; named in honor of the number Mackey wore. The 88 Plan provides up to $100,000 annually for former players suffering from dementia, Alzheimer's disease, ALS, and/or Parkinson's disease. More than 166 players have benefited. John Mackey died in 2011; he was sixty-nine.[18]

1980s: More of the Same

Following the expiration of the 1977 collective bargaining agreement, there was further labor unrest in 1982. That year, a new television agreement resulted in a massive increase in revenue to the owners. The five-year broadcast deal was worth $2.1 billion; $13.6 million annually per team. This was an increase of $7.8 million for each team annually. The NFLPA believed that the players deserved a fair share of the NFL's windfall and demanded that player salaries and pension be pegged to 55 percent of gross revenues. Unsurprisingly, the owners were not interested in giving the players a majority share of gross revenues. One owner stated that such an idea was "alien to American business." The association then revised its demand. Instead of an across-the-board majority share, the NFLPA wanted league revenue to "be divided among players based on years of service, playtime and individual and team performance. The proposal was designed to pay players based on performance, not on how high a player was drafted or how well he was expected to play." It was a novel approach, but the owners rejected this proposal as well, and were preparing for a fight. They secured a $150 million line of credit to help mediate the effects of any potential strike. For their part, because negotiations were not progressing in any meaningful way the players were prepared to go on strike, to begin during week three of the season.

Retired Los Angeles Rams defensive end Gary Jeter later stated, "In 1982, there were some bitter feelings on both sides. . . . We hadn't seen the owners' books and when we finally were able to see them, we were upset at the percentage (of revenue) we were receiving. It wasn't fair. Guys were willing to sit out the whole season. We weren't making any money. We were called professional ballplayers, but we weren't being paid like professional ballplayers. There was no severance. We didn't have as good a pension. Overall benefits weren't as good." On September 21, following the Monday Night game, the players struck. In response, the owners locked the players out of their respective team facilities. For the first time in NFL history, games were cancelled during the regular season. During the strike, in a compromise deal the owners offered a $1.6 billion package. While this was amenable to the NFLPA, there was dispute over how the money would be divided. The strike lasted fifty-seven days and was marked by relatively strong player solidarity, at least initially. The players held their own All-Star games and even made noise about starting their own league to rival the NFL, although the latter was largely just talk. The two All-Star games, held in Washington and Los Angeles, were marked by weak attendance, which, along with the threat of injunction, led to no further games being played. As the strike progressed there was increasing disquiet from a minority of players regarding lost salary and Garvey's leadership. This led to some players imploring the NFLPA to end the strike. Dallas Cowboys quarterback Danny White actually attended meetings with the Cowboys general manager. As NFLPA staffer Doug Allen later noted, "In '82, we had a very vocal minority of players that were adamantly opposed to what we were doing. And some of them were very highly visible and got a lot of attention. So we wasted a lot of energy and emotion internally in the majority trying to deal with the minority." Eventually, two developments led to a resolution.

First, it became apparent that the entire season would be canceled unless games resumed by early November. An entire season lost was not palatable to either the owners or the players. Second, the owners' proposed $1.6 billion package, with $1.28 billion in guaranteed money that would cover the 1983–1987 seasons, seemed a lot better to the NFLPA than forfeiting the season without a deal in place. The owners' proposal amounted to approximately 50 percent of total NFL revenue. The players returned to work while the negotiations continued and games resumed on November 21. An agreement was reached on December 5. Besides the previously announced package, benefits to the players included severance pay and increases in the minimum salary, pensions, preseason pay, and injury protection. Moreover, the owners paid the players $60 million which covered a large part of wages lost due to the strike. However, the free agency question remained unresolved and the system agreed to under the 1977 collective bargaining agreement remained largely in place with only very minor modifications. This was the same system that had led to only one instance of a player changing teams where draft compensation was involved in five years.

The outcome was not a good one for the players, and the overwhelming consensus was that the owners had won. Conversely, in trying to put a positive spin on the outcome the NFLPA claimed that while the collective bargaining agreement "did not change the NFL system in any significant respect, it instead increased the price the owners would have to pay to continue that system, and it assured that players would have accurate information when they attempted to negotiate their salaries within that system." At the end of the shortened nine-game season, the Washington Redskins defeated the Miami Dolphins in what was called the Super Bowl Tournament.

The 1982 strike was to be Ed Garvey's final meaningful accomplishment as NFLPA executive director. Following the general disquiet about his leadership during the strike his position had become untenable. In 1983, Garvey quit the position to seek a career in politics. He was replaced as executive director by Gene Upshaw, the NFLPA president since 1980, who let it be known that he wanted the players to choose the NLPA's policy objectives.[19] Listening to the members and getting their input is essential to any union, and this was a positive development for the NFLPA.

It is undeniable that the 1977 and 1982 agreements did not live up to player expectations. This is especially true in regard to free agency. While in theory there was (limited) free agency for all, in practice very little player movement had occurred. Considering that the Mackey case had resulted in the ruling that the NFL violated the Sherman Act with the Rozelle Rule, the NFLPA should have been focusing on player mobility. The union under Garvey simply "fumbled the ball." Demonstrating the inadequacy of the free agency rules for the players, while they were in existence, between 1977 and 1988, approximately 1,500 players became eligible for free agency; only two players managed to join new teams.

For the players, one positive outcome of the agreements was a dramatic increase in their salaries. However, while average player salaries increased from $90,412 in 1982 to $230,000 in 1987, this was largely due to competition from the United States Football League, which began operating in 1983 and led to players being offered higher salaries by their current clubs as inducements not to jump to the rival league. In fact, the increase in player salaries had very little to do with the 1982 agreement, despite claims by the association. The NFLPA argued that while the 1977 and 1982 agreements were not as good as the players had sought, it would have been unrealistic to expect great results in the short term, due to the power and solidarity of the owners. Thus, it had been necessary to modify some of their demands to achieve victory in the long term.[20] This was a positive way to look at less than stellar achievements. The NFLPA was to have its victory, but this was not to be achieved via a work stoppage.

As was becoming the norm, in the lead-up to the 1987 collective bargaining negotiations there was labor disharmony. When the NFLPA polled its members in 1986, free agency was the players'—and thus the NFLPA's—number one priority, since, as noted above, during the lifetime of the current contract only one out of five hundred "free agents" had been offered a deal by another club. However, the level of animosity between the players and the owners was lower than it had been in the lead-up to the 1982 strike, and few acrimonious words were being employed by either side. Thus, one might have thought that there would be no chance of an industrial dispute breaking out.

For the owners, the threat of the United States Football League (USFL) had passed. It had folded due to mismanagement, the difficulty of fighting the incumbent, and, most of all, heavy losses amounting to an average of some $3.3 million per team in 1983 alone. Ultimately, the USFL's total losses ended up being approximately $180 million, and the league ceased operations in 1986 due to its inability to land a major television contract once ABC was no longer willing to broadcast its games. Once again, this left the NFL owners in a dominant position, which they exercised by rejecting the players' demands.

The negotiations were going nowhere, and very little was agreed to. Moreover, serious negotiations had not even begun until late August, with the season fast approaching. Arguably, if the USFL had still been in operation the owners would have done almost anything to prevent a work stoppage, as this would have given increased exposure to the rival league. The players gave the NFLPA strike authorization, although, quite ominously, the strike vote was a long way from unanimous. The issue of free agency was the overwhelming priority, but the association also wanted an increase in the minimum salary, as well as large increases in owner contributions to the pension fund. In regard to the pension, the NFLPA asked for a $25 million increase, while the NFL was offering $12.5 million. As for minimum salary, the NFLPA demanded $90,000 for rookies and $320,000 for thirteen-year veterans. The owners countered by offering $60,000 for rookies and $180,000 for thirteen-year veterans. Thus, in addition to free agency the two sides were far apart on all issues. The owners, led by their hardline spokesperson Jack Donlan, who had also been the owners' spokesperson in 1982, prepared to hire replacement players to fill the places abandoned by the striking players.

Quite surprisingly, the NFLPA was not really prepared for a strike. It had failed to learn any lessons from the aborted 1982 strike. For instance, there was no strike fund and/or line of credit for the players. However, the AFL-CIO supported the NFLPA by urging its members to boycott games as well as forming picket lines at the grounds. Nevertheless, the fans, referees, and media generally supported the owners.

For the first, and hopefully the last, time, regular season games were played by replacement players. While television ratings started out quite high for the new season, likely due to viewer curiosity, they declined as the strike continued. Despite the public's siding with the owners, they did not want to watch subpar players. Average attendance was only 17,000 for week 1, and 25,000 for week 2, which represented only 28 and 41 percent of the usual attendance for NFL games. Nonetheless, the owners remained unified. The unity of football owners was unlike that of baseball owners, in that it was almost guaranteed that a number of owners would break ranks during conflict with the MLBPA. The unity displayed by the football owners was certainly not matched by the players. On the first day of the strike, two high-profile players crossed the picket line, and throughout its duration the players continually abandoned the strike. By the time the strike was over, eighty-nine players, approximately 16 percent of NFL rosters, had crossed the picket lines and played regular season games alongside replacement players, including future Hall of Famers Joe Montana, Tony Dorsett, Steve Largent, and Lawrence Taylor. Faced with these obstacles and the fear that more players would abandon the strike, after twenty-four days the NFLPA called it off. The players returned to work without having achieved any of their demands.

At least, they thought they would be able to play in that weekend's games. But the owners had set a deadline of October 14 for the players to return to work. As the NFLPA abandoned the strike on October 15, the owners did not allow the players to participate in the weekend's games. The owners claimed that they did this because there was a risk of injury to the players. The NFLPA filed a suit with the NLRB on the grounds that the players should have been allowed to play. It took until 1994, but finally the NLRB ruled in favor of the players and awarded back pay of $30 million to be divided by approximately 1,300 players. This did somewhat soften the blow of the strike, during which the players had lost almost $80 million. In another postscript, this one not beneficial to the association, the NFLPA lost its dues checkoff. Rather than have them automatically deducted from player salaries, the NFLPA had to personally ask each member to pay his dues. Following the total failure of the 1987 strike, this was not an easy matter. The players completed the season without a collective bargaining agreement in place.

In looking back at the strike, former Minnesota Vikings general manager Mike Lynn summed up the feelings of many people: "I didn't think any part of it was fun or funny or hilarious. . . . It was embarrassing. It was a bad, bad part of the history of the National Football League. The relationship between owners and players should never come to something like that." Relationships between players also had to be mended. Tim Irwin, the player representative for the Vikings, stated, "It made me angry. . . . Some of the guys crossing the line were superstars making the bucks. It was selfish."[21]

Why the NFLPA thought that going on strike would have been beneficial to the players is uncertain. Even a cursory glance leads one to realize that the players were far from united and the NFLPA did not have a plan for the strike. The owners were never going to capitulate as, unlike the players, they were united. It was a misguided action that further undermined player solidarity and cost the players money. It almost seems as though the NFLPA during this time was prepared to go on strike every time a collective bargaining agreement expired, and even with a new leader it followed in that misguided tradition without thinking the issue through. However, if one tactic does not succeed try another one. The next tactic was the same one that had led to the overturning of the Rozelle Rule; namely, go to court.

On the day the 1987 strike ended, the NFLPA filed an antitrust lawsuit against the NFL on antitrust grounds in the United States District Court for the District of Minnesota. The suit was filed on behalf of the players by then-president of the NFLPA Marvin Powell, and in January 1988, the court ruled in favor of the players. The NFL quickly filed an appeal. However, they were worried that the appeals court might rule against them, and unilaterally imposed what was known as "Plan B" (this Plan B is different to the NFLPA's Plan B mentioned above).

Under this plan, it was initially proposed that each team could protect either forty-two or forty-four players, depending on where the team had finished the previous season. However, after the NFLPA requested an injunction against the plan due to its allegedly only allowing free agency to players that teams declined to re-sign, the NFL modified Plan B. Under the final version, every team could subject its best thirty-seven players to the current free agency rules whereby if a player was offered a deal to switch teams, the player's current club had the right of first refusal, and if they did not want to retain the player they would receive draft picks in return.

Thus, an additional 142 players were now eligible for free agency compared to the number cited in the initial proposal. A player not included in the protected thirty-seven could change teams between February 1 and April 1 without compensation for his former team; that player was granted free agency. After April 1, the original team had exclusive rights to negotiate with the player. This was somewhat of a token gesture by the NFL as the teams still could protect their most valuable assets while granting free agency to lesser players. Such an action might also have the effect of potentially undermining solidarity between these players and the star players.

Plan B showed that free agency did lead to increased player movement and a dramatic increase in player salaries. The NFLPA compiled a report that noted, "Over 1,100 players have been deemed unrestricted under Plan B. Almost a third changed Clubs each year. Those 413 players changing Clubs negotiated contracts with averages per year 61% higher than their previous contract series. Virtually all received a signing bonus; the average value was $48,000.00. That average rose 40% in 1990—from $40,000.00 in 1989 to $57,500.00 in 1990." Plan B was a great benefit to the non-stars of the NFL. Average player salaries increased from $230,000 in 1987 to $354,000 in 1990. Nonetheless, such a system, while a step in the right direction, was still not palatable to the NFLPA. It continued to fight in court, helped in a large part by a dramatic increase in group licensing revenue, which increased from $2 million in 1988 to $11 million in 1990. The increase was achieved because most players "signed Group Licensing Authorizations, granting exclusive rights to the NFLPA."

While things were looking promising for the players, they received a setback on November 1, 1989, when the Eighth Circuit Court of Appeals reversed the lower court's decision in *Powell v. NFL*. The appeals court ruled that because the NFLPA was a union it could not sue the league for antitrust violations. The judgment stated, "The labor arena is one with well established rules which are intended to foster negoti-ated settlements rather than intervention by the courts. The League and the Players accepted this 'level playing field' as the basis for their often tempestuous relationship, and we believe that there is substantial justification for requiring the parties to continue to fight on it, so that bargaining and the exertion of economic force may be used to bring about legitimate compromise." The court was in essence arguing that as a union, the NFLPA, and the NFL, agreed to a certain set of rules; the level playing field.

The decision basically gave the players two options: either keep the union going and attempt to achieve free agency for players via col-lective bargaining, or decertify the union and sue the NFL on antitrust violations as individuals. The latter course was hinted at by the majority of judges and outright suggested by the dissenting opinion. Considering the NFLPA's abject failure at collective bargaining, there was only one option to consider, and in response to the court's hints, more than 930 of the approximately 1,500 NFL players signed a petition stating that neither the NFLPA nor any other body could collectively bargain on their behalf. On December 5, 1989, all twenty-four player representatives voted in favor of the NFLPA decertifying itself and instead becoming a professional association. Having decertified, the NFLPA only had to prove one thing in court if it filed an antitrust suit against the NFL; namely, that the NFL's rules restricted player movement.[22]

While *Powell v. NFL* was occurring, another court case related to antitrust issues was being heard: *Brown v. Pro Football*. NFL teams decided to limit the amount practice squad players could earn to $1,000 per week. The NFLPA opposed this restriction of salary and took the NFL to court on antitrust grounds. The association was initially successful as in 1991 the district court determined that as the limitation on wages did not occur as a result of arm's-length collective bargaining, the NFL was not protected by a nonstatutory labor exemption, that is, the NFL was not excused from antitrust laws in this case because the league had imposed a wage restriction outside of collective bargaining. However, in 1996 the Supreme Court reversed the district court's decision, finding that the nonstatutory labor exemption did apply because the imposition of the wage controls:

1. Took place during and immediately after a collective bargaining negotiation;

2. Grew out of, and was directly related to, the lawful operation of the bargaining process;

3. Involved a matter that the parties were required to negotiate collectively; and

4. Concerned only the parties to the collective bargaining relationship.

The *Brown* case was important because the court ruled that players could only take the respective leagues to court on antitrust grounds if their unions were decertified, no longer in existence, or recognition has been withdrawn.[23] While the NFLPA was not successful in the *Brown* case, it was a lot more successful in other cases occurring at the same time.

Labor Peace and Free Agency

The start of the new decade saw the average player salary rise to over $350,000, but the NFLPA was no longer a union and there was no collective bargaining agreement in place. As for the NFL, it had a new television contract for the next four years worth $3.65 billion, or an annual windfall for each team of $32.6 million, an increase of $15.9 million. The first few years of the decade were to be good for the players and the NFLPA. In March 1990, as previously noted, the NFL was assessed damages of $30 million because it had refused to allow players who participated in the 1987 strike to return to the first weekend's games after the conclusion of hostilities. Moreover, in the spring of 1990, eight players—Freeman McNeil, Don Majkowski, Tim McDonald, Niko Noga, Mark Collins, Lee Rouson, Dave Richards, and Frank Minnifield—sued the NFL, claiming that Plan B restricted player movements and thus antitrust laws. The case was to be known as *McNeil v. NFL*.

The NFL tried to get the court case thrown out by claiming that the NLRB had yet to formally decertify the NFLPA as a union under labor law. However, the court ruled, "The existence of a bargaining relationship does not depend on NLRB certification, but rather depends on whether a majority of the employees in a bargaining unit supports a particular union as their bargaining representative." The lawsuit was free to continue. While it did not participate in the lawsuit, the NFLPA covered the players' costs. However, hampering the NFLPA was that the NFL was attempting to poach players from the NFLPA's licensing group to add to its own licensing arm, NFL Properties. Eventually, more than seven hundred joined NFL Properties, including many stars such as Jim Kelly, Warren Moon, Dan Marino, Phil Simms, John Elway, Boomer Esiason, Troy Aikman, Jim Everett, Randall Cunningham, Michael Irvin, and Ronnie Lott. By withdrawing, not only were the players taking money away from the NFLPA, they were putting their own self-interest ahead of the collective interest at a time when the issue of free agency was reaching a climax. Nonetheless, in *McNeill v. NFL,* in what was becoming a tradition, the United States District Court for the District of Minnesota ruled in 1991 in favor of the players. The court reasoned that because the NFLPA was no longer a union, the NFL was subject to antitrust laws, and the league would have to defend itself in a jury trial beginning in June 1992. The NFL petitioned the appeals court to review the decision, but it declined to do so.[24]

In June, the jury was made up exclusively of women, most of whom did not consider themselves sports fans. Not everyone was happy with the makeup of the jury; Denver Broncos owner Pat Bowlen stated he did not want "eight women who are basically domestic housewives [to] decide the future of the National Football League." Considering his sexist outburst, even though Bowlen was meant to be a witness during the trial, it was not a surprise he did not appear. Indeed, no owners testified during the proceedings.

Throughout the trial, the NFL was forced to reveal its financial data. Despite the owners' pleading financial hardship and claiming that free agency would cause them financial turmoil, the data revealed that the teams were profitable and doing a lot better than was generally thought. After a fifty-two day trial, on September 10, 1992, the jury found that Plan B had stifled player movement more than was necessary and caused economic injury to the players. However, they restricted their finding to the cases of Richards, Rouson, Minnifield, and Collins, whom they awarded $543,000 each, which was trebled to $1.63 million due to the actions being in violation of antitrust law. Thus, it was not a total victory for the players.

Nonetheless, one week after the trial the NFLPA followed up with another lawsuit. Philadelphia Eagle Keith Jackson was protected under Plan B, but still had not signed a contract. He and three other players requested an injunction against Plan B and, as was the "tradition," Judge Doty of the United States District Court for the District of Minnesota ruled in favor of the players and issued a five-day restraint on Plan B before the case would be considered further. In other words, the players were unrestricted free agents for at least five days. During this period, Jackson signed a new four-year contract worth $6 million, having previously earned $350,000 a year. Two other players also signed new contracts, while another was unconditionally released from his club and allowed to negotiate with whatever team he desired. Thus, as there were no unsigned or non–free agent players still involved in the case, the NFL requested that the court dismiss the case as moot, which the court duly obliged.[25] Following the McNeil and the Jackson verdicts, Plan B was on shaky ground.

It remained in place for the 1992 season, but its death knell was close. In October 1992 Philadelphia Eagles star Reggie White filed a class action lawsuit against the NFL claiming antitrust violations. The lawsuit covered "all players who have been, are now or will be under contract to play professional football for an NFL club at any time from August 31, 1987, to the date of final judgment in this action and determination of any appeal therefrom, and all college and other players who as of August 31, 1987, to the date of final judgment in this action and the determination of any appeal therefrom, have been, are not, or will be eligible to play football as a rookie for an NFL team." The owners were worried; if the court found for the players, damages would be trebled due to their having violated antitrust law. Some owners wanted to modify Plan B enough that the McNeil and Jackson verdicts would not be applicable to the new plan, so the players would have to continue filing new lawsuits. Basically, they were hoping that the NFLPA would run out of money and be unable to continue funding the players' challenges to the system. However, before there was an outcome in the *White* court case, the NFLPA and the NFL engaged in a series of negotiations in November 1992, and a compromise was eventually reached in January 1993.[26]

As part of the compromise, owners agreed to a form of free agency, but in return they wanted a salary cap. The NFLPA accepted this on the condition that it would only be implemented if player costs exceeded 64 percent of defined gross revenue; defined gross revenue was approximately 95 percent of total NFL revenue. The salary caps for the remaining years of the agreement were set at 64 percent of defined gross revenue in 1994, 63 percent in 1995, and 62 percent for the remainder of the agreement.

Although there was now a salary cap, it was porous in nature. As Backman notes, the agreement permitted "a team to prorate the dollar amount of a signing bonus over the course of a player's contract, and only the prorated or allocated portion counts against the Cap during each contract year." In addition, teams could use individual and team bonuses at the end of the year "to avoid the Cap ceiling during a given year." Thus, while the owners wanted a salary cap, they also did not mind loopholes in it that permitted them to go above the cap if they deemed it necessary to sign and/or retain certain players. In a tradeoff for agreeing to a salary cap, the agreement stated that players' salaries had to be at least 58 percent of defined gross revenue. Players' getting a majority of NFL revenue was, obviously, no longer "alien to American business."

Under the new free agency rules, teams were allowed to exempt one so-called franchise player for the duration of his career. However, that player had to be paid at least the average of the top five salaries for his position or 120 percent of his previous year's salary. Starting in 1993, a team would be able to match another team's offer for a "transition player." If the player did eventually sign with another team, the original team was awarded compensation. On each roster, two players in 1993, and one player in 1994 who was in the last year of his contract, could be labeled a transition player. All other players were allowed free agency after five years of service time in the NFL. But if the salary cap limit was reached, players with four years' service were eligible for free agency. The salary cap was indeed reached in 1993, so more players were granted free agency.

The new free agency rules led to more than one hundred players per year changing teams during each year of the agreement except in 1995. More players changed teams in the first year of the agreement than in all other previous years combined. As expected, free agency also led to increased player salaries. In 1995, the average salary increased to $584,000 and by 2000 it was $787,000, a tenfold increase from 1980. The number of million-dollar contracts increased from 120 in 1993 to more than 520 in 2000. In addition, the NFL paid $195 million in damages for antitrust lawsuits, including *White v. NFL.*

As there was no further antitrust litigation in the works, the NFLPA, following authorization from a majority of players, once again became a union. This led to a new seven-year collective bargaining agreement being reached on May 6, 1993. The players voted 952 to 34 in favor of the agreement. In addition to the free agency rules, all player pensions were increased by 40 percent, with former players who had played prior to 1959 receiving a pension for the first time. Players also received improved health and severance insurance. The NFL also benefited from increased television revenue. It signed a new agreement covering 1994–97 worth $4.4 billion, an annual income per team of $39.2 million.[27]

Despite some misgivings, both sides were relatively satisfied with the 1993 collective agreement and free agency rules. NFL commissioner Paul Tagliabue stated that "[t]he clubs recognized they'd have to be pragmatic and accept free agency in some form and the Players Association recognized that they would have to accept some mechanism to allow the teams to maintain some kind of structure to operate and the league to grow." Likewise, Upshaw noted, "Before, the best players were frozen and couldn't move. Now the starters can find out what they're worth in the marketplace. We forced the traditionally cheap teams to spend, and we increased benefits drastically."

Of course, not everyone was happy with the NFLPA agreeing to a salary cap. Former MLBPA head Marvin Miller was always strongly opposed to a salary cap. In 2011 he claimed, "No legitimate union could ever agree to a salary cap. In my mind, if a union did that, if would be grounds for decertification, for membership to go court. They were not representing their goal in the law: to improve the wages, hours and working conditions of its members." Nonetheless, as both the players and the owners were content with the 1993 collective bargaining agreement, or at the very least tired of constant labor disputes and lawsuits, it was extended in 1998 and again in 2001 with only minor modifications related to minimum salary and disciplinary issues. During this period, NFL annual revenue increased from $1.7 billion in 1993 to $6.1 billion in 2005. Likewise, the salary cap increased from $34.6 million per team in 1994 to $85.5 million in 2005. By 2005, the average player salary was $1.4 million, although much of that derived from the wages of star players. While the average player salary increased by almost $1 million between 1995 and 2005, the median salary only increased by $268,000, to $569,000. Thus, even though all players benefited from the modified free agency rules, the greatest benefit went to the superstars and not your so-called lesser players.[28]

While both sides were happy to extend the 1993 collective bargaining agreement twice, the NFLPA was concerned that there was an increase in revenue not counted as defined gross revenue. As Quinn notes, defined gross revenue "included home and visitor shares of gate receipts and national and licensing revenues, but not venue revenues such as parking, concessions, sponsorships, and luxury seating income. Furthermore, personal seat license revenues used for stadium construction were also not included." During the 1990s and 2000s a number of new stadiums were built, and "owners specifically emphasized maximizing revenues that were not counted toward DGR or shared with other teams. Consequently, the percentage of total revenues going toward player pay fell from 70.8% in 2000 to 62.3% in 2005." This was the main sticking point in finalizing a new agreement. Nonetheless, in 2006 the NFLPA and the owners negotiated a new collective bargaining agreement after weeks of sometimes hostile negotiations. In the end, neither side wanted further labor strife at a time when the NFL's visibility, popularity, and marketability were continually on the rise.

Under the 2006 agreement, the salary cap was now calculated on the basis of all football-related revenue minus $1 billion, rather than defined gross revenue. By way of comparison, player salaries had been 55.1 percent of football-related revenue in 2005, but under the new agreement they received 58.4 percent of football-related revenue. The cap was set at $102 million in 2006 and $109 million in 2007. Signing bonuses were still allowed to be prorated. In a benefit to the players and the richer teams, the number of years a signing bonus could be prorated was increased by one year, to five in 2006, to six in 2007, and then reduced back to five in 2007. This meant that the players' income was approximately 14 percent above the salary cap limit. The owners voted thirty to two for the deal. Pittsburgh Steelers owner Dan Rooney stated at the time, "It was a compromise by all parties and I think that makes it great." The NFLPA was also happy with the outcome, especially as it meant somewhere between $850 million to $900 million going to the players over the life of the agreement. In addition, there was also revenue sharing; the fifteen most profitable teams every year would contribute to a fund that would be divided among all teams, which in turn would be used in part to pay players' salaries. NFLPA attorney Jeffrey Kessler claimed that "[t]he union is delighted. . . . The new CBA is a big leap forward for the players and means a fairer system for all. It also means seven more years of labor peace. Fans can now forget about the lawyers and owners and enjoy football."[29] Unfortunately, there would not be seven years of labor peace.

The 2011 Lockout

In 2008, the salary cap increased further, to $116 million. For the highest-revenue team, the Washington Redskins, this only amounted to 35 percent of their revenue; but for the lowest, the Detroit Lions, it was 56 percent. There was concern from the owners that the disparity was increasing between the high-revenue and low-revenue teams, which led the owners to opt out of the collective bargaining agreement in 2008 although it was not due to expire until March 2011. NFL commissioner Roger Goodell, in an e-mail to Gene Upshaw, outlined the reasons why the NFL was opting out of the deal, citing high labor costs, problems with the rookie pool, and the teams' inability to recoup bonuses from players who refused to perform and/or otherwise breached their contracts.

While the increasing gap in revenues was undoubtedly a factor for some owners, and the disparity between the richest and poorest NFL teams did increase in 2009, another reason the owners opted out was that they believed they could get the NFLPA to agree to concessions. The NFL claimed, "The current labor agreement does not adequately recognize the cost of generating the revenues of which the players receive the largest shares; nor does the agreement recognize that those costs have increased substantially—and at an ever increasing rate—in recent years during a difficult economic climate in our country." However, a 2009 study by *Forbes* estimated that of the thirty-two NFL teams, nineteen were worth more than $1 billion, with the lowest valuation belonging to the Oakland Raiders, who were worth "only" $797 million. Only two teams, Oakland and the Seattle Seahawks, showed negative operating income for 2008. Moreover, in 2006, the NFL had signed a six-year television contract with its broadcast partners worth $22.41 billion. That amounted to $3.735 billion per year or approximately $117 million annual revenue for each of the thirty-two teams. NFL revenues had also increased by 12 percent for the period 2007 to 2009, even though the United States was experiencing a severe economic downturn.[30]

The players were due to receive approximately 59 percent of $7.5 billion, as guaranteed them under the 2006 collective bargaining agreement. However, by opting out of the agreement, the owners sought to force the players to accept $1 billion in concessions, or approximately

18 percent of the revenue pool. The owners wanted to use the money they recovered to build new stadiums. Their argument was that new stadiums would lead to increased revenues in the future, which would benefit all concerned. Considering that the average NFL player's career lasts 3.5 years, the majority of players were thus being asked to sacrifice a great deal for the future generations of players. This in turn assumes, of course, that the owners would actually pass the increased revenue on to the players. In view of the history of labor relations in the NFL, it might be assumed that such an action would occur only after major conflict and/or court cases.

In addition to the concessions, the NFL wanted to increase the length of the regular season to eighteen games from the current sixteen. In return, the number of preseason games would be reduced by two. While in theory the number of games would remain the same under this plan, preseason games have always been largely meaningless affairs in which the majority of regular players only participate for one half or less. Moreover, the intensity level is a lot lower. By increasing the regular season schedule, the NFL was asking the players to play more meaningful games, despite the increased likelihood of injury, and to do so for less money. Such a situation was obviously not palatable to the NFLPA or the players. In response, the NFLPA offered $138 million in concessions. It would also be willing to accept an eighteen-game season as long as rosters were increased by either one or two players to fifty-four or fifty-five and game day rosters increased to either forty-eight or fifty from the current forty-five. Moreover, the NFLPA wanted practice squad rosters to increase by two, to ten.

While expanded rosters would mean increased employment opportunities for players, as well as more members for the NFLPA, the expansion of the schedule would still mean that an overwhelming majority of players would play more meaningful minutes every year. As we shall see below, NFL players' health, especially in regard to head injuries, is increasingly becoming an area of concern. It is certainly arguable whether the NFLPA should have supported the NFL's desire for more games under any circumstances, especially since in a 2010 poll NFL players voted against increasing the schedule by a margin of 84 to 16 percent.[31]

During the negotiations, an important court case was coming to an end. American Needle sued the NFL, claiming that NFL Properties' ten-year agreement with Reebok violated Section 1 of the Sherman Act because it was a conspiracy. While a lower court found that the NFL was a single entity, the Supreme Court ruled that the NFL could not get total single-entity status. Instead, each case brought against the league would have to be determined on its merits. This ruling was crucial as the NFL was claiming that despite there being a number of teams the league was a single entity, and as such it could not conspire and in turn should be exempt from antitrust laws. It was also important to the players, as the ruling allowed the NFLPA the opportunity to decertify, allege that the NFL was acting as a cartel, and sue the NFL for violation of antitrust laws, as it previously had in the *McNeil* court case.[32] The Supreme Court's ruling strengthened the NFLPA's bargaining position.

In an attempt to reach a compromise, the NFL dropped its demand for $1 billion in concessions. Instead, it asked for $650 million in concessions and then, as the negotiations were going down to the wire, stated that it wanted the players to give up "only" $325 million. With the two sides unable to reach a compromise, and to prevent the NFL from imposing a lockout, on March 11, 2011, the NFLPA decertified, mere hours before the 2006 collective bargaining agreement was set to expire, on the premise that because the association was no longer a union the players could take the NFL to court on antitrust grounds.

The NFL released a statement criticizing the NFLPA's maneuver. The league stated, "At a time when thousands of employees are fighting for their collective bargaining rights, this union has chosen to abandon collective bargaining in favor of a sham 'decertification' and antitrust litigation. This litigation maneuver is built on the indisputably false premise that the NFLPA has stopped being a union and will merely delay the process of reaching an agreement." The NFL prepared for a fight by extending its television deal and guaranteeing itself $4 billion, which it would receive even if no games were played. The NFLPA argued that the league had accepted a worse television deal just for the guaranteed funds, to which the NFL replied that the money was only a loan and would be repaid with interest. Eventually, following a series of court cases during the lockout, it was ruled that the NFL did indeed accept less money than it should have, thereby placing its own interests above the players' and causing the players economic harm. This could have resulted in hundreds of millions of dollars in damages, and it gave the NFLPA leverage in the negotiations during the lockout.

Eventually, no damages were awarded to the players, as the case was dismissed as soon as the NFL and NFLPA finalized a new collective bargaining agreement. Of course, the court cases were still to happen. And on March 12, 2011, the NFL locked out the players. In response, several star players, including Tom Brady, Drew Brees, and Peyton Manning, filed a class action lawsuit against the NFL. The players attempted to get an injunction against the lockout on antitrust grounds. While the players were initially successful and the lockout was suspended for one day, the NFL appealed the decision to the Eighth Circuit Court of Appeals. The appeals court temporarily stayed the order on April 29, which meant the lockout could resume. This was reaffirmed on July 8, as the appeals court ruled that the lockout could continue.

However, the NFL and the NFLPA continued negotiations during the court cases and the lockout was nearing an end. Throughout the lockout there was very good solidarity between the players and the NFLPA kept the players informed on how the negotiations were progressing. This was in marked contrast to previous lockouts and strikes and certainly helped the NFLPA's bargaining efforts. The players also benefited because the public generally sided with them. The players were not making excessive demands; they did not want to be forced to accept wide-ranging concessions. The players were willing to play for the same wages and conditions as under the previous contract. It was the owners, despite the size of their profits, that wanted more. This resonated with the public, because across America companies were demanding concessions from their workforces irrespective if the company was profitable or not. As Pittsburgh Steeler Troy Polamalu stated, "It's unfortunate right now. I think what the players are fighting for is something bigger. A lot of people think it's millionaires versus billionaires, and that's the huge argument. The fact is, it's people fighting against big business. The big-business argument is, 'I got the money, and I got the power, therefore I can tell you what to do.' That's life everywhere. I think this is a time when the football players are standing up and saying, 'No, no, no, the people have the power.'"

Also helping the NFLPA's cause was that it had secretly secured insurance in the event that there was a work stoppage lasting the entire 2011–12 season, which would have paid every player approximately $200,000. A source told Sports Illustrated that the "Players Association leadership looked into this as a last possible resort to keep players together in case games would be missed. . . . It was never intended to be used as a bargaining chip or negotiating point until things became critical." The NFLPA revealed the previously secret insurance deal to the owners in July. The insurance money, combined with any potential damages awarded to the players due to the NFL agreeing to a substandard television deal, would have helped player unity in the event the lockout continued. This revelation was another possible impetus to get the owners thinking about the settlement. On July 14, the two sides announced that an agreement had been finalized. After 127 days, the longest work stoppage ever in the NFL, the lockout had come to an end. Crucially, despite the length of the lockout, no regular season games had been lost.[33]

The new collective bargaining agreement was a 10-year deal from which neither party can opt out. Thus, there is a guarantee of no work stoppage until at least 2021. Importantly for the players, the season remains at sixteen games, but there is an option to extend it to eighteen games if the NFLPA desires it to be so. In regard to revenue, the salary cap was set at $120 million for the 2011 season; it had been $128 million in 2009. However, for the 2012–2020 seasons a new system was devised to determine the amount that goes to players. Previously, players received approximately 59 percent of the money in the revenue pool. From the 2012 season onward, players will receive 55 percent of media revenue, 45 percent of licensing revenue, and 40 percent of local team revenue. As Quinn notes, the salary cap "must average at least 47% of total league revenue over the life of the CBA. Owners no longer take $1 billion off the top, but teams now receive credit for actual stadium investments, up to 1.5% of revenue each year." Teams can also borrow 1.5 percent of salary cap money from a future year. Finally, teams must average at least 89 percent of the salary cap for the 2013–16 and 2017–20 periods. On the basis of the new salary cap rules, players received approximately 51 percent under the 2006 agreement. In the 2011 agreement, players only received 47 percent, quite a large reduction. Minimum salary was set at $375,000 for rookies in 2011, a 17 percent increase from 2010; players with two years of service were guaranteed $450,000; those with three years' service, $600,000; four to six year veterans, $685,000; seven to nine year veterans, $810,000; and ten-plus year NFL veterans will receive at least $910,000 a year. The minimum salary across all categories increased by $15,000 in 2012 and 2013, and did so again in 2014. In a big win for the NFLPA, all players will now be eligible for the NFL's health plan for the rest of their lives. Previously they could only be part of the health plan for five years after their career was over. Considering the injuries NFL players accrue, this is a major positive. The big losers were rookies, who will receive vastly reduced salaries, with the money instead going to veterans and retired players. Players drafted in the first round are limited to four-year contracts with an option for a fifth year. Players drafted in all other rounds must sign a four-year deal. The reduced salaries for rookies are demonstrated by comparing the number one picks in the 2010 and 2011 drafts.

As Deubert, Wong, and Howe note, the number one pick in the 2010 draft, Sam Bradford, signed a six-year, $76 million deal with the St. Louis Rams. The contract could end up being worth as much as $86 million, with $50 million guaranteed. In contrast, the number one pick in the 2011 draft, Cam Newton, signed a four-year, $22,025,498 deal with the Carolina Panthers. If the Panthers exercise the option year, the deal will be worth $36 million over five years. Nonetheless, most first and second round draft picks received an increase in the guaranteed portion of their contracts. Indeed, more and more players at every level are receiving at least part of their contracts guaranteed, which is a very positive development. In this regard, in a win for the NFLPA, a player with a multiyear contracts who suffers a season-ending injury is indemnified against being cut from the team and will receive up to $1 million for one year and up to $500,000 after a second year following the injury. Likewise, under the terms of the agreement, the NFL created a Legacy Benefit Fund that will help players who played before the 1993 season, as well as their widows and other survivors. The Benefit Fund will be funded to the tune of $620 million over the course of the collective bargaining agreement.[34]

Overall, there were no clear winners or losers from the 2011 collective bargaining agreement, but the owners achieved some concessions they were after, and if it had been a boxing match they probably would have "won on points." While the NFL did gain concessions from the players in the form of a pay cut, the league was not able to extend the season to eighteen games. Likewise, considering the past failures of the NFLPA to achieve decent collective bargaining agreements for its members following work stoppages, that it was able to prevent an extension to the schedule and to minimize salary reductions is a positive. In addition, there was very good player solidarity throughout the duration of the lockout and the star players were often at the forefront of the struggle, which certainly helped in the NFLPA's bargaining efforts. That the NFLPA also kept in constant communication with the players also helped. This was the first work stoppage in NFL history where the players did not undermine the NFLPA's bargaining efforts. Considering that the average career for a player is only 3.5 years long, the unity they displayed throughout the lockout was quite impressive, and for that alone, the lockout must be considered a positive step for the NFLPA and the players. After all, not everything should come down to dollars and cents. There are things more important; arguably the most important is the players' health and safety.

Head Injuries in the NFL

Football is a violent sport. There is no disputing that. While the players wear padding and helmets, injuries occur in almost every game. Moreover, injuries also happen quite often in practice. Broken bones, hamstring strains, and the like can heal. However, for players suffering head injuries, specifically concussions, the result may be a lifetime of pain and misery. It is estimated that in the NFL, players suffer hundreds of concussions per year.

In 2012, NFL teams reported that their players suffered 240 concussions. A study found that more than 60 percent of NFL players suffer at least one concussion during their playing careers. However, not all teams adequately report the number of concussions incurred by their players. Such an approach jeopardizes player safety.

Andre Waters estimated that he suffered numerous concussions over the course of his NFL career. He stopped counting when he reached fifteen. In 2006, Waters killed himself. In a posthumous examination, his brain "resembled that of an octogenarian Alzheimer's patient." The examining doctor concluded that the damage "was caused or expedited by successive concussions he suffered playing football." Unfortunately, Waters is only one of the growing list of former NFL players who have committed suicide before turning fifty. In another sad tale, Steve Hendrickson was a championship player for the San Francisco '49ers. He was a special teams madman, seemingly having no concern for his body in the way he flung himself around. During his playing career he suffered fifteen grade 3 concussions. A grade 3 concussion is one in which the player blacks out. Today, Hendrickson suffers from mood swings and depression. He has been unable to work for the last six years. He claims, "I would swear I got up and went to work, but I was asleep. . . . When I did show up, they'd tell me what to do, and I'd say, 'You never taught me that.' They'd look at me and say, 'We taught it to you yesterday.'"

Unfortunately, examples like Waters and Hendrickson are all too common. In a study commissioned by the NFL on 2,552 former NFL players aged between thirty and forty-nine, it was found they suffer memory-related diseases at a rate nineteen times higher than males who did not play in the NFL. Likewise, retired NFL players who had played in the league for at least five years were more likely to suffer Alzheimer's or Lou Gehrig's disease. In a study of 334 players who played between 1959 and 1998, Alzheimer's was the contributing factor in seven deaths and Lou Gehrig's disease was the contributing factor in seven more. For 334 random members of the general public, each disease would be a contributing factor in only two deaths. While the sample size is relatively small, the lead researcher called the findings statistically significant. Indeed, it is likely an increasing number of former and current NFL players are suffering from CTE. CTE is Chronic Traumatic Encephalopathy, a "degenerative disease that effects the brain and [is] believed to be caused by repeated head trauma resulting in large accumulations of tau proteins, killing cells in regions responsible for mood, emotions, and executive functioning. Basically it is a condition that appears only after a long time of abuse to the brain." Unfortunately, CTE can only be diagnosed once a person is dead. Due to the increasing concern about players suffering concussions, the NFL implemented rule changes regulating when players can return to the field after an injury and where players may hit each other.[35]

However, a lot more can and should be done. As concussion expert Chris Nowinski argues, "We can prevent them with rule changes, recognize them better and treat them better. . . . But the bigger change in dramatically reducing how we practice the game. Seventy-five percent of hits happen in practice when no one is keeping score. If this is bad for you, we should eliminate them from practice and save hits for the game. If we did that, we would lower everyone's exposure by 50 percent." In a positive step, the 2011 collective bargaining agreement eliminates twice-a-day practices where the players are padded up and also limits full-contact practice to only fourteen days during the season. Moreover, the offseason program for the players has been reduced by five weeks. This will result in fewer injuries and, hopefully, prolong NFL careers.

The agreement also outlined the formation of a Neuro-Cognitive Disability Benefit for players who played for at least one season after 1994. This is in addition to the 88 Plan that was previously discussed. Under the Disability Benefit scheme a player suffering from a Neuro-Cognitive disability may receive at least $3,000 a month for up to fifteen years. Moreover, beginning in the 2013–14 season there have been "Unaffiliated Neuro-trauma Consultants" on the sidelines for each game. The independent consultants, who are not paid by the particular teams, will determine whether a player should undertake the concussion test in the locker room.

These are positive developments. However, if a player receives compensation through the Neuro-Cognitive Disability Benefit scheme he must agree never to sue the NFL. This is of particular importance to the NFL because more than 4,500 former players have sued the league on the grounds that it failed to protect them from concussions. Over two hundred suits were filed against the NFL and consolidated into one court case being overseen by the Federal Court in Philadelphia.[36] The case, which was settled in August 2013, was then revised following U.S. District Court Judge Anita Brody's deeming the proposed settlement figure inadequate, due to there being a limit on the amount players could receive. Under the proposed settlement, the NFL agreed to pay approximately $765 million, with $675 million going to more than 4,500 players. The overall settlement includes $75 million for scientific tests and $10 million for further research. The most a player with Alzheimer's may receive is $5 million. Players who are diagnosed with CTE will receive a maximum of $4 million. Players who have dementia will receive up to $3 million. While it may seem a lot of money, the settlement works out to be $23.9 million per team, payable over the course of twenty years. The majority of players in the lawsuit will receive less than $100,000 apiece. Crucially, by settling the case, the NFL has not admitted any responsibility, and it is unlikely the league will have to make public when it knew concussions were a problem and whether it covered up this information. In response, NFLPA President Kevin Mawae stated, "The NFL doesn't have to say anything, admit any wrong doing, or even apologize . . . the same league that once called players 'cattle' and themselves the 'herders' have just put the herd back into the pen."

The NFL's concern about what it knew about concussions and when it knew it was further demonstrated when its broadcast partner ESPN backed out of a partnership with PBS to produce a documentary on head injuries in the NFL. While both ESPN and the NFL deny that the league influenced the decision, it would be very foolish for either of them to admit it publicly. *The New York Times* reported that the NFL pressured ESPN to abandon the partnership with PBS.[37]

In the end, despite the NFL taking some steps in the right direction when it comes to concussions and head injuries, there is still a long way to go. The NFL should shelve any plans to increase the regular season schedule. An increase in the schedule, while certainly lucrative to all concerned, would come at the cost of increased injuries to the players, shorter careers, and more concussions. In the end, what is more important, profit or people?

4

NBA

The Rise and Fall of the NBPA

The National Basketball Association (NBA) has become a global phenomenon; players from around the world now ply their trade under its auspices. Its initials are instantly recognizable in almost every country on Earth. Unlike the other three big American professional sports, which have attempted, and generally failed, to capture the imaginations of people around the globe, basketball is truly an international sport. Michael Jordan, the NBA's most famous player ever, is a multinational legend, instantly recognized by hundreds of millions of people in places as diverse as Australia, the United Kingdom, and China.[1]

In China, thanks largely to the exploits of Jordan, and more recently former Houston Rockets player Yao Ming and other Chinese players who made it to the NBA, basketball is fast becoming the number one sport, played by an estimated three hundred million people. The Chinese people, like most fans of the game, love the sheer athleticism of the NBA.

NBA players, both past—Julius "Dr. J" Erving, Earvin "Magic" Johnson, Larry Bird, Michael Jordan—and present—Kobe Bryant, Kevin Durant, Lebron James—are graceful and majestic, with individual skills that the general public can only regard with awe. Indeed, the NBA in recent years has moved away from presenting a team-oriented game to showcasing one wherein the individual skills of the players are increasingly on display. Whether the focus on individualism makes the game better depends, of course, on one's preference.

Despite this individualism, NBA players, like players in other sports (and employees around the globe), all want fair wages and decent working conditions. Unlike players in MLB, the NFL, and the NHL, NBA players have never engaged in a league-wide strike to put economic pressure on the owners to achieve these ends. Their collective voice, the National Basketball Players' Association, has been in existence since 1954, and until recently it was assumed that the absence of any walkout or other serious public confrontation between labor and management during those sixty years indicated a harmonious relationship. In fact, the relationship between the NBA and its players has often been tumultuous, and although there was never a work stoppage before 1995—and this one was caused mostly by a civil war within the players' union—there have been a number of lawsuits over the years filed by the players against the league, and since the 1990s a noticeable increase in hostile rhetoric expressed by both sides.

Hostilities culminated in the 2011 lockout, which led to huge economic losses for the players and the season almost being abandoned. As much as one might admire the individualism of the players on the court, this same individualism in recent years has cost them at the bargaining table. Like their brethren in the NFL and NHL, NBA players have often lacked solidarity during conflicts with management, which has led to concessions resulting in less than fair compensation for their labor. Players' individualism and athletic skills may have enabled them to play in the global phenomenon that is the NBA, but their lack of teamwork has cost them in the arena of labor struggle.

The Birth of the NBA and the NBPA

The NBA was formed in August 3, 1949, by the merger of the National Basketball League (NBL) and the Basketball Association of America (BAA). The NBA considers the BAA, which came into existence in 1946, as the precursor to the modern league. The NBA's official Web site lists the three seasons of the BAA before the merger as part of NBA history. In the BAA's first season, the average player salary was between $4,000 and $5,000, with a salary cap in place of $55,000. A few top stars earned substantially more. Detroit Falcon Tom King earned $16,500; however, he also was the team's publicity director and business manager. Likewise, Philadelphia Warriors player Joe Fulks earned a decent wage: his salary was $8,000. The merger had the effect of stopping the bidding wars between the two rival leagues for college players. *The New York Times*, in one of its few articles on the NBA in 1949, noted that the merger would prevent contracts being handed out to "big-time" college players that were excessive and threatened the livelihood of many teams.

In contrast to the relative restraint of the BAA owners in their first season, the period between 1947 and 1949 saw some players rewarded handsomely. For example, the best player of the decade, George Mikan of the Chicago American Gears, signed a five-year contract worth more than $60,000, Rochester Royals player Bob Davis signed a four-year $50,000 contract, and in 1947 future Hall of Famer Jim Pollard signed a one-year deal with the Minneapolis Lakers worth $12,000.[2]

Nineteen forty-nine, the first season of the NBA, saw seventeen teams compete for the title, with the Minneapolis Lakers defeating the Syracuse Nationals four games to two to be crowned the first NBA champion. However, in the following year the NBA was down to eleven teams, then ten teams in 1951, nine in 1953, and by 1954 the league consisted of only eight teams. Quite simply, the early years of the league were not a success. Considering the struggles of the NBA as a whole, then, it was not a surprise that the players were also having a rough time. Before the formation of the National Basketball Players' Association (NBPA), they did not have a minimum salary, a pension plan, health benefits, a per diem, and when the number of NBA teams had been cut by more than half there were a lot fewer job opportunities for players.[3] In other words, while the star players were looked after, most players were playing for the love of the game rather than economic rewards.

The NBA's number one player, Bob Cousy, was not content with the situation. In 1954, when the players were forced to compete in twenty-one consecutive exhibition games, he wrote to the star player on each of the other teams—Philadelphia's Paul Arizin, New York's Carl Braun, Rochester's Bob Davies, Baltimore's Paul Hoffman, Fort Wayne's Andy Phillip, Syracuse's Dolph Schayes, Milwaukee's Don Sunderlage, as well as Pollard—seeking support for the formation of a union. There was near-unanimous support for the idea, with only Phillip against the idea, probably because the Pistons' owner was staunchly antiunion. With this overwhelming mandate, in 1954 the NBPA formed, with Cousy as president.[4]

At the 1955 NBA All-Star Game, Cousy met with NBA president Maurice Podoloff and presented him with a series of demands. They included the elimination of the $15 so-called "whispering fine" that referees could inflict on a player during a game for talking or protesting a decision, as well as a request that players from the defunct Baltimore Bullets receive the salaries that they were still owed. Podoloff agreed to provide two weeks' salary for the Bullets' players and arranged to meet with the association within a fortnight to discuss the other issues.

However, despite his promise to meet with the players, Podoloff, and the owners, ignored the NBPA for the following two years. In this regard they were no different than owners in other major sports: when faced with a players' union/association for the first time, they ignored it in hopes that it would go away.

Eventually, after two years of inaction on the part of the NBA, Cousy and the NBPA had enough. The players were annoyed by the no strike clause in their contracts and in January 1957 met with representatives of the American Guild of Variety Artists regarding the possibility of the NBPA's becoming affiliated with them. In fact, Cousy did not want the players either to strike or to become affiliated with a union. He later noted that "[e]veryone knows that's [striking] so illegal . . . it's laughable. But we want to be heard and if joining a union, which we hate to do unless we have to, is the only way of being heard . . . then that's it!" Nonetheless, the threat was a sufficient cause for concern for Podoloff and the owners that they recognized the NBPA in April 1957.

The NBA committed to the formation of an arbitration procedure for player grievances; players received meal money of seven dollars a day, an increase of between one and two dollars; for a trial period, referees could no longer fine players during a game; and the league agreed to meet annually with the NBPA. The spokesperson for the union's player representatives, St. Louis Hawk and future Hall of Famer Ed Macauley, stated, "We believe this is extremely fair—we believe the players will be happy with this." Likewise, Cousy later claimed, "My biggest win was getting the meal money bumped from $5 to $7. Getting that concession made me a hero."[5]

While he was laughing when he made that statement, it is doubtful that the players considered Cousy anything resembling a hero. The NBPA's demands were not excessive in the least; it is hardly surprising that the league agreed to them. There was no request for a minimum salary, a pension, and/or health insurance. Cousy was quite conciliatory with the owners. He was generally happy with the little they would provide; after all, the players were, in his words, playing a "child's game." Cousy said in 1959 that the "owners have been extremely fair with us money-wise. Frankly, I don't know of one player who is dissatisfied with his salary." Such a statement is quite remarkable. Moreover, Cousy was wrong about how satisfied the players were; in fact, they were generally displeased by the performance of both Cousy and the NBPA, as was demonstrated by the refusal by many players to pay the ten dollars in dues they owed the NBPA in 1957. Cousy claimed that only forty-one players actually did pay, which frustrated him to such an extent that in 1958 he resigned as NBPA president. He was replaced by his Boston Celtics teammate Tom Heinsohn.[6]

Heinsohn was not as conciliatory toward the NBA and the owners Cousy had been. To begin, he pushed for the formation of a pension plan for the players, which came to fruition with the NBA's acceptance, in January 1961, of a scheme by which the owners would match the players' yearly $500 contributions. The pension plan would be available to any player with five years' service time in the NBA. However, the NBA reneged on the deal and engaged in a series of stalling tactics, which was successful for a number of years.

During this period, Heinsohn hired Lawrence Fleisher as the NBPA's general counsel. This appointment was to prove to be a master stroke. Fleisher, like Marvin Miller, viewed the situation as a struggle that pitted the players against the owners and the NBA, a case of "us versus them." He continually harangued the owners over the pension and pushed the union in a more militant direction. Before the start of the All-Star Game in January 1964, the players demanded that the owners put the pension approval in writing, even though the plan had already been signed off on by new NBA president Walter Kennedy. The start of the game was delayed by almost thirty minutes while the players held a meeting to decide whether to play after Kennedy had insisted it would be impossible for the owners to sign the pension approval at that time, although he agreed to call them on the phone. An unnamed player stated, "We were ready to refuse to play . . . because we feel the owners have been putting off a pension plan and have not been fair about it." Eventually, the players decided to participate, and the East beat the West by a score of 111–107.

The players made it known that if the pension plan was not approved at the owners' meeting in May 1964, further steps could be taken, including some star players refusing to sign contracts for the following season. This annoyed the owners, and Heinsohn's boss, Boston Celtics owner Walter Brown, labeled him the "No. 1 heel in sports." While he may have been a heel to the owners, Heinsohn was a "good guy" to the players.

In May, the owners approved the pension deal. Under the terms of the plan, the pension was in the form of a thirty-year endowment insurance policy for each player worth $2,000. The owners would contribute half and the players the other half.[7] The pension approval was to be Heinsohn's great success. He stepped down as NBPA President in 1966 and was replaced by Cincinnati Royals player Oscar Robertson.

Robertson continued to pursue the more militant strategy first started by Heinsohn; he was ably helped in this regard by Fleisher, and in 1967 the NBPA negotiated the first collective bargaining agreement in NBA history. Following the All-Star break in January, Robertson sent NBA president Walter Kennedy a letter outlining the NBPA's demands; chief among these were an increase in owner contributions to the pension plan, a reduction in the number of games, health benefits, and a minimum wage. In regard to the pension plan, the owners offered to increase the policy to $4,000 per player, and to pay 75 percent of the cost. However, only players who signed a contract in September 1967 would be eligible for a pension, and previous service time would not count. A ten-year veteran would receive a minimum of $500 a month. Robertson noted that as a seven-year veteran, if he retired under the terms the owners were proposing his pension would only be $75 per month. In contrast, the NBPA wanted all current and former ten-year veteran players to receive $600 a month. With no action taking place on the owners' part, in early March, at a news conference, Fleisher stated, "First, we are immediately filing with the National Labor Relations Board to be the first player union certified with the NLRB. . . . Second, we will not participate in any playoff games this year." Helping the NBPA's bargaining effort was that the players were solidly behind it: 117 out of 120 players supported striking if their demands were not met. Both the NBA and the media continually emphasized that any strike would be illegal, as all players were under contract. In response, Robertson said, "So what if we're bound by our contracts. . . . Workers at General Motors can take a vote to go on strike–I don't see why we can't." Following thirty-six hours of negotiations between Fleisher and Kennedy, and two hours before the league's self-imposed deadline, an agreement was reached.

The key terms of the collective bargaining agreement included: the owners acceptance of the NBPA's demand that the pension be increased to $600 a month, with ten-year veterans receiving it once they had been retired for thirty years; a health and medical plan for the players; a $20,000 life insurance policy for each player; and days off before and after the All-Star Game. The NBPA was very happy with the outcome. Fleisher stated, "Never since the turn of the century has a group of athletes joined together and remained united under such trying circumstances. . . . That loyalty has now been amply rewarded." Likewise,

Robertson affirmed that "I'm very well pleased. I had been hoping for this all along." Through strong leadership, a militant approach, and, most crucially, united players, the NBPA had achieved a successful collective bargaining agreement.[8]

For the NBPA, success continued to follow when, before the start of the 1968–69 season, the union negotiated a minimum salary agreement with the NBA. For the 1968–69 season, the minimum wage for rookies was set at $10,000; this would rise to $12,500 in 1969–70 and $13,500 in 1970–71. Current NBA players received $12,500 for 1968–69, with an increase to $13,500 in 1969–70. Thus, the long-term trend of ever-increasing salaries continued. Whereas in 1956–57 the average salary had been only $6,000, by a decade later, in 1966–67, it had more than doubled, to $13,000, and the year after that it jumped dramatically to $20,000.[9]

In October 1970, after months of meetings without any of the acrimony of the previous round of negotiations, the NBPA and the NBA came to terms on a new collective bargaining agreement. The two sides released a statement noting, "Both Commissioner Kennedy and Mr. Fleisher were in agreement that the new terms were arrived at during harmonious sessions and both also expressed the belief that the negotiations between both parties this year had reached a new level of mutual understanding." Under the terms of the agreement, the minimum salary increased to $15,500 for the 1970–71 season, with a further increase to $17,500 for the following season. The latter figure was at the time the highest minimum wage in American professional sports. The daily meal per diem also increased $3, to $19. In addition, the playoff pool, which is divided between teams who have made the playoffs, rose from $400,000 in 1968–69 to $700,000 in 1970–71, with a further $25,000 increase over the following two years.[10] What was significant about this collective bargaining agreement is that the two sides came to terms even though they were battling in court on a different matter.

Nineteen sixty-seven witnessed the formation of a rival to the NBA; namely, the American Basketball Association (ABA). The ABA was the brainchild of sports entrepreneur Gary Davidson, who also went on to form the World Hockey Association. Rather than attempt to directly challenge the NBA, the ABA situated teams in as many cities as possible that did not have existing NBA teams. While initially the majority of the ABA teams employed second-rate players, eventually several NBA players jumped to the rival league. Also, the NBA would only draft players who had completed college; the ABA observed no such restriction, which led to its signing, among others, future stars Moses Malone and Julius "Dr. J." Erving. However, a true bidding war for players never eventuated.

In 1969, the ABA and the NBA began merger talks, and in 1970 the eleven ABA teams agreed to pay a combined $11 million to join the NBA. However, the NBPA was against the merger, reasoning that it would lead to less competition, with fewer hiring opportunities and, potentially, lower salaries for players. The union filed an antitrust lawsuit opposing it and succeeded in persuading the federal court to issue a preliminary injunction against the merger. In response, the NBA and the ABA tried to get Congress to issue an antitrust exemption for basketball. However, their efforts failed.

Legal wrangling delayed the merger for a number of years, but finally, in June 1976, the last obstacles were removed and the NBA and ABA united. The ABA had been a money pit for its team owners, who lost approximately $50 million over the course of the league'sexistence, and by 1976 only six of its teams remained in operation. Four of them—the Denver Nuggets, Indiana Pacers, New York Nets, and San Antonio Spurs—joined the NBA, after paying $3.2 million apiece. This brought size of the NBA to twenty-two teams at the beginning of the 1976–77 season.[11]

The Reserve Clause in the NBA

In 1955, in *Washington Professional Basketball Corporation v. National Basketball Association*, a group led by Morris Fox sued the league on antitrust grounds. In May of that year, Fox's group thought they had persuaded the Milwaukee Hawks to relocate to Washington, D.C. Instead, the team moved to St. Louis. Fox's group then tried to buy the Baltimore Bullets and were unsuccessful. In response, they filed a $1 million antitrust lawsuit against the NBA, claiming that the league had colluded and prevented them from buying the Baltimore franchise. The suit was unsuccessful, as the United States District Court ruled that there had been no contract between the two parties that could have been violated. However, the court also ruled that because the NBA conducted business across state borders and sold broadcast television rights, it was subject to the Sherman Act.[12]

Even though the court had ruled that the NBA was bound by the Sherman Act, the league still had a reserve clause, whose legality was affirmed by the courts in three separate cases in the 1960s. The first case involved Dick Barnett, who tried to switch from the NBA's Syracuse Nationals to an American Basketball Association team for the 1961–62 season. Even though Barnett did not have a contract with Syracuse, the club contended that they had an oral agreement. The Court of Common Pleas of Ohio found in favor of the Nationals, ruling that there need to be reasonable regulations in place to protect all concerned.

The second court case involved Lou Hudson attempting to back out of a contract to join the ABA team in Minnesota following his departure from the St. Louis Hawks in the NBA. As it happened, Hudson had his option year with the Hawks remaining. The court ruled that Minnesota did not have "unclean hands" in its negotiations with Hudson and that, as such, he was not obligated to join the ABA.

The third case involved Rick Barry. Barry was under contract to play for the NBA's San Francisco Warriors for the 1966 season, and as with all NBA contracts, Barry's had an option year that bound him to the team for the following year. However, Barry signed a three-year contract to play for the ABA's Oakland Oaks beginning in the 1967–68 season. The Warriors took Barry to court and the California Court of Appeals ruled that Barry had to play for San Francisco or he had to sit out his option year and not play with any other team. As part of his ruling, Superior Court Judge Robert J. Drewes stated, "It has been held that substantially identical league practices and contract provisions prevalent in professional football are not illegal as promoting monopolies, either as to cities or as to players. Further upon this record, the restraint on the defendant's [Barry's] freedom to contract imposed by the reserve clause appears to this court to be reasonably necessary to provide the stability and continuity required for the efficient management of such an enterprise." However, at no point in the decision did the court rule that the reserve clause tied a player to a team for the duration of his playing career. Instead, the reserve clause only tied a player to a team for a reasonable amount of time.[13] Of course, the definition of a "reasonable" time was uncertain and might vary from court to court, but in the Barry case the judge's opinion pointed to the conclusion that it comprised just the option year. Within a decade, the reserve clause in any form in basketball would be consigned to history.

As noted above, in 1969 the NBPA, headed by its president, Oscar Robertson, filed a class action lawsuit in an attempt to block the merger between the NBA and ABA. In addition, the lawsuit alleged that the reserve clause, the player draft, as well as uniform player contracts were all in violation of antitrust laws. Uniform player contracts permitted teams to set the terms of the contracts they offered players. A player had to play for the team until he was traded or sold, and if the player refused to play, the club could terminate his contract and prevent him from playing for another team. Under the reserve clause, the contract could be renewed unilaterally by the team for an option year, with a 30 percent reduction in pay. However, in 1971, the NBA proposed that the unilateral renewal be at the same salary as the previous year, with the reserve clause only applicable for an option year, after which, if the player changed teams, his former club was entitled to compensation. Initially, the player's former team could demand the compensation they wanted. If the two teams could not come to an agreement, the NBA commissioner would determine what the compensation should be. In this, it was similar in scope to the NFL's Rozelle Rule.

The NBA was obviously trying to get Congress to approve an antitrust exemption and at the same time to force the NBPA to drop its antitrust lawsuit, so that the merger with the ABA could proceed. When the NBPA rejected the league's proposal, the NBA unilaterally imposed the compensation rule and option year.[14] Despite this, the NBA was unable to convince Congress to grant basketball an antitrust exemption.

Despite the hostility engendered by the antitrust lawsuit, in 1973 the NBPA and the NBA successfully negotiated a new three-year collective bargaining agreement. Under the terms of the agreement, the minimum salary was increased to $20,000; at that time it was the highest in all American professional sports. Players could now receive their pension at age fifty, with benefits increasing to $720 a year for each year of service. Thus, a ten-year veteran would receive $7,200 a year at age fifty, while a fifteen-year veteran received $10,800. Players could have their grievances heard by an independent arbitrator rather than the NBA commissioner. Fleisher claimed that the NBPA "got most of the major issues in collective bargaining to the point where we're [NBPA and NBA] on what I'd call equal footing. Sure we'd like some things better, but that's normal." One area where Fleisher was not willing to compromise was the reserve clause. He declared that "any kind of a reserve or option system is illegal. It violates basic rights. We haven't negotiated this. We've always taken the position that it's illegal. . . . But there's nothing to negotiate."[15]

However, despite the reserve clause, most NBA players were not struggling financially. As previously noted, for the 1967–68 season, the average salary had grown to $20,000, representing approximately 30 percent of team gross revenue, and shortly, due to both the increased power of the NBPA and the rivalry with the ABA, it increased even more dramatically, reaching $90,000 for 1972–73. This was 66 percent of team gross revenue. In 1977, player salaries as a proportion of team gross revenue would peak at 70 percent.[16] While it is easy to blame greedy players wanting more, no one was forcing the NBA owners to grant them such a healthy percentage of gross revenue. As for the reserve clause, while some limitation on player movement might have been necessary, the system employed by the NBA was illegal, a fact that was to be affirmed in court.

In October 1975, the United States District Court ruled that the reserve clause, the player draft, and the uniform contract were all in violation of the Sherman Act. The court stated that: "Some degree of economic cooperation which is inherently anti-competitive may well be essential for the survival of ostensibly competitive professional sports leagues." However, it further noted that the "college draft, a perpetual reserve clause, boycotts, and a proposed merger, absent Congressional approval, or a non-competition agreement are illegal." Not surprisingly, the NBPA was ecstatic. Fleisher wrote a memo to the players stating that the judge's decision is "sensational, brilliant, and devastating to the NBA . . . and while the NBA will probably continue to fight us, it is a major victory that can only strengthen our position enormously." Following the ruling, the players could have filed a class action lawsuit against the NBA for damages, which, if the suit were successful, would have incurred what the NBA's counsel admitted would have been payments "almost too astronomical to contemplate," especially in view of the fact that because of the antitrust context of the violations, any damages awarded by a jury would be tripled.[17] However, before the matter could go that far, the NBPA and NBA negotiated a settlement.

Under the settlement, which was reached in 1976, the NBA paid $4.5 million in damages to approximately five hundred players, plus $1 million in legal fees. The two sides also signed a new collective bargaining agreement. Starting immediately, the option clause would only be applicable to rookie contracts. The compensation agreement imposed by the NBA in 1971 would remain in effect until the end of the 1980–81 season, but beginning in 1980 a new system would be put into place wherein if a player received an offer from another team, the player's current club had the right to match the offer, the so-called right of first refusal.

Another crucial aspect of the new agreement was that the draft remained in place, but with one major change. If a player was drafted but did not want to sign with the team that drafted him, he could sit out a year until another team selected him in the following year's draft. In addition to the change in the free agency rules, the minimum salary was increased from $20,000 to $30,000; players received $75 per month toward their pension as well as (for the first time) cost of living adjustments; meal money increased from $19 to $24 with a further increase to $26 by the end of the contract; better medical and dental coverage were offered; and life insurance increased from $35,000 to $50,000. Finally, there was an increase in the playoff pool and All-Star game payments.

Overall, the 1976 agreement was good for the players monetarily, and they also gained the right to free agency. By the 1979–80 season the average player salary had further increased, to $173,000. The media proclaimed it a near-total victory for the players and an unconditional surrender by the owners. Fleisher stated that "[w]e are happy and delighted with the agreement." Likewise, new NBPA president Paul Silas declared, "The main thing is that now we can concentrate totally on basketball and not worry about the possibility of a strike. . . . This will make for happier times for all of us." Quite ominously, however, and foreshadowing things to come, new NBA commissioner Larry O'Brien noted that "[m]y feeling is that this is an equitable resolution, which is shared by the cast majority of owners, but not all of them."[18] While the players had been overwhelmingly successful in the Robertson lawsuit and subsequent settlement, there were warning signs that the owners would eventually want to regain some of their lost power.

Labor Relations in the 1980s

The collective bargaining agreement having expired at the end of June, the 1979 season began without a contract in place. In the face of increasing payrolls, team owners were attempting to impose a limit on individual salaries beginning in the 1980–81 season. For their part, the players were asking for a share of the NBA's cable television revenue, something the owners staunchly opposed. Due to the deadlock over these issues, there was talk of players going out on strike during the playoffs, but it was lightly regarded by all. NBA commissioner O'Brien noted, "There have been no threats or rancor on either side. . . . A player walkout would be difficult for the league, but I don't believe it will happen." He was correct. Two days after the proposed strike threat surfaced, the NBA and the NBPA negotiated a new three-year collective bargaining agreement. The minimum salary was increased by $5,000 to $35,000, there was an increase in the daily meal money, and in the final year of the agreement NBA rosters increased from eleven to twelve players. In return, the NBPA agreed to drop a lawsuit against the NBA demanding a share of the league's cable television revenue, and to eliminate no-trade clauses from players' contracts.

It was a good couple of days for O'Brien, as in addition to negotiating a new contract with the union, he got the owners to agree to a team in Dallas joining the NBA. Likewise, the contract was beneficial for the players. While they had to make some concessions, there were now more job opportunities for players, and salaries continued to increase at an incredible rate. For the 1980–81 season the average salary was $189,000. This grew to $218,000 in 1981–82, and $246,000 for the 1982–83 season. Free agency had certainly paid off for the players. On the other hand, by 1983 player salaries accounted for more than two-thirds of team revenue; teams were losing an average of $700,000, and the league as a whole approximately $15 million a year.[19] This situation was clearly unacceptable for the owners, and they approached the July 1982 negotiations for the new collective bargaining agreement determined to play hardball.

Representing the league's side were O'Brien and the chief spokesperson for the owners (and future NBA commissioner), David Stern. Representing the players were Fleisher and new NBPA president Bob Lanier, of the Detroit Pistons. The owners sought to reduce rosters from twelve players to ten; they demanded that players fund their own pensions, health and life insurance, and severance income and fly economy rather than first class; they asked for 75 percent of the income from players' sneaker endorsements; and they insisted on the elimination of guaranteed contracts. Fleisher claimed that the "big hangup is that the owners are taking a position of taking back all the benefits we've gained since 1967. . . . I assure you, we're not going to give them up."

In response to the owners' demands, the NBPA wanted increased benefits, all contracts to be guaranteed, and a share of television revenue. In October 1982, O'Brien stated that if the two sides could not come to an agreement the NBA would unilaterally implement some of its demands such as the reduction of rosters, players flying coach, and players paying for their pensions, health benefits, and insurance. The NBA owners justified their position by claiming extreme financial hardship, although among them there were still high rollers such as Philadelphia's Harold Katz, who was willing to sign Moses Malone to a six-year, $13 million contract with all the money paid up front.[20]

The negotiations continued into the new year with the sides no closer to an agreement. Now the owners offered to cap player salaries at 40 percent of the NBA's gross revenue up to $250,000 and 30 percent above that. Such a low ceiling was rejected outright by the NBPA, but they indicated a willingness to accept player salaries at 55 percent of gross revenue with the proviso that the teams must spend the maximum amount on salaries and benefits. Tired of the growing impasse, the NBPA imposed a deadline of April 1 for a contract to be reached or the players would go out on strike. This would eliminate the last few weeks of the regular season as well as the payoffs. As CBS was planning to televise the majority of the playoff games, a strike at that time would cost the NBA a large part of its $22 million contract with the network. In contrast, by waiting until April 2 to strike, the players would have already received 90 percent of their income. Milwaukee Bucks player representative Junior Bridgeman astutely argued, "In baseball nothing got settled until they set a deadline, and the same thing happened in football. So maybe now that we set one, something will happen for us."

As was the case with labor-management conflict in other sports, the general public generally sided with the owners. One aspect of the NBA players' strike threat that did not affect public response to job actions in the other professional sports was the color of the players' skin. Fleisher noted, "Seventy percent of the players in this league are black. So you're getting people saying, 'Not only are they highly paid, but they're *black* too.' We realize it isn't going to be an easy job."

Nor was it an easy job negotiating with the owners. The NBPA initially was willing to accept a salary cap and a percentage of gross revenue beginning in 1987, following the end of the Robertson settlement. After the talks in March, it agreed to a salary cap, beginning the following season, of approximately $3.5 to $4 million. In contrast, the owners had wanted a cap of somewhere between $1.8 and 2.5 million, but with the strike deadline fast approaching they were now willing to cap player salaries at 50 percent of NBA gross revenue, up from the 40/30 percent levels they had proposed at the beginning of the year.[21] Last-minute negotiations proved beneficial, and after twenty-six meetings over the course of nine months, a new collective bargaining agreement was finalized on March 31, 1983.

Under the terms of the agreement, player salaries would be 53 percent of NBA gross revenue. Crucially for the players, this would include network and cable television revenue. The salary cap was set at a minimum of $3.6 million in 1984–85, $3.8 million in 1985–86, and $4 million for the 1986–87 season. The five teams with the current highest player salaries had their payrolls frozen until existing player contracts expired, as they were already above the salary cap. The minimum salary was increased to $65,000 with further increases of $5,000 a year for the following two years. The number of players in the league was set at 253, a decrease of only three players from the previous season. Overall, the agreement was acceptable to all concerned, with the owners voting twenty-two to one in favor of it and O'Brien calling it "a landmark labor agreement in professional sports." The owners had wanted large concessions and for the most part the NBPA had protected its members. Fleisher noted that "[i]t's hard to have sympathy with someone who makes that much money. But they [the public] would have to realize that we weren't trying to get more. They [the league] put us up to the wall." The owners had played hardball, and the reason the players had been largely able to resist making concessions while still being able to maintain free agency, their pensions, health benefits, insurance (and not give the owners 75 percent of their shoe endorsement money) was that the players were united. They did not want to give up what previous generation of players had fought to achieve. As NBPA president Bob Lanier stated, "I am getting along in years, and I may not reap the benefits of this agreement, but we have worked on behalf of the younger brothers and those who are still to come. Guys like Oscar Robertson and Paul Silas sacrificed for me. We won because the guys stuck together."[22]

In November 1983, Larry O'Brien stepped down as the NBA's commissioner (the NBA's head became known as commissioner from 1968). He was replaced by David Stern, an appointment that was to have far-reaching implications for the players in the 1990s.

The 1983 collective bargaining agreement expired in June 1987, by which time the average salary had increased from $246,000 to $440,000. While there was a salary cap in place, NBA revenues increased due to higher television contracts and a 31.3 percent increase in attendance, which benefited the players in the form higher salaries. With the agreement set to expire in June, negotiations began in February. The NBPA and the players wanted an increase in revenue share, as well as the removal of the salary cap, the draft, and the teams' right of first refusal. In an attempt to hasten negotiations, in June the NBPA and the NBA agreed that no player contracts would be signed between June 17 and October 1 unless a new agreement had been negotiated. Stern claimed that "[b]y Oct. 1, either we'll have a good agreement or we won't have any excuse for not having one." However, by October 1 an agreement had not been reached, and the sides were still far apart on the issues.

While there was talk of a possible strike, the NBPA decided on another course of action; namely, it filed a class action lawsuit against the NBA on antitrust grounds. It argued that the salary cap, college draft, and the right of first refusal policy were in violation of the Sherman Act. Considering that the union had relatively recently agreed to these terms it was difficult to imagine that they would be successful in overturning them. However, Chicago Bulls player representative John Paxson argued that when the players had agreed to the salary cap in 1983 the NBA had been floundering, with the real possibility of a number of teams folding. "Now that the league is prospering," Paxson said, "we'd like a little back in return." In response, the NBA's general counsel Gary Bettman, who later became the head of the National Hockey League and imposed a series of lockouts, stated, "It's unfortunate the players have decided to litigate, instead of negotiate. However, we are very comfortable with our legal position and believe that ultimately we're going to make a deal."

While both the NBPA and the NBA were hoping for a quick resolution to the court case, this was not to be. The U.S. District Court judge turned down the players' request for a summary judgment while also refusing the league's request to dismiss the lawsuit. Thus, both sides were looking at a long trial. Following the judge's decision, the players refused the NBA's request to resume negotiations,[23] having decided on a different tactic.

In February 1988, in order to enhance their chances of successfully prosecuting the antitrust lawsuit, the NBPA player representatives voted unanimously to decertify the union, thereby forfeiting their collectively achieved pension and per diem benefits, which would now have to be negotiated individually. While the player representatives were in favor of the tactic, its adoption required approval by 60 percent of the union's rank and file members, whose support was hardly assured. For instance, Boston Celtics stars Larry Bird and Kevin McHale were quoted as saying that they would probably cross the picket line in the event of a strike. Such public statements undermined solidarity and the NBPA's position, betraying a lack of unity that was a precursor to what would come to pass in the following decade. By late February, however, while the NBPA was still polling its members about the decertification, the negotiations resumed, and by April a contract was successfully negotiated.[24]

Under the terms of the 1988 agreement, the salary cap was set at 53 percent of the NBA's designated league-wide revenue. The 1988 draft was reduced from seven rounds to three, with subsequent drafts to consist of only two rounds. The right of first refusal only applied to a player's first contract or at the end of a negotiated extension and in the first year of the agreement would not apply to seven-year veterans, in the second year to players with five years' experience, and in 1993–94 to four-year NBA veterans. In addition, players received increases in their pension, per diem, and insurance, with players who had retired before 1965 now being eligible for the pension plan. The minimum salary was doubled, from $75,000 to $150,000. The NBPA was happy with the agreement; as Fleisher noted, it "continues to leave NBA players as the highest-paid athletes in team sports." This was to be Fleisher's last major struggle for the NBPA as he resigned soon afterward.

For the most part, the NBA was also happy with the settlement, although one unnamed Eastern Conference coach stated his belief that under the agreement players would be uncoachable. He announced, "You're going to have to give guys four- or five-year deals to get them to stay with your team, and unless he is a superstar you know that he's gonna take a year or two off somewhere down the line." One wonders whether the coach would have made the same claim if the majority of the players in the NBA had been white. According to the prevailing stereotype, white players were gritty and hardworking compared to African Americans, who were lazy and relied on their natural talents. It's the sort of pernicious fallacy that when repeated often enough comes to be accepted as fact, and to his credit David Stern responded immediately, saying, that it was an "almost racist approach. . . . What's uncoachable? Is Bruce Springsteen uncoachable? Does he tank because he pulls down $1 million for a show? Is Michael Jackson uncoachable? If that happens, it only says something about the way teams select players, how they indoctrinate them and motivate them."[25]

Notwithstanding that it exposed the racist opinions of one unnamed coach, the collective bargaining agreement was beneficial to all concerned. The NBA was in the middle of a boom period, and player salaries continued to escalate. For the 1993–94 season the average player salary was almost $1.56 million, with the NBA's gross revenue increasing to $945 million from $135.2 million a decade earlier.[26] Moreover, unlike all the other major sports in America, there had still not been a work stoppage in the NBA. While at times there were court cases, strike threats, and a potential decertification, both the players and the NBA had realized that it was in their best interests to have no interruptions during a season. Even though the players might have earned more with a well-timed strike and the owners could have undermined some of the players' gains with a lockout, both sides had recognized that the first work stoppage could lead to a slippery slope of conflict. However, this era of peace was about to come to an end, and an era of lockouts was set to begin.

1990s: A Decade of Lockouts

In June 1994, the 1988 collective bargaining agreement expired. In response, the NBA filed a lawsuit seeking its continuation until a new agreement was reached, and specifying that the salary cap, draft, and right of first refusal were not in violation of antitrust law. In July, Judge Kevin Duffy found in favor of the league, as the provisions had been negotiated in good faith in a collective bargaining agreement. His ruling was reaffirmed by the court of appeals in January 1995. During the collective bargaining negotiations, the owners sought a hard salary cap of $22 million rather than the flexible one that was currently employed. The difference between the two was that under the NBA's system if the players' share of designated league-wide revenues exceeded the 53 percent at which the cap was set, they would receive the higher amount. Under the hard cap sought by the league, players would receive the cap amount and no more. In addition, the owners wanted to impose a limit on rookie salaries.

On their part, the NBPA wanted an end both to the salary cap and the college draft, as well as unrestricted free agency. The players, however, were willing to accept a soft salary cap of $27 million. Although there was talk of a lockout and the two sides were still far apart, in October 1994 the NBPA and NBA announced that the season would not be disrupted by a lockout or strike.[27]

In April 1995, with talks still in progress, the NBPA's executive director, Charles Grantham, resigned. While it was a labeled an amicable departure in the press, he acknowledged that there were "irreconcilable differences" with the NBPA's executive committee, seemingly caused by the continuing deadlock over the new collective bargaining agreement and Grantham's hardline approach to the negotiations, albeit he modified his stance to the extent that he would accept a soft salary cap, a reduction of the draft to one round, and an extension of up to three years on contract limits for rookies. Nonetheless, Grantham was replaced by the NBPA's counsel Simon Gourdine.[28]

In May, talks between the NBA and the NBPA resumed, with the league threatening a lockout following the playoffs if an agreement was not reached. In June, the two sides were close to an agreement, but a group of dissident players and attorneys/agents began steps to decertify the union. Ironically, Marc Fleisher, the son of Larry Fleisher, was one of the dissenting attorneys. They were unhappy that the NBPA was not keeping the players informed during the negotiations and fearful that any proposed deal would not be beneficial to the players.

The dissidents were also upset by the fact that the player representatives would be the only ones who would get to vote on the deal, not the rank-and-file players, although this had always been specified in the NBPA's bylaws,[29] With a strong advocate such as Larry Fleisher representing them, it had been a less than burning issue, but Simon Gourdine had yet to earn the players' unquestioning trust. Seeking to bypass the negotiations, the dissident players, led by Michael Jordan and Patrick Ewing, as well as player agent David Falk, hoped to bring a successful lawsuit against the NBA on antitrust grounds. However, within twenty-four hours the NBPA and the NBA announced a new collective bargaining agreement.

Under the agreement, the soft salary cap would remain at place but at an increase first from $15.9 million to $23 million and eventually to at least $28 million by the end of the contract. The players' share of NBA designated league-wide revenue was set at 57.5 percent, with a luxury tax to be introduced if player salaries exceeded 63 percent during the first two years of the agreement or 60 percent in the final four years. A team that exceeded the salary cap would be taxed on any amount above a 10 percent increase to veterans' contracts. There would be no tax in 1995–96, 50 percent in 1996–97, and a 100 percent tax from that point forward. The luxury tax was largely introduced to prevent teams from re-signing their veteran free agents outside the salary cap; the so-called Larry Bird Rule. In addition, there would be a rookie wage scale applied to a player's contract during his first three years, following which he could become a free agent. Players would receive $200 million in guaranteed licensing revenue over eight years, compared to $3.8 million they had received over the previous nine years. The owners voted unanimously to approve the agreement, but following the decertification attempt the NBPA player representatives postponed their vote. In response, the NBA locked out the players.[30]

Charlotte Hornets player representative Kenny Gattison blamed Falk for the lockout: "I think this whole thing has been manufactured by David Falk. . . . He gets kinda bent out of shape because he expected our union to keep him abreast of what's going on. We didn't feel it was our responsibility to have every agent in the country know what was going on." Likewise, both Stern and Gourdine blamed the agents and were unhappy that their influence had reached this stage. Gourdine stated, "We believe this work stoppage could have been avoided . . . had certain agents restrained themselves from trying to dictate union policy for our players."

In addition to their attempt to decertify the union, Jordan, Ewing, and five other players launched a class action lawsuit against the NBA on antitrust grounds. Jordan argued, "We're not being greedy here. We're not trying to make sure the league starves or doesn't become successful. If the league is not successful, we can't be successful and we endanger our own position. But we know the league is very successful. We just want an equal opportunity to make our value." In large part as a response to the decertification attempt, in August the NBA and the NBPA modified the initial terms of the collective bargaining agreement. The major change for the players was the elimination of the luxury tax, although the Larry Bird Rule remained in effect for players who had been on a team for three years. However—and it proved to be crucial a few years later—the agreement included a provision that allowed the owners to renegotiate the agreement if salaries exceeded 51.8 percent of basketball-related income.

Previously, the players had received a percentage of defined gross revenue; this was left in place in the 1995 agreement. However, there had often been disagreement on what it entailed. Indeed, in 1992 the NBPA had won a $60 million settlement from the league as compensation for underpayment based on what constituted defined gross revenue. Under the revised agreement, players received a percentage of *basketball-related* income, which was broader in scope than defined gross revenue. The players had accepted a lower percentage than under defined gross revenue, 48.04 percent compared to the 57.5 percent initially negotiated, but the percentage was now based upon basketball-related income.

Despite the new agreement, in September 1995 the decertification vote was still scheduled. If it was successful it likely would prolong the work stoppage, which Commissioner Stern vowed would continue, even if meant jeopardizing the start of the new season, if a new contract was not reached. Both the NBPA and the dissident players tried to sway the rank and file. Both camps went to great lengths trying to get the players to vote for their side. General managers sent faxes to players telling them not to decertify the union and to accept the agreement. The NBPA and the NBA agreed to pay for transportation for players to the polling stations.

The dissidents sent all players an eight-page letter outlining the reasons they should decertify the union. Moreover, they sent a videotape to the players. As *Sports Illustrated* noted, Atlanta Hawks player Grant Long received a copy. On it, "The dissidents argued that union executive director Simon Gourdine and union president Buck Williams had negotiated two bad deals. The first one, which was abandoned in the face of intense opposition, included a team luxury tax that, it was argued, would have put a drag on salaries. In the dissidents' view the current proposal was only slightly better. Long watched and listened as Jordan, Ewing and Reggie Miller told him that the best way to get a fair deal was to eliminate the union. Under antitrust rules, that would allow the players to seek an injunction against the owners' two-month-old lockout. The teams would then be forced to open their doors to the players, and without the leverage of a lockout the league presumably would negotiate a deal more favorable to the players." Before he watched the tape, Long had been going to vote against decertification; after watching it he was undecided what to do.

Tactics such as these divided the players and had the effect of undermining confidence in the union leadership no matter the outcome, which was evident in the decertification vote. By a margin of 226 to 134 the players voted against decertification, thereby approving the collective bargaining agreement negotiated by the NBPA. The CBA was approved by the player representatives by a vote of 25 to 2, and by the owners by a margin of 24 to 5. However, this was not a "victory" to be celebrated; there was a rift in the union, and player solidarity was divided. As New York Knick and executive vice president of the NBPA Charles Smith claimed, "We have divided players. . . . Some have taken it personally. There used to be a sense, even when you saw retired players, that we all had a bond. Now the bond boils down to, 'Were you for the union or against the union?' We have to resolve that. We have to get all the key players involved in the union. The guys who were against the union had some valid points, but the way they went about it was not the correct way to do things. At some point, we have to settle our differences."[31]

In January 1996, still trying to heal the wounds of the internal conflict, the player representatives voted to replace Simon Gourdine as NBPA executive director, despite the fact that the executive board had offered him a two-year contract the previous December. He was replaced by G. William "Billy" Hunter, with Patrick Ewing, a client of David Falk, becoming president of the NBPA. The decertification attempt had caused a rift in the union and undermined player solidarity, and the lockout made Stern and the owners realize that the same tactic could work in future conflicts. Indeed, the next lockout was less than one year away.

Despite the collective bargaining agreement's having been ratified by both owners and players, by June 1996 the NBPA still had not signed off on the contract. There was conflict over the language in the agreement, and whether the NBPA would be able to control group licensing, and in addition the union wanted another $31 million for the players. When negotiations reached a deadlock, Stern and the owners locked out the players. However, the lockout was to last less than two hours before a compromise was reached. The NBPA was able to obtain the majority of the $31 million it sought; it also received $90 million from the television contract with the TNT network, to be included in basketball-related income, and the union was granted permission to run exhibition games as well as receive money from licensing fees to go toward a strike fund.[32]

While this lockout was minor and is largely forgotten today, the next lockout was anything but that. As previously noted, the NBA was authorized to reopen the 1995 collective bargaining agreement if players' salaries exceeded 51.8 percent of basketball-related income. The NBA would not have been able to do this under the first agreement signed with the union in 1995; it was only included in the revised contract that was negotiated following the decertification attempt. In March 1998, with players' salaries accounting for 57 percent of basketball-related income, the NBA owners, by a vote of 27 to 2, terminated the 1995 collective bargaining agreement effective June 30. Stern stated, "What we're seeing now is a system where salaries continue to rise, teams are becoming unprofitable and ticket prices are continuing to rise. . . . The players said to us (in the current agreement), 'If it does not work come back to us and we'll negotiate a new one.' Here we are. We need a better system." In response Billy Hunter noted, "It is unfortunate the owners have chosen to forfeit three years of guaranteed labor peace at a time when the industry is so obviously healthy." The league demanded that the players' salaries account for no more than 48 percent of basketball-related income and sought to impose a hard salary cap as well, which would effectively eliminate guaranteed contracts. However, while claiming financial hardship and alleging that half of the teams were losing money, the NBA signed a new television deal worth $2.64 billion. This resulted in each team's annual share more than doubling, to $23 million. Moreover, *Forbes* contended that only ten of the twenty-nine NBA teams were losing money. Considering the NBA's demands, it was not surprising that the NBPA rejected them.

One of the main problems that the NBPA faced was that superstars received the bulk of the money. For example, in 1997 the top nine players received 15 percent of all player salaries, while approximately 30 percent of the players received the minimum salary. The union accepted that something had to be done about this.[33] Nonetheless, following halfhearted negotiating efforts that led nowhere, on July 1 the owners locked out the players. Not all owners were in favor of the lockout. Both Portland Trail Blazers owner Paul Allen and Boston Celtics owner Paul Gaston voted against locking out the players, and several large-market teams such as the Knicks and the Lakers wanted the players to return to the court as soon as possible.

During the lockout, the league continued to receive income from its television contracts; if the games were not played the league would have to return the money, but they had three years to do so, without interest. The players, on the other hand, received no income during the work stoppage, as the regular season had not begun. This situation obviously favored the owners. The NBPA did manage to secure lines of credit from banks, and financial support from unions in baseball, football, and hockey in addition to the money it received from group licensing. During the lockout, Hunter claimed, "The players are strongly united in their opposition to the elimination of a soft cap. . . . That's not negotiable. We're prepared to work out some kind of compromise as long as it doesn't involve a hard cap. That's the main issue. There are other solutions to their problems. There are no teams in the red, the issue is guaranteed profits."

The NBPA proposed a luxury tax, which was ironic considering Ewing and Falk had been adamantly against this in 1995 and it had played a part in dividing the union. The union also proposed that annual salary increases be tied to the NBA's growth. Despite these concessions by the players, the lockout continued, and the NBA cancelled the start of the season for the first time in its existence. While Hunter claimed the players were united, the earlier rift in the NBPA weakened the players' position. In November, Stern tried to play up the rift by arguing that player agents Falk and Arn Tellem were trying to prevent any deal from occurring because they cared more about the superstars than majority of the players. At the time, Falk represented almost one-half of the NBPA's nineteen-man negotiating committee, including Ewing, Juwan Howard, Alonzo Mourning, and Dikembe Mutombo. The negotiating committee had the power to decide whether a proposal was acceptable and, if so, present it to the other four hundred players to vote upon. Falk himself wanted to be on the committee and to take more of a role during the lockout. This was rejected by Hunter and the NBPA. Stern questioned why the negotiating committee had all the authority to decide on an agreement, but in the summer more than 250 players had voted to give the negotiating committee this power, so its authority was established.

Nonetheless, some players were concerned that Falk's clients had too much power. New Jersey Net Jayson Williams claimed, "Any time you have a monopoly—in that the stars people listen to are Falk guys— it's not good for everyone." He further stated that he wanted to be on the negotiating committee, "but they didn't want me. They wanted all of Falk's guys as the leaders." Whether this was "sour grapes" or not, such public displays of disunity did not help the players' cause. Moreover, other agents questioned the role of Falk. Harold MacDonald, who represented Derrick Coleman and Terry Mills, stated, "Every time I see Patrick [Ewing] say something, it's almost like watching the Energizer bunny. . . . I'm just waiting for Falk to put in another battery, and off Patrick goes again. Hardly any influence? Give me a break." Whether Falk really had as much influence as publicly claimed—and his influence was disputed by the NBPA—such accusations undermined the resolve of the players.

Trying to increase the divide between the players even further, Stern let it be known that the NBA wanted to raise the minimum salary to $350,000 for rookies and up to $1 million for ten-year veterans. In return, players with high salaries could receive only an annual 5 percent increase, with top free agent's salaries being limited to 25 percent of the salary cap for players with six or fewer years' experience, 30 percent for six to nine-year veterans, 35 percent for veterans with ten or more years, and with annual 10 percent increases across the board. Nearing the cutoff point for the season to go ahead, Stern sent the players a nine-page proposal outlining the owners' position. The owners backed away from a hard salary cap; the Larry Bird Rule would remain (though with some limits for the top earners) but annual increases would rise to 12.5 percent with other players receiving 7.5 percent annual increases; and the minimum salary would increase for veteran players but would decrease for rookies and players with limited time in the league. In addition, Stern set January 7 as the deadline for an agreement to be reached or he would cancel the season.

The NBPA rejected Stern's proposal, but the players began to break ranks. Kevin Willis of the Toronto Raptors called for the players to be able to vote on Stern's latest offer. He stated, "The majority would vote for the owners' latest proposal, just to start playing ball again." Willis's agent Steve Woods, who had an antagonistic relationship with the NBPA and was later decertified for speaking out against the union, claimed, "A secret ballot is something the union is adamantly against because they would feel it would tear a hole in their blanket of unity. . . . The players' union unity is based more on peer pressure and collective egos rather than on reasonable minds coming to a reasonable conclusion." Despite the claims of Willis and his agent, it was likely the owners' proposal would be rejected, even though this would have led to the cancellation of the season.

Player solidarity was further jeopardized when more than twenty players, including stars of the magnitude of the Detroit Pistons' Grant Hill and the Los Angeles Lakers' Shaquille O'Neal urged retired NBA great and former NBPA president Isiah Thomas to become involved once again with the union. Thomas criticized Falk, as he believed he was trying to take over the union, and claimed, "I think there's a system and a process in place that should allow the players to vote on their deal. However, if that process doesn't take place, I'll step up and support them, as they've asked me to." By this point, the infighting among the players and the looming loss of the season were enough to persuade the NBPA and Stern to agree to engage in further talks and work for an agreement. When it was reached, the players voted overwhelmingly in favor of the agreement; they were happy just to get back onto the court.[34]

Under the terms of the contract, there was an individual cap on players' salaries. The maximum a player could receive was $14 million per year if he had over ten years' experience. Likewise, players with less than 10 years' experience could only receive between $9 million and $11 million. Free agents who re-signed under the Larry Bird Rule would receive a maximum annual salary increase of 12 percent. Moreover, the players agreed to an escrow tax of 10 percent of their salaries in years four to six of the agreement if income devoted to salary was above 55 percent of basketball-related income.

The agreement also contained provision for a luxury tax, which the NBA termed a "team tax," beginning in 2003. If the escrow amount was not sufficient to control team spending the luxury tax would implemented when the players' share of basketball-related income exceeded 61.11 percent: "The luxury tax threshold is one over the number of teams (1/29 for 2003) times 61.11 percent of league BRI as determined at the end of the season." A team above the threshold pays a 100 percent tax for any amount above the threshold.

The owners were not as successful in obtaining a hard salary cap. The soft cap remained in place, with exceptions; as Staudohar notes, "Any team can sign two additional players each season, one at the league average salary and the other at the league median salary, even if the team is over the salary cap. And there is no limit on total salary spending by the 29 teams in the first 3 years of the agreement." Rookie contracts were to be in effect for three years, with a team option in year four, and with teams having the right of first refusal in year five. In a victory for the players, there would be no limit on salaries for the first three years of the contract; from that point forward players would receive 55 percent of basketball-related income, a 5 percent increase over what the owners had previously offered. Moreover, minimum salary increased on a sliding scale from $287,500 for rookies up to $1 million for players with more than ten years' experience. Since both the union and the owners had wanted the minimum salary to be increased, this was not the great victory it first appears to be.[35]

Overall, the lockout was a clear victory for the owners. Salaries were curtailed, with an individual salary cap being implemented for the first time in professional sports in America. However, during the 1999–2000 season, players received 62 percent of basketball-related income, with it reaching 65 percent in 2000–01, a new record. For the 2001–02 season the salary control mechanisms came into effect. Under the terms of the agreement, 10 percent of players' salaries were withheld in escrow to be redistributed to the owners. Nevertheless, players received approximately 57 percent of basketball-related income and for the next three years, the rate was about 60 percent. Then, beginning in 2003, as player share of basketball-related income was above 61.11 percent, the luxury tax kicked in. For 2003, sixteen teams were above the threshold and were taxed a combined $173.32 million, while in 2004 twelve teams were above the limit and the tax amounted to $157.21 million. It is worth recalling that at the start of the lockout the owners had wanted the players to receive a maximum of only 48 percent of basketball-related income and had eventually settled for 55 percent. Thus, while individual salaries were curtailed, there was now a more equitable distribution among all players,[36] so that the end result was not as bad as it might at first have appeared. Nevertheless, the owners had once again been shown that the players would lack unity in the face of a lockout, that the NBPA was still divided between the haves and the have-nots, and that as a consequence the union could be forced to accept concessions it would have resisted in the past.

The 2005 Agreement and the Power of Stern

The 1998 collective bargaining agreement was set to expire on July 1, 2005. There was talk that the owners once again wanted a hard salary cap, although during negotiations they proposed only that players receive 57 percent of basketball-related income, that players be at least twenty years of age before they join the league, and that salaries and the maximum length of contracts be reduced. The owners were prohibited from commenting on the negotiations lest they incur heavy fines from the league. *Forbes* estimated that eleven of the thirty teams were losing money, but the least valuable team, the New Orleans Hornets, was worth $225 million and the average worth of all teams had increased by 9 percent since 2003–04. The National Hockey League's season had just been lost to a lockout, and both Stern and Hunter vowed that this would not happen in the NBA. Stern stated, "I may be combining a sort of reality with hope, but I think there will be a deal . . . by the end of the season. We're going to spend three days a week [negotiating in March] until we either can't stand each other or we can make a deal." Likewise, Hunter claimed, "Our players are making a substantial sum of money. The league appears to be thriving, and we would be foolish to not make every effort to make a deal. I'm trying to accomplish an agreement before the close of the season—the sooner the better." However, the negotiators failed to reach an agreement in March and the possibility of a lockout increased, although Stern and the owners were taking a less hardline approach compared to 1998.

Once again, the league blamed players' agents for preventing a deal and in May broke off talks with the NBPA, although they were resumed shortly thereafter. During the hiatus, the NBA tried to mount a public relations campaign blaming the top players and their agents for blocking a deal. Stern claimed that he was convinced that if an agreement was not reached a lockout could occur. Considering that it was up to the owners to impose a lockout and that Stern could have easily persuaded them not to, it was apparent that he was trying to convince the players that a lockout would occur if they did not accept the owners' proposal. It did not come to this. In the middle of June, the two sides began talking again, and a settlement was reached on June 21.[37]

Under the terms of the six-year agreement, the salary cap was set at 49.5 percent of basketball-related income for the 2005–06 season, increasing to 51 percent for the remainder of the contract. In regard to exceptions to the cap, "For the 2005–06 season, the Mid-level exception will be $5 million. In subsequent years, the Mid-level exception will equal 108% of the average player salary for the prior season." As stated in the agreement, "The escrow level will be 57% [the same as the 2004–05 season]. This percentage will be guaranteed to the players, so that if total player costs before deducting escrow monies from the players are less than 57% of BRI, the difference will be paid by the league to the players." In regard to the escrow amount, "The maximum percentage of player salaries and benefits that can be withheld from the players for purposes of meeting the 57%" was 10 percent of players' salaries to be redistributed to the owners in the first year of the contract, 9 percent in years two to five, and 8 percent in year six. Thus, with all the exceptions included, the most the players could receive was 57 percent of basketball-related income.

Minimum salary occupied a sliding scale, ranging from $398,762 for rookies to $1,138,500 for ten-year veterans; by the 2010–11 season, this would be increased to $473,604 for rookies and $1,352,181 for ten-year-plus veterans. Larry Bird Rule players could receive a maximum six-year contract with annual increases in salary of 10.5 percent; all other players were eligible to receive five-year contracts with an 8 percent annual salary increase. To be eligible for the draft, a player had to be nineteen years old and one year removed from high school.

In addition, teams had to spend at least 75 percent of the salary cap, and there was a luxury tax of $1 for every dollar a team was above the threshold. In regard to the luxury tax, the amount collected was distributed evenly to all teams. However, if a team went over the threshold, even by $1, they were not eligible to receive any money collected from the tax; instead, the amount the luxury tax violators would have received went to league purposes. Commenting on the agreement, Stern said, "I will say we agreed almost all the way along that this business would suffer greatly from a lockout and that the deal reflects . . . a 50-50 deal. . . . Half of it went our way. Half of it went their way, and the central economics really remain the same." In a similar vein, Hunter stated, "It's a compromise deal. . . . When you look at professional sports, I don't think there's any better system in place than the one that exists with us. So we were inclined to not move too far off of that."[38] Both Stern and Hunter were correct in their assessments. The agreement was a compromise deal that largely benefited both sides. Undoubtedly, the lost NHL season was at the forefront of both the NBA and the NBPA's minds and neither side truly wanted a work stoppage; the agreement reflected that. The NBPA had not been able to recover its lost strength, having failed again to win back the concessions it had agreed to in the 1998 agreement, although it did well in resisting further concessions in 2005. What the NBPA was not able to resist, however, was the increasing power of Commissioner Stern.

Unlike the collective bargaining agreements in MLB, the NFL, and the NHL, the NBA agreement grants the commissioner a wide range of powers, as does the NBA's constitution. Beginning in 2004, Stern began to use the commissioner's power to a much greater extent than previous commissioners had. He began by cracking down on what he perceived as the NBA's chief image problem, highlighted by a fight involving players and fans during a game between the Indiana Pacers and the Detroit Pistons, namely, public perception that professional basketball was primarily an African American game.

As part of Stern's image makeover, beginning in 2005–06 the NBA implemented a dress code for the players, under which "[p]layers are required to wear Business Casual attire whenever they are engaged in team or league business." Players attending a game but not playing must wear a sports coat, dress shoes or boots, and socks. The following items are banned when players are on team or NBA business: sleeveless shirts, shorts, T-shirts, jerseys, or sports apparel; any headwear except under certain circumstances; "chains, pendants, or medallions worn over the player's clothes"; sunglasses while the players are indoors; and headphones except when the player is on the "team bus or plane, or in the team locker room." It is an extensive list, and invites the question whether a player's attire off the court is relevant to the league's business, that is, falls within the commissioner's purview or whether this dress code constituted a form of social engineering. Quite simply, Stern was attempting to appeal to conservative white fans by implementing a dress code that buried any traces of so-called hip hop (read: African American) culture beneath what he defined as a more "professional" public wardrobe.

Stern imposed the code unilaterally. Although he did discuss it with the NBPA, he did not seek the union's approval before implementation, nor did he receive it. Arguably, the NBPA has grounds to overturn the dress code, because it should have been agreed to in a collective bargaining agreement. However, it has not chosen to do so.[39]

In addition to the dress code, in 2006 the NBA unilaterally introduced a new basketball, again without consulting the NBPA or the players. The ball was substandard in many aspects and it led to numerous complaints. The NBPA filed a grievance with the NLRB, believing that Stern had overstepped his powers. However, before the board could rule on the matter, in an embarrassing retreat, Stern and the NBA withdrew the new basketball. These and other episodes, such as investigating whether it was possible to ban players from certain nightclubs, mandating what players can wear on the court, blocking certain trades in deference to the so-called (and self-defined) good of the game, as well as wielding a disposition to dish out heavy fines to players, coaches, and management, all served to demonstrate that Stern was determined to ensure his legacy before he retired.[40] This was clearly demonstrated by his handling of the 2011 lockout.

The 2011 Lockout

Even though the 2005 collective bargaining agreement was not due to expire until June 30, 2011, the NBA submitted a proposal for its renewal to the NBPA in January 2010. Once again, the NBA owners were claiming financial hardship. Stern argued that the league was going to lose approximately $350 million in the 2010–11 season and had lost money every year since 2005. Because of their losses, the NBA owners were proposing a hard salary cap, a 38 percent reduction in player salaries, which would amount to between $750 million and $800 million, a reduction in the length of player contracts, and the elimination of all salary cap exceptions such as the Larry Bird Rule. The reduction the owners sought would result in players receiving 40 percent of basketball-related income.

The NBPA disputed the extent of the financial woes of the league, but was willing to accept a reduction in the players' share of revenue, although not to the extent the owners wanted. While the NBA claimed that twenty-two of its teams were losing money, a *Forbes* investigation revealed that only seventeen teams were, and that the net worth of the teams had increased to an average of $369 million, a 1 percent increase from the previous year, but 2.9 percent lower than the two years before that. However, as *Forbes* notes, "Our estimations are based on the team's current economics (unless ground has been broken for a new building) and do not include the value of real estate." This was demonstrated when both the Golden State Warriors and the Washington Wizards were sold for more than their *Forbes*-estimated worth. Indeed, the new owner of the Warriors, Joe Lacob, was not in the slightest concerned that the franchise, which was hardly successful, would be a money loser for him. He stated soon after buying the team in 2010 that "[t]his is an incredible business opportunity. . . . Look, sports franchises appreciate 10% a year on average over three decades, the last three decades. There's no reason to think this won't appreciate in value. So that is the least of my worries."[41] Thus, while teams were losing money, the situation was not as bad as the NBA claimed, and the majority of owners could recoup any losses through selling the team at a vastly higher price than they had bought it for. Moreover, owners were not forced to offer players contracts that led to the teams losing money; they did so voluntarily.

The owners displayed a united front, and to sustain this, Stern let it be known that he did not want them talking to the media. In 2010, he fined Washington Wizards' owner Ted Leonsis $100,000 for publicly advocating a hard salary cap. Stern stated, "We're negotiating and that was one of our negotiating points . . . but collective bargaining is a negotiating process, and that was not something that Ted was authorized to say and he will be dealt with for that lapse in judgment."[42] In other words, Leonsis was not permitted to publicly advocate a hard salary cap even though Stern acknowledged that it was being negotiated on. Such disciplinary measures were also handed out during the lockout that was to follow.

There were disagreements among the owners when it came to revenue sharing. Under the 2005 agreement, some of the money in the luxury tax pool was being redistributed to the have-not teams. Not surprisingly, the economic powerhouses in the NBA were not open to any idea of comprehensive revenue sharing such as existed in MLB and the NFL. The NBA argued that revenue sharing was between the owners and outside the parameters of a collective bargaining agreement, while the NBPA argued that the idea of revenue sharing was tied to the players having a salary cap.[43]

Despite on-and-off negotiations, by May 2011 the two sides were still far apart. The owners still wanted a hard salary cap of $45 million per team, although they were willing to phase it in rather impose it immediately. Stern was claiming in the media that if an agreement was not reached there would be a lockout, not explicitly threatening the players with one so much as accepting it as a fait accompli. This was a similar situation to the 1998–99 lockout.

The owners did not have to lock out the players if an agreement was not reached by June 30; they threatened to do so as a bargaining tactic. With the June 30 deadline nearing, the owners modified their demands. Instead of a hard cap they now proposed a "flex cap" and a ten-year agreement. Under the flex cap, the salary cap would be set at $62 million, a figure that represented the assumed median for all teams. If the actual median exceeded $62 million, the players would have to accept salary reductions. For example, for the 2010–11 season the Los Angeles Lakers' player payroll was a league-high $91 million while the Sacramento Kings only spent $44 million.

The owners' goal was for players to receive approximately 50 percent of a newly defined basketball-related income for the 2011–12 season, thereby reducing their salary and benefits to approximately $2 billion, compared to $2.17 billion for the prior season. The NBPA claimed that under the owners' proposal, by the middle of the ten-year contract, the players' share of basketball-related income would fall to around 45 percent and then farther, to 35 percent for the final three years of the contract. The union countered by offering the owners a five-year contract containing $500 million in savings. The players' share of basketball-related income would fall, but only from 57 percent to 54.3 percent.

Following the NBA's proposal, a journalist asked Hunter to estimate, if the two sides had been one hundred miles apart before the owners' new proposal, how widely they were separated now. Hunter replied, "ninety-nine." In a show of solidarity, more than forty players attended last-minute negotiations between the NBPA and the NBA wearing T-shirts with STAND printed on them, as in, "United we stand, divided we fall."[44] On June 28, the owners authorized a lockout to take place if a new agreement could not be reached. It could not, and the lockout began on July 1.

During the lockout, both sides tried to portray that they were united. However, cracks appeared on both sides. Before the lockout began, the NBA sent a memo to the owners stating that they could be fined up to $1 million if they discussed the lockout or any player during the work stoppage. Michael Jordan, who now owned the Charlotte Bobcats, was fined $100,000 for arguing in the Australian press that revenue sharing was a good idea for all concerned, as well as discussing Australian NBA player Andrew Bogut. In addition, Stern fined Miami Heat owner Micky Arison $500,000 for discussing the lockout on Twitter and implying that it should be abandoned. It is interesting to note that Arison was fined five times as much as Jordan; Arison wanted the lockout to end, Jordan wanted what the NBA wanted, revenue sharing. And while Arison sought an end to the lockout, all the small and medium-sized teams were unhappy with the fifty-fifty offer. There was disunity between them and the large market teams. The small and medium-sized teams' owners wanted a majority share of revenue.

If the players had remained united they might have profited from owner disunity, and the lockout might have ended sooner with them receiving a better deal than otherwise would have been the case. However, it is alleged that there was disunity between Hunter and NBPA president Derek Fisher. During the lockout, Hunter vowed that the union would not accept less than 52.5 percent of basketball-related income, while in the press it was claimed that Fisher was willing to agree to Stern's proposal for a fifty-fifty split. Fisher denied the accusation, and wrote to the players stating as much, but he did not deny that he agreed to a fifty-fifty split until the end of the letter, and he never mentioned Hunter either directly or indirectly. Trying to maintain unity Hunter, at least publicly, supported Fisher. Nevertheless, as one unnamed player told the press, "Right now, everyone has to choose sides: Billy or Derek. . . . How the [expletive] did it come to this?" There was further disunity when a number of players began publicly lobbying on Twitter for the NBPA to make a deal. Boston Celtic Glen Davis wrote, "Take the 51% man and let's play" and Cleveland Cavalier Samardo Samuels stated he would be happy with a fifty-fifty split, while Houston Rocket Terrence Williams wrote, "Hey @TheNBPA Let's play BALL enough with the stare off."[45]

This disunity was not helping the NBPA and, capitalizing on this, Stern insisted that if an agreement was not reached by November 9 the owners would no longer offer the players a fifty-fifty split but rather only 47 percent of basketball-related income. In response, the NBPA indicated that it was willing to accept the equal split if the owners were willing to concede some ground on free agency. This resulted in Stern backing away from his threat and negotiations continued.

On November 14, with the lockout in its fifth month, the NBPA utilized a familiar tactic: it decertified. However, unlike in the past, the NBPA declared a "disclaimer of interest," which the players had previously authorized. Under a disclaimer of interest, which is a top-down approach, there does not have to be a decertification vote, and in this instance it meant that the union decertified itself almost immediately. Following the decertification, two lawsuits were filed against the NBA on antitrust grounds; one in California and one in Minnesota. Eventually, the suits were merged and the case was docketed to be heard in Minnesota. While it might be months or years before the court cases were decided, the NBPA was attempting to get the owners to concede some ground, and in that regard negotiations continued.[46]

Once again there was a lack of solidarity evidenced among the players. Glen Davis argued that there was a lack of communication between the NBPA and the rank and file. He also complained, "It seemed like we just had a couple of issues, and now we have to go to court. . . . You don't want to waste that amount of money going to court." Sacramento King DeMarcus Paul stated, "Some of the young players I talked to, it's not about the money. . . . We just want to go out there and play ball." Likewise, Samardo Samuels claimed even though he did not like the NBA's latest proposal he would have voted for it. He noted, "A lot of people in the league are panicking. . . . You're talking about missing paychecks. Those paychecks you're missing are going to add up and guys have families and responsibilities and bills to pay."[47] Comments like these didn't help the NBPA's negotiating position, and just twelve days after the union decertified an agreement was reached that was not favorable to the players.

Under the terms of the ten-year agreement, players received 51.5 percent of basketball-related income in 2011–12 and would get between 49 and 51 percent for the years that followed. Thus, Hunter's vow that the NBPA would not accept less than 52.5 percent proved hollow. Ten percent of player salaries were designated to be held in escrow every year. Teams had to spend 85 percent of the salary cap for the 2011–12 and 2012–13 seasons, and 90 percent of the salary cap for the remaining seasons covered under the agreement. The luxury tax was increased, especially for repeat offenders. However, unlike in previous agreements, where offending teams did not receive any share of the collected tax, in the 2011 agreement nonoffending teams may receive up to 50 percent of the total amount. While the agreement does not specify what the NBA will do with the remaining 50 percent, it appears that it may go to league purposes and/or be distributed evenly among all of teams.

A revamped revenue sharing plan was agreed to that was a lot more comprehensive than in the past, with its full details unveiled in January 2012. Under the new system, "Each team then receives an allocation equal to the league's average team payroll for that season from the revenue pool. If a team's contribution to the pool is less than the league's average team payroll, then that team is a revenue recipient.

Teams that contribute an amount that exceeds the average team salary fund the revenue given to receiving teams." Another term of the agreement granted Larry Bird Rule players only a maximum five-year contract with annual increases in salary of 7.5 percent; all other players could receive four-year contracts with a 4.5 percent annual salary increase. Minimum salary remains the same for the first two seasons as it had been in 2010–11, with incremental increases for the remaining years. Crucially, while it is a ten-year agreement, either the owners or the players can choose to opt out as early as 2017. Considering recent history, one would think that it is almost a given that that will occur. Fisher proclaimed, "For myself, it's great to be a part of this particular moment, in terms of giving our fans what it is that they so badly wanted and want to see." He did not smile when he said this. Indeed, no one representing the players at the news conference when the settlement was announced praised the agreement, nor should they have.[48]

Quite simply, the deal was not one to be celebrated by the NBPA; the players were happy to go back to work but they were doing so with a greatly reduced share of revenue. Moreover, players on minimum salary were hit hard with a wage freeze for two seasons. In the end, while the players could play ball again, the owners won in every other area. Following the settlement, the NBPA recertified and the players as well as the owners approved the agreement.

The owners were pleased with the results, and this was further reflected in the NBA's financial position. *Forbes* estimates that the average NBA team in 2012 was worth $509 million. This was a massive 30 percent increase from the previous season. The average operating income of an NBA team increased to $11.9 million, the highest level since at least 1998, when *Forbes* began investigating NBA team worth and revenue. The "least" valuable NBA team, the Milwaukee Bucks, was worth $312 million, with the New York Knicks leading the league with a net worth of $1.1 billion. The Knicks and the Lakers are the first two NBA teams worth more than $1 billion. Regarding operating income, only eight teams lost money in 2012, compared to fifteen teams in 2011. This was due in part to the new revenue sharing plan and, of course, the reduction in player costs.

There were even better results for owners in 2013. Operating income doubled to 23.7 million, with only four teams losing money. Reduced labor costs and revenue sharing, which saw $120 million transferred from high-revenue teams, has greatly benefited low-revenue teams. The average NBA team is now worth $634 million, a 25 percent increase from 2012. The Knicks are now worth an estimated $1.4 billion. More-over, in October 2014 the NBA signed a new nine-year, $24 billion television contract with ABC/ESPN and TNT. The deal tripled the previous television contract. The owners' cries of financial hardship no longer will ring true, if they ever did.[49]

The fallout from the lockout saw Billy Hunter unanimously sacked as NBPA executive director by the player representatives. He was accused of conflict of interest and mishandling union finances, and is currently under investigation by the United States government. Following the vote, Fisher stated, "Going forward, we'll no longer be divided, misled, misinformed."[50] However, even if the NNBPA is united this does not mean the players are. Economist David Berri points out that there is a short career span for an NBA player, the majority of games are won by a select few players, and by the time an NBA player peaks, in his mid-twenties, he knows whether he will be a star or not. These factors combined mean it is likely that nonstars will not remain united, or care about star players. He states, "[T]he players cannot stay united, and that means the NBA owners tend to win. In other words, we should not be surprised that across the past three decades the players have agreed to a cap on league payroll, team payroll, rookie pay, and individual pay."[51] It is hard to disagree with his claims. However, the players' lack of unity in the most recent negotiations and lockout also led to a freeze on minimum pay for two years and only gradual increases after that.

If the players are fragmented, not only will star players be forced to accept concessions, but all players. As the players generally have a short career span, it is essential for them to maximize their earnings while they can. If they are divided, this will not happen. This is the biggest challenge the union faces going forward. If the players' solidarity remains weak and divided by different factions, the NBPA will continue to engage in concession bargaining and the players will earn less than they otherwise would. But while on the basis of their recent performance it is easy to assume that the players will remain divided, it is important to remember that NFL players, who have on average shorter career spans, remained united during their 2011 lockout after years of showing weak solidarity. NBA players were united in the past; they can become united once again, even though it will be difficult. For the players to regain the solidarity they lost, the first step is to remember what the slogan STAND meant on the T-shirts some of them wore just before the 2011 lockout began: United we stand, divided we fall.

Labor Struggles in the NHL

The Rise and Fall of the NHLPA

Hockey, like football, is a quick and graceful game with moments of bone-crunching violence. This violence sometimes manifests itself in unofficially condoned fights. Considering this, one would think it would be difficult for players to achieve the solidarity necessary for them to achieve fair wages and working conditions. For decades, this was true, and the players had no collective voice while the owners and the National Hockey League (NHL) had the overwhelming share of power. Then, for a while, the players were united, which led to their being handsomely rewarded for their skills. However, in recent years, every time a collective bargaining agreement has expired the owners have demanded huge concessions from the players, backed up by the threat of a lockout; this has occurred in 1994, 2004, and 2012. Every time, the players, led by their collective voice the National Hockey League Players' Association (NHLPA), have tried to resist, but during each lockout, the players have become divided and solidarity has faltered. This has led to the players losing many of their hard-earned gains.

This chapter will look at the labor struggles in the NHL and the rise and fall of the NHLPA. It is not easy to feel sympathy for these multimillionaire players. After all, from the perspective of a person earning a minimum wage and struggling to get by, who would not want the salary NHL players have? However, as in the NFL, the players pay a high price to bring enjoyment to their fans. Concussions are a major problem in the NHL and while the league has instituted measures designed to reduce their number, they are insufficient, and the players continue to endanger their health and mental well-being. There might be people who aspire to the salary of an NHL player, but nobody would want the deteriorating health that goes along with it.

The Birth of the NHL and the NHLPA

Although hockey's origins are obscure, the modern version of the game was invented in Canada, and this is reflected in the birth of the NHL. The National Hockey Association formed in 1909 with teams from eastern Canada. The Pacific Coast Hockey League was created two years later comprised of western Canadian teams as well as teams from the United States. Beginning in 1912, the champions of the two leagues held a championship series, with the winner being awarded the Stanley Cup, named after Frederick Arthur Stanley who had been the governor general of Canada. At a dinner of the Ottawa Amateur Athletic Association in 1892, the host quoted a letter from Lord Stanley stating, "I have for some time been thinking that it would be a good thing if there were a challenge cup which should be held from year to year by the champion hockey team in the Dominion of Canada. There does not appear to be any such outward sign of a championship at present, and considering the general interest which matches now elicit, and the importance of having the game played fairly and under rules generally recognized, I am willing to give a cup which shall be held from year to year by the winning team." Initially, it was awarded to the best amateur side, but beginning in 1912 the best professional team was presented with the Stanley Cup.

The National Hockey Association ceased to exist in 1917, and was replaced by the National Hockey League. The NHL was initially comprised of five Canadian sides: the Montreal Canadiens, Montreal Wanderers, Ottawa Senators, Quebec Wanderers, and the Toronto Arenas. The NHL expanded to the United States in 1924, when the Boston Bruins joined the league. The rival Pacific Coast Hockey League folded in 1924. The NHL's only other rival in its early years was the Western Canada Hockey League; formed in 1921, it had ceased to exist by 1926. By 1942, the NHL was compromised of the "original six" teams: Boston Bruins, Chicago Blackhawks, Detroit Red Wings, Montreal Canadiens, New York Rangers, and Toronto Maple Leafs (the former Arenas). The NHL expanded in 1967 by doubling its size, and then added another six teams in 1974. By 2000, there were thirty teams, including ostensibly non-hockey cities such as Raleigh, North Carolina, Nashville, Tennessee, and Phoenix, Arizona.[1]

In the early years of the NHL it was difficult to convince the top amateur players to turn professional, as most had good jobs and the highest paid professional player only earned $900. However, by 1925 some star players were rewarded handsomely for their efforts. This was in large part due to expansion into the United States; the highest-paid player, Pittsburgh's Lionel Conacher, had a three-year contract worth $22,500. Other players also did well: Dunc Munro received $7,000 per year, Billy Burch $6,500, while Joe Simpson earned $6,000 per year. Beginning in the 1925–26 season the NHL introduced a salary cap to limit wages growth and ensure team stability. The cap for the twelve-player roster was $35,000. By 1932–33 the cap had increased to $70,000, but there was also an individual salary cap of $7,500. Previously, some players had been earning $11,000 per year. The salary cap was eliminated in the late 1930s, following the end of the Great Depression.[2]

The first player strike in the NHL occurred during the 1924–1925 season. The number of games during the regular season had been increased by six, to thirty. However, player salaries did not increase. In addition, the players were obliged to begin preseason earlier than in the past, and they had to pay their own way until the regular season began. This led to some disquiet among the players. The Hamilton Tigers players were due to play the winner of the Canadiens and Toronto St. Patricks series for the Stanley Cup; however, Tigers players demanded an extra $200 to play in the championship series or they wouldn't play at all. Neither players nor management were willing to compromise, which resulted in the Canadiens being awarded the NHL's championship following their semifinal victory over the St. Pats. The Hamilton players stated, "We would be more than pleased to represent Hamilton again in the NHL for the benefit of the fans who have so generously patronized our games. . . . But this is final: We do not ever intend to ever play again for the present management." Hamilton management responded by announcing that they would sell all the players.[3]

Following the first strike in the NHL, wages increased over the next two decades, but the players did not receive any benefits. However, beginning in 1947 the players gained a pension plan. The plan was the brainchild of Jack Adams, a former player and the current manager of the Detroit Red Wings. He stated in January 1947 that he "talked with Detroit players over the years regarding arrangement of a satisfactory pension plan, and this year for the first time I have broached the subject to President Clarence Campbell and the directors of the National Hockey League." Unlike in other sports where a players' association had to fight with their respective league to agree to a pension, the NHL approved the pension plan without any hint of labor-management dispute. Indeed, the owner of the Chicago Blackhawks, Bill Tobin, claimed he was "for it

100 per cent." In addition to the pension plan being beneficial for the players, he believed it would be good for the owners, as "they wouldn't have to see their players going around desperate after completing their professional careers." Under the plan, players contributed $900 per year and the NHL staged an annual All-Star Game from which two-thirds of the revenues would go to the players' pension. The NHL also contributed twenty-five cents out of every ticket sold for the playoffs. Players would be eligible to receive the pension once they turned forty-five. Defending the large outlay from the players, NHL president Campbell argued that as a hockey player's career only lasted between five and six years the contributions needed to be higher than that of someone whose profession might result in a twenty or thirty-year career.[4] Even with the achievement of the pension plan, the players still were not represented by a union or players association. This changed in 1957.

The NHL Players' Association (NHLPA) came into existence in 1957, after months of secret negotiations. The players were outraged that they had not received any share from the 1956 television deal between the NHL and its broadcast partner, CBS. Detroit Red Wings player Ted Lindsay contacted Cleveland Indians pitcher Bob Feller, as the MLBPA had just negotiated a deal for MLB to fund a pension plan from revenue from the All-Star Game and World Series. Feller introduced Lindsay to MLBPA's law firm, Lewis & Mound. With Norman Lewis involved with the baseball union, Milton Mound became engaged in the proposal to organize hockey players, and on February 11, 1957, the players announced the formation of the NHLPA. Lindsay claimed that all but one player, who was later identified as Toronto Maple Leaf Ted Kennedy, joined the association and contributed $100 in startup funds. Among their demands, the players sought an improved pension plan, $10 a day meal money, training salary of $35, and a no-trade clause for players with six years' service time.

The players were not particularly militant in their approach and were happy with the current minimum salary of $6,500, which was $500 more than in baseball. However, the average hockey salary was only $9,500 compared to $13,500 for baseball. NHLPA President Lindsay said, "We don't have many grievances. . . . We just felt we should have an organization of this kind." In response, NHL president Campbell claimed, "In light of Mr. Lindsay's statement, it would be interesting to know what rights, interests, or privileges require the protection of a formal organization." He also stated that "there was nothing which the players of the NHL could accomplish through a union or association

which could not just as easily be secured by direct, informal represen-
tations to the league or its member clubs." While Campbell took the
diplomatic road, some team owners and officials blasted the decision by
the players. Detroit general manager Jack Adams called Lindsay a cancer,
while Toronto Maple Leafs owner Con Smythe, who was conciliatory in
public, interrogated his players in private and looked in his dictionary
for the meaning of the words *communist* and *communism*.[5]

The NHL refused to negotiate with the NHLPA. Campbell told the
owners, "I don't think there is any substantial group of players for it at
all. But whether the best way to handle them is to hit them on the nose
and secure a knockout, or let them die out is a matter for your decision."
The owners decided to hit the players on the nose. Both Lindsay and
Maple Leafs player representative Jim Thomson were traded to Chicago.
In response, the players association filed a $3 million antitrust lawsuit
against the NHL, the six NHL teams, as well as Madison Square Gar-
den. NHLPA vice-president Doug Harvey noted that the players "have
always felt that matters between us could be settled amicably. But since
club owners have remained adamant about [not] meeting with us, we
were forced to take this action with full support of our membership."
The lawsuit stated that the players were "deprived of their natural and
lawful right to sell their services to the highest and most acceptable
bidder. . . . As a result of the defendants' monopolistic position, their
economic power and control over this important industry, and over all
who labor in it, is complete and absolute."

However, the players were not united. In November Detroit Red
Wings players unanimously voted to withdraw from the NHLPA. They
were opposed to the antitrust lawsuit and claimed they were not con-
sulted on the action. The Red Wings players stated that they could
achieve many of their demands through talks with Detroit's management
and suggested other players do the same. The NHLPA suffered another
blow in January 1958 when, after meeting with management and being
satisfied with the response to their grievances Montreal Canadiens players also stated their willingness to withdraw from the NHLPA. Despite
these setbacks, the NHL owners agreed to meet with thirteen representatives from the NHLPA, but with no lawyers present. At the same
time, the association withdrew its antitrust lawsuit against the league
and its teams.[6]

After thirteen hours of negotiations, the owners agreed to raise the
minimum salary to $7,000 and increase pension benefits, with owners
matching players' contribution. This amounted to approximately a 60

percent increase in player pensions. The playoff pool was also increased, by almost $1,000 per player. Players also received improved hospitalization benefits, exhibition games would be limited, and players would receive compensation for moving and other expenses if they were sold or traded. The owners also agreed to the formation of a players and owners council that would meet regularly to discuss any issues. In return, the NHLPA agreed to drop all lawsuits against the NHL and its teams.

The gains made by the players were modest. The minimum wage was already unofficial policy, the pension increases were still dependent on players contributing more to the scheme, the players-owners council had no authority to compel the owners or the NHL to do anything they did not want, and television revenue, the issue that had led to the formation of the NHLPA, still remained in the hands of the owners. Moreover, the owners and the NHL still refused to recognize the NHLPA. Lindsay claimed that the NHLPA would not disband and would "continue actively as it has done up to now."[7] However, the NHLPA faded to obscurity until 1967.

After a decade of inactivity, Alan Eagleson revitalized the association. Eagleson was a lawyer and player agent who represented one of the great NHL players, Bobby Orr of the Boston Bruins. Eagleson used his position to talk to the players during the 1966–67 season about reforming the dormant NHLPA. While they were reluctant, eventually Eagleson convinced enough players and the association once again came to life, with Eagleson its executive director even though he remained a player agent. Somewhat surprisingly considering their reaction to the NHLPA in 1957, this time around there was less hostility from the NHL and the owners. This was in a large part due to the Teamsters being interested in organizing players in professional sports, including hockey. As the owners did not want a powerful union such as the Teamsters representing the players, an Eagleson-led NHLPA appeared to be preferable. Indeed, NHL president Campbell stated, "I don't like unions, but I'm glad it's Eagleson at the head of the Players' Association rather than somebody else."

Eagleson claimed that the goal of the NHLPA was for the players to achieve better conditions, and "not to put a gun to the heads of the owners."[8] The early successes of the Eagleson-led NHLPA included the minimum wage being increased to $10,000 in 1967, as well as the owners in 1969 agreeing to submit to salary arbitration if a player and team could not come to an agreement. Also, the owners agreed to wholly fund the players' pension rather than requiring the players to contribute a certain amount, and to guarantee it for ten years. Moreover, players received

life insurance, including total and permanent disability and dismember-
ment up to $50,000 and the owners agreed to discuss the reserve clause,
which Eagleson called a "milestone in itself" and claimed helped delay a
players' strike for at least one year.[9] The players benefited initially under
Eagleson's reign, and achieved more success off the ice during the 1970s,
although not as great as it might have been.

WHA, Free Agency, and
Collective Bargaining in the 1970s

In 1971 Gary Davidson, the founder of the American Basketball Association, turned his attention to hockey. With Dennis Murphy, he formed
the World Hockey Association (WHA). Neither Davidson nor Murphy
were hockey fans; they viewed the sport as a way to make money. The
first twelve-team season began in 1972–73.

Like many incumbents when faced with an upstart, the NHL did
not take the WHA seriously at first. However, after the WHA had
drafted a number of excellent prospects and NHL players began jump-
ing to the new league, the NHL began paying more attention. The
WHA was great for the players. In 1971–72, the average NHL salary
was approximately $31,000; the average WHA salary for its first sea-
son was approximately $53,000. The competition led to NHL salaries
rising dramatically in 1972–73; soon, the average NHL player's salary
was $44,000.[10] Moreover, the formation of the WHA led to a drastic
modification of the reserve clause.

As in the other professional sports, the NHL employed a perpetual
reserve clause tying a player to a particular team until he was traded or
sold. The formation of the WHA led to several NHL players attempting to disregard the clause and join the new league. Eventually, seven
separate court cases related to WHA teams signing NHL players were
combined into the federal case *Philadelphia World Hockey Club, Inc. v.
Philadelphia Hockey Club, Inc.* The WHA argued that the NHL's perpetual reserve clause, among other measures related to player mobility,
was antitrust in nature. Federal court judge Higgenbotham ruled that
the NHL was in violation of the Sherman Act because it engaged in
interstate commerce, the reserve clause was for perpetuity, and the clause
did not come about through good faith bargaining between the league
and the NHLPA. He stated that there was a "mutual understanding and
conspiracy by the NHL and its affiliated minor leagues to maintain a

monopolistic position so strong that the NHL precludes effective competition by the entry of another major professional league." He went on to argue that "[t]o grant the National Hockey League an exemption in this proceeding would undermine and thwart the policies which have evolved over the years in disposing of labor-management and antitrust disputes. I cannot compatibly reconcile the National Hockey League's monopolistic actions here with the labor exemptions from the Sherman Act."

Following the ruling, in 1974 the NHL and the WHA reached an out-of-court settlement that was approved by the judge. The NHL agreed to pay the WHA $1.75 million in damages, the WHA was allowed to use NHL arenas, there would be fifteen exhibition games between teams from the two leagues, and they would respect each other's reserve clauses. The NHL's reserve clause was replaced with a one-year option.[11] The settlement was good for the WHA and for players in both leagues.

The 1975, NHL-NHLPA collective bargaining agreement further modified the option clause. Under the terms of the five-year agreement, the NHLPA approved the NHL's implementation of a version of the Rozelle Rule, which had been unilaterally imposed by the league in 1973 in an attempt not to be found in violation of the Sherman Act. The difference between the one adopted in the NHL and the original Rozelle Rule in the NFL was that in the NHL if the two sides could not agree on compensation for the player who wanted to switch teams once his option year was finished, an independent arbitrator decided on the matter, rather than the NHL president. In addition, players and teams could enter into contracts that did not contain an option year.

The collective bargaining agreement also saw the players receive 50 percent of revenue from international competitions and pensions increase by 50 percent; players now received $750 per year of service, an increase from $500. In a positive development for the players, their contracts were now guaranteed. Future NHL President John Ziegler noted at the time that "[u]nder the old contracts . . . there was a clause that said management could give a player two weeks' notice and fire him if they felt his play wasn't up to an acceptable standard. We struck that clause, and immediately every contract was guaranteed. It was a monumental change." However, he regretted the implementation of guaranteed contracts, later stating, "Players knew their contracts were guaranteed. It was clear to general managers and coaches that in numerous instances the players weren't giving. They had to send some guys home and still they had to pay them. That created a big chunk of liability." Nonetheless, that the NHLPA accepted a form of the Rozelle Rule even after Judge Higgenbotham ruled that the reserve clause in the NHL was in violation of the Sherman Act was a large concession to the owners.

The NHLPA's acceptance of a version of the Rozelle Rule was the first time in American sports history that a union or players association agreed to such a rule. The president of the NHL players group claimed that the NHLPA accepted the compensation agreement for free agents because hockey players had the option to jump to the WHA if they did not receive a good offer from a NHL team. Not surprisingly, the owners were happy with the arrangement. Chicago Black Hawks owner William Wirtz stated that it was a "Homeric agreement" and the negotiations were conducted "with an attitude of understanding by the players and Mr. Alan Eagleson" and that the players understood the importance of the compensation clause to the "structure and stability of the entire league." The owners had a right to be happy; between the signing of the agreement and 1982 only three compensation cases were sent to the arbitrator to rule upon. Teams were hesitant to sign free agents because, as in the NFL under the Rozelle Rule, they were uncertain what the compensation would be if the case went to the arbitrator. Moreover, following discussions between Eagleson and Ziegler in September 1977, they agreed to end guaranteed contracts. Teams could buy out a player's contract at one-third of its value, with the player becoming an unrestricted free agent. In return, the NHL agreed to set up a dental plan for players, coaches, and general managers, and paid off a $600,000 debt the NHLPA had incurred in ensuring that players for the insolvent Cleveland Barons received money owed to them.[12] In sum, by agreeing to submit to the Rozelle Rule, the NHLPA effectively prevented player mobility and artificially reduced player salaries, as well as collaborating in the elimination of guaranteed contracts.

During this period, the NHLPA likely would have been able to achieve a lot more for the players if it had been willing to be much more militant. However, Eagleson followed a path of company unionism, where the NHLPA adopted a friendly attitude toward the owners. Eagleson had a cozy relationship with the owners and this continued under John Ziegler's presidency of the NHL, beginning in 1977. The two had such a comfortable working relationship that future NHL president Gil Stein observed, "It does not take a great stretch of imagination to believe that when Eagleson and Ziegler led their respective troops into collective bargaining negotiations, the results might have been pre-ordained." He further noted, "Eagleson would first make a number of demands on behalf of the players, including, of course, those Ziegler and he had already agreed would likely, at the end of the day, be granted by the NHL. . . . And once the deal was struck, the owners treated the player reps and their wives to a lavish banquet."[13]

The WHA folded in 1979, with four of its teams joining the NHL. The four clubs paid the NHL $6 million as a joining fee that was redistributed to the NHL teams, and following the merger, Eagleson requested half the money the WHA's teams had paid to the NHL teams for the union. The NHLPA had always opposed a merger as it would likely have resulted in lower salaries for the players. It was largely due to the competition between the two leagues that the average player salary in the NHL had increased from $31,000 for the 1971–72 season to $90,000 in 1977–78 season. However, after Eagleson had privately consulted with the association's president, Phil Esposito, and convinced him that a court case would hurt the NHL and that the owners were willing to compensate the players with improved benefits rather than increasing salaries, the NHLPA agreed to the expansion.

The NHL did not call the WHA teams' entry into the league a merger in an attempt to prevent any future antitrust lawsuits by the NHLPA. By allowing the expansion to proceed, the NHL and the NHLPA extended the life of the 1975 collective bargaining agreement, with some changes. Under the revised agreement, the players' pension fund was increased; players received $1,000 for each year of service, an increase from $750. In addition, the disability, life insurance, and dental plans were doubled in value, with the playoff pool also increasing. In regard to free agency, the NHL's version of the Rozelle Rule remained in place. While Eagleson may have publicly proclaimed that the players wanted a large windfall from the merger, what the players achieved was a standard extension to the collective bargaining agreement with improved benefits. However, Eagleson defended the gains made by the NHLPA. He believed his "job, as I saw it, was to keep the players working. . . . There was no sense being confrontational when the bucket you wanted to share wasn't that big. NHL revenues were inhibited by the lack of a major TV contract. The WHA was as dead as a ghost. . . . I had a lot of players in the WHA—they were my clients—and a lot of them weren't getting paid. My argument was, if we can bring in four more teams with twenty-five or thirty jobs each, it's not that bad a deal."[14]

Collective Bargaining in the 1980s
and the Fall of Eagleson

The previous collective bargaining agreement was set to expire at the end of the 1983–84 season, but the players could opt out of the agreement following the 1981–82 season as long as they notified the owners of their intent to do so by February 28, 1981. The NHL, unlike the other big three sports, had a system in place where collective bargaining was within the domain of the owners-players council that met every February and June to review the issues and had the power to make changes if necessary. Thus, each of the collective bargaining negotiations in 1975, 1982, and 1986 focused principally on a specific issue. In 1982, the issue was free agency. In February 1981, Eagleson claimed, "The players indicated they are firm in their request for free agency as an item of our negotiations with the owners." Considering how few players were changing teams under the system that was in place, the owners were happy with the status quo. By July, Eagleson and the NHLPA were now no longer demanding total free agency, but agreed that teams could receive draft picks as compensation for losing players. With negotiations still at a standstill by October, the NHLPA was exploring the possibility of obtaining strike insurance from Lloyds of London.[15] However, the likelihood of strike was low, and talks continued into the new year. By early August 1982 a deal was close, and it was duly agreed upon in the middle of the month.

Under the terms of the agreement there was a substantial change in the free agency rules. A team had the right of first refusal if a player was offered a contract by another team. If the former club did not match the contract offer, the compensation they received was tied to a player's salary. If his new contract amounted to less than $85,000, no compensation was given to his former team; if he earned between $85,000 and $99,999, the former team received a third-round draft pick; if he earned between $100,000 and $124,000, the compensation was a second and third-round draft pick. If he earned between $125,000 and $149,000, the compensation was a first-round draft pick or a player from his former team, but that team could protect eight players including the person switching teams. If a player earned between $150,000 and $199,999, compensation included either both a first and second-round draft pick or a player from the other team, but with the proviso that the latter team could protect six players, including the person switching teams.

Finally, if a player earned $200,000 or above, the compensation was two first-round draft picks or a player from the other team, but the team could protect four players, including the person switching teams. Players who were thirty-three or more were accorded unlimited free agency, while the old system remained in place for players under twenty-four or with less than five years' service time.

The NHLPA was happy with the free agency rules. NHLPA president Tony Esposito claimed that total free agency would ruin the NHL. Eagleson himself believed that total free agency would reduce the number of teams in the league to twelve, and that "the job of a players' association is to keep its membership as high as it can." The collective bargaining agreement "protects jobs, does a lot for the rank and file and gives the owners security in making long-range plans." The new system led to more free agents, but the majority of them were players for whom no compensation was required because they were earning less than $85,000 or had been let go by their teams. Approximately 15 to 20 percent of free agents were players who were earning $150,000 or less. For the duration of the 1982 collective bargaining agreement, no free agent changed teams under circumstances where the higher levels of compensation would have been invoked.[16]

Another area where hockey players lagged behind their contemporaries in other sports was in wages growth. Between the 1977–78 and 1984–85 seasons, players' wages only increased from $90,000 to $149,000. By the end of the 1985–86 season, when the 1982 collective bargaining agreement expired, salaries had only increased another $10,000, to $159,000. This was in part due to the cozy relationship between the NHLPA and the NHL. It was also, in part, due to the NHL's inability to land a good television contract. From 1956 until 1975 the NHL had an agreement with, at different times, both CBS and NBC to broadcast a certain number of games. However, hockey was not a ratings winner. This led the NHL focusing on the cable industry to broadcast its games. In 1985, it signed a $20 million, three-year agreement with ESPN to broadcast thirty-three games, the All-Star game, and the Stanley Cup playoffs.[17]

This was the situation leading into the 1986 negotiations for a new collective bargaining agreement. Once again, despite being on record numerous times in the past that it did not want total free agency, the NHLPA was now arguing, at least publicly, that the players wanted it. The NHLPA also wanted a one-time payment of $30 million to help fund a post-career program for retired NHL players, as well as improvements to the pension scheme. As there had been during the previous set of negotiations, there was strike talk in 1986, but it was just that: purely talk. There was very little likelihood that the NHLPA under Eagleson would engage in a collective action such as a strike. Indeed, a new collective bargaining agreement was announced in July 1986 without any hint of acrimony, at least publicly.

Under the terms of the agreement, the free agency rules were modified to the slight benefit of the players. Players earning less than $110,000 were now unrestricted free agents. This effectively raised the unofficial minimum salary to $110,000 compared to $85,000 under the old agreement. For players earning above that figure, a player from the other team could no longer constitute part of the compensation deal; only draft picks and money were involved. At the highest level of player salary, $400,000 or above, the compensation for losing a free agent was two first-round draft picks, with the picks having to be among the first seven of the draft, plus $100,000. Because this scenario promised to be unlikely, a cash consideration would be applied if the team did not have two picks within the first seven slots. The only other change to the previous rule applied to older players. They now received total free agency if they were thirty-one or older and their contract had expired, a two-year reduction.

In addition to the changes in the free agency rules, player pensions were doubled and former players who had played in four hundred games or more in their careers would receive a lump sum of $250,000 Canadian once they turned fifty-five. However, only players who played during the 1986 season or after qualified for the lump sum payment. The lump sum payment was part of the post-NHL careers program that would be administered as well as funded by the NHLPA. Although the association had entered the negotiations seeking $30 million, it settled for an owners' contribution consisting of a one-off payment of upward of $15 million. Trying to put a positive spin on the agreement, NHLPA vice-president Tim Kerr stated that "it was a fair deal. . . . Sure, we'd like free agency, but we're not like football, baseball and basketball. We don't have the TV contracts like that. I think what we did was get the best deal for the most players. Most guys will get more money, especially at the low end. And we got a great pension. All right, so we still don't have real free agency, but this deal makes it a lot better than it was before."[18] The pension increase was, in theory, certainly beneficial to the players, as was the lump sum payment. However, once more it was likely that the NHLPA could have done better. Indeed, there were rumblings from the players regarding Eagleson's leadership.

In 1989, there was a challenge to Eagleson's rule led by former NFLPA boss Ed Garvey and agents Ron Scaler and Rich Winter. More than two hundred NHL players contributed $100 each toward a study of Eagleson's performance. The study found that the NHLPA had not benefited the players to any great extent during the 1980s, and Eagleson's conflicts of interest had negatively affected the players' finances. It also noted, "Eagleson may be the most overpaid executive in the labor movement in North America. Not even the president of the two-million member Teamsters union comes close to Alan in wages, benefits, pension and expense accounts." Moreover, it was revealed that just before negotiations for the 1986 collective bargaining agreement Eagleson had demanded a new six-year guaranteed contract, with his salary paid in U.S. dollars, and a U.S. $50,000 per year pension for life. He'd given the player representatives five minutes to decide; unsurprisingly, he got what he wanted. The report concluded: "What we found can only be described as a scandal."

Following the report's release, a fiery meeting was held, which led to the association's executive board telling Eagelson that in order to remain head of the NHLPA he could no longer be a player agent, must allow an audit of his previous three years' tax returns and all future ones, must personally guarantee approximately $2 million in loans he had made using NHLPA's funds, and must take a leave of absence from his law firm. Eagleson agreed to follow the requests, and he remained head of the NHLPA.

Eagleson announced that he would step down on December 31, 1991, once he had groomed his deputy Bob Goodenow for the position of executive director and, hopefully, had successfully negotiated a new collective bargaining agreement. Clearly demonstrating how exclusively the NHLPA had become Eagleson's domain, it had only three employees, including Eagleson, before Goodenow was hired.

In the same year that Eagleson resigned, seven former NHL players filed a lawsuit seeking damages of $25 million in relation to the pension plan. Due to the high interest rates of the 1970s and 1980s the plan had generated a large surplus for a number of years. Rather than increase the amount going to retired players, between 1982 and 1985 the owners used the surplus to fund the plan for current players. The Ontario Court of Justice sided with the players, and the ruling was upheld by the Supreme Court of Canada. The Ontario Court of Justice noted that Eagleson had made no effort to stop the owners' raid and that this demonstrated "moral shortcomings." The players were eventually awarded almost $50 million, a windfall for hundreds of former players who saw their annual pension tripled to $30,000. During this period, while the NHLPA's executive board had only asked Eagleson to make some changes in order to remain head of the association, the FBI, the U. S. Department of Labor, and the Canadian government were viewing the charges levied in the report much more seriously. Following a two-year investigation, in 1994 Eagleson was indicted by a grand jury on racketeering, misappropriation of NHLPA funds, receiving kickbacks on NHLPA disability insurance, embezzling money from the NHPA by "submitting $250,000 in claims for such things as theatre and ballet tickets, tickets to the Wimbledon tennis tournament, gifts for customs officials, dinner parties for Canadian judicial and political figures, golf and ski trips and for rental fees on properties he owned," and defrauding two NHL players, among other charges. He accepted a plea bargain and paid a fine of $700,000 and served six months of an eighteen-month prison sentence.[19] As of 2014, Eagleson was still unrepentant about his actions.

The NHLPA under Goodenow was vastly different than the one under Eagleson. Indeed, it was under his tenure that the players went on strike for the first time.

The NHLPA under Goodenow

Once he became NHLPA executive director, Bob Goodenow made an effort to meet hundreds of players to forge solidarity in preparation for any future dispute with management. He was determined to take a much more adversarial position in collective bargaining and to strive to achieve more for the players than Eagleson had been prepared to do. During the negotiations in 1992 for a new collective bargaining agreement, players sought changes in the free agency rules, better pensions, and a salary arbitration system like baseball's, where an independent arbitrator decided on the outcome. In contrast, the owners wanted to limit salaries, tighten free agency, as well as receive a greater share of the trading card revenue earned by the players.

The recent expansion of the NHL had led to an injection of cash. Indeed, the average player salary had increased from $184,000 in 1987–88 to $369,000 for the 1991–92 season. In part this was due to the players having overwhelmingly agreed to the NHLPA's publicly releasing player salaries beginning in 1989, despite Eagleson's vehement opposition. This allowed player agents and the players themselves to more accurately determine how much they should be earning. It also forced owners to engage in bidding wars to secure prized players. The number of players earning million dollar contracts went from two to sixteen within two years after salary disclosure; by 1991, the number had grown to thirty-three.

The increasing salaries led the owners to claim financial hardship. A player involved in the 1992 negotiations remembered that the owners had cried poor during negotiations for the previous collective bargaining agreement. "We were duped," he said. "We were told that with Minnesota, St. Louis and Winnipeg all in bad shape then, jobs would be lost if the players pushed too hard. The players became afraid and made concessions. Well, our premise this time is a dramatic change. The league is reasonably solid and profitable. The large amount of salary increases in the last few years have raised suspicions, and we want to know how that came about, where that money came from." The 1991–92 season had begun without a contract in place, and as the playoffs approached there was still no agreement.

With negotiations still at a deadlock, the players voted 560–4 in favor of a strike beginning on March 30, 1992, if an agreement was not reached. The timing of the strike was tactical. As it was near the end of the season, the players had already received the bulk of their salaries, but the majority of the owners' revenues were derived from the broadcasts of playoff games, so presumably they had more to lose.

In preparation for a strike, teams began to look into the possibility of signing replacement players. NHL president Ziegler stated that players were receiving approximately 63 percent of league revenue and that the NHL would lose $9 million for the 1991–92 season, but there was disagreement on how the revenue was calculated, and the NHLPA claimed the NHL would actually make a profit of $24 million. Ziegler further argued that the owners and the players had a great relationship, which the new NHLPA leadership was violating by using lawyers who knew little about hockey and even less about the hockey business during the negotiations. Of course, Ziegler failed to mention the he himself was an attorney and both the NHL and the NHLPA had used lawyers in the past.

Adding fuel to the flames was New Jersey Devils owner John McMullen, who stated that he did not give the players "too much credit for too much intelligence," and expected them to make a mistake by going out on strike. Whether it was a mistake or not and whether the players lacked intelligence, they did indeed go out on strike, beginning on April 1. Washington Capitals player Mike Liut, who was a member of the bargaining committee, declared, "We decided we'd learn the issues, develop the issues, argue the issues among ourselves. . . . We decided we weren't going to be an apathetic group anymore."[20]

Compared to subsequent work stoppages in the NHL, the 1992 strike was a minor one that lasted only ten days. During the strike, the players remained largely united. Chicago Black Hawks player Keith Brown noted, "In other contract agreements, I never even voted and never knew the issues. . . . I just went along. Now, players see how important it is to be involved and informed. We know more than ever before." In contrast the owners were divided. Nine out of the twenty-two were willing to agree to the players' latest offer, but they were opposed by others who wanted to play hardball. As a result, negotiations continued throughout the strike, with each side offering its proposals only for the other side to reject them.

On April 7, the players rejected the NHL's final offer. Ziegler, trying to hold back tears, claimed it was a "sad day, my friends, a sad day." Trying to convince the press and the public that the proposal the NHLPA rejected was heavily in the players' favor and that the owners had surrendered to the players, he stated, "If it will make the players happy, I'd be willing to call it an unconditional surrender. . . . All they have to do is go back and play hockey." Ziegler gave the players until April 9 to accept the deal or he would call off the season. However, the players rejected Ziegler's ultimatum. At that point, the hardline owners wanted to cancel the season, but the other owners urged restraint. The moderates won out, and the owners agreed to a final meeting with the NHLPA on April 10, at which an agreement was reached.[21]

Under the terms of the 1992 collective bargaining agreement, the players had input into the choice of arbitrators and it was agreed that all arbitrations would be completed before the season began. There was a one-year reduction, from thirty-one to thirty, in the age at which a player could become an unrestricted free agent. In addition, there was a reduction in the compensation given to a player's former team when he switched teams. The rules allowed more fringe players to switch teams, but star players were generally "stuck" with their teams until they turned thirty.

The playoff pool was increased to $7.5 million from $3 million. The players were also successful in keeping the rights to their own likeness, but they yielded the rights to the owners to promote games, and their share of revenue from commercial ventures remained at 68 percent. In a win for the owners, the regular season was extended by four games, to eighty-four.

The contract was scheduled to expire on September 15, 1993, after only two years, despite the NHLPA's having requested a three-year deal. This was a concern to some players, as they believed the owners would seek revenge for the strike. Indeed, following the settlement Quebec Nordiques President Marcel Aubut stated, "This is not a victory for the owners because we will lose a lot of money with the deal we have made."[22] While the agreement was not a victory for the owners, neither was it an overwhelming win for the players, and in time the fear that the owners would want to take "revenge" for the strike came to fruition.

The 1992 agreement was to be Ziegler's last major contribution as NHL president. He was forced to resign by the owners in June, and on February 1, 1993, he was replaced by Gary Bettman as head of the NHL, with the title of the office changed from president to commissioner. Bettman had been a senior vice-president and general counsel of the NBA.

The 1993–94 season was played without a collective bargaining agreement in place. As a signal that Bettman was determined to unify the owners, he threatened fines of up to $250,000 for any owner who discussed collective bargaining negotiations in public. The players were willing for the 1994–95 season to be played under the terms of the previous agreement. Since the 1992 strike, the average salary had increased to over $500,000 and the number of players earning $1 million and above had more than tripled. The rise in salaries was due to salary disclosure, arbitration, as well as the expansion of the NHL into five new markets. While there was a large increase in the number of teams, the number of NHL-caliber players did not rise accordingly, and star players were at a premium. Moreover, under Goodenow, the NHLPA's objective was to make the players financially secure. Liut quotes Goodenow as telling the NHL that "the players should earn enough to be financially secure for life when they retired. . . . That was an unbelievable statement. People couldn't fathom it. Bob set out to make it happen." However, the dramatic rise in salaries was not in the best interests of the owners, and they urged the NHLPA to engage in concession bargaining.

In August 1994, the NHL initially proposed that NHL rosters be reduced from twenty to nineteen, that salary arbitration be eliminated along with the $250,000 lump sum payment agreed to in the 1986 agreement, that players pay for their own transport to preseason training camps and to return home after the season, that players contribute to their medical insurance, and that highly paid players pay for their own life, health, and disability insurance They also wanted the elimination of contracts under which NHL players sent to the minors still received their NHL salaries, the elimination of meal money both during preseason training and on the road, and the reduction of the playoff pool from $9 million to $2 million. The NHL claimed that its proposal would save the league $20 million annually, while the NHLPA argued the savings would be between $50 million and $70 million.

The league's proposal was not well received by the NHLPA and the players. NHLPA president Mike Gartner stated, "It is certainly warfare. . . . They obviously want to fight. Why would they be doing something like this unless they were trying to provoke us?" During collective bargaining negotiations it is customary for each side to put forth proposals that the other side will not agree to, but with room for compromise. The NHL's opening proposal did not do this; it was a hardline approach. In addition to the previous demands, during the negotiations the NHL also requested a rookie salary cap and a payroll tax.

The NHL wanted the wealthier teams to redistribute some of their wealth to the less well-off teams. In response, the NHLPA proposed a 5 percent tax on salaries and revenue, estimated to be approximately $40 million, to be redistributed to small-market teams. This was rejected by the owners. The NHLPA told the players to prepare for a lockout. Edmonton Oilers player representative Bill Ranford noted, "The guys are all supposed to have saved their money for the possibility that this would happen. . . . We were told before the summer to get ready for this." Bettman claimed that if an agreement was not reached before the start of the season, the NHL would lock the players out. "The absence of a collective bargaining agreement leaves us no choice," he said. "To have the season start and then have it taken away [by a strike] would not be fair to the fans, the players or the teams." While it is debatable, the fans would probably prefer some hockey rather than the prospect of no hockey at all, and there was no guarantee the players would strike. Bettman and the owners were playing hardball and were prepared to lock out the players if the NHLPA did not agree to major concessions. Their hardline approach was clearly demonstrated when they rejected the NHLPA's last-minute proposal that they would play the season without a contract in place and would not strike during the regular season and the playoffs. Bettman stated, "We need a player-employment system that avoids making this a league of haves and have-nots. . . . This situation must be addressed, and addressed now."[23] Unable to come to an agreement, the owners locked out the players before the 1994–95 season could get underway.

During the lockout, the NHLPA agreed to concede on some points. The union was willing to accept a rookie salary cap as long as there was no version of a luxury tax. The proposal was rejected by the owners. The NHLPA later agreed to a salary cap for rookies of $1.2 million for their first season, but the owners wanted a rookie salary cap of $700,000. The two sides moved slightly closer together later, when the NHLPA agreed to a cap of $1 million, although the owners wanted it to be $800,000.

The lockout continued, with Bettman periodically reducing the length of the season. He claimed that if an agreement was not reached in time to play a fifty-game season, the entire season would be canceled. Not helping the owners' cause was that even though they constantly stated that they were losing money, they refused to provide any documentation for their claims. Further helping the players was that there was some disunity among the owners. Bettman continually tried to claim that the version of a payroll tax the owners wanted was not a salary cap. However, Detroit Red Wings owner Mike Ilitch disagreed. "It's a cap," he said. "That's what we're after here. They're using other fancy terms, but that's what it boils down to." In contrast to the hawkish approach of Ilitch, Pittsburgh owner Howard Baldwin opposed the lockout and was privately trying to get it to end. The players were largely united during the lockout, although not always New Jersey Devil Stephane Richer publicly claimed that the majority of players would agree to one of the owners' offers if they could vote on it.

In late December, the owners agreed to withdraw their demand for a payroll tax. This concession greatly increased the chance that a deal could be made. Still, the lockout continued into 1995, but an end was near. Arguably, the owners were willing to slightly back down from their hardline approach because they had recently signed a $155 million five-year contract with Fox to broadcast a number of regular season and playoff games. (By way of comparison, the NFL had recently signed a four-year deal worth $1.6 billion.) Under the television agreement, Fox shared coverage with ESPN. Fox was scheduled to broadcast the All-Star Game, but due to the lockout the game was not played. If the lockout continued, the playoffs would be lost and the owners would not receive any revenue from their broadcast partners, as well as making a less than auspicious start to their relationship with Fox. An agreement was reached in early January 1995. The lockout had lasted for 104 days, and the regular season was cut from eighty-four games to forty-eight.[24]

Under the terms of the six-year agreement, there was a rookie salary cap for players under twenty-five years old. For 1995–96, it was $850,000, rising annually to $1,075,000 in the 2000–01 season. Free agency rules were tightened, with players younger than twenty-five no longer eligible for restricted free agency. The age at which players could gain free agency rose from thirty to thirty-two during the first three years of the agreement, and was then reduced to thirty-one for the remaining years. Players could only achieve free agency after completing their second contract with a team.

Salary arbitration was modified so that teams could reject three awards of $550,000 or above over a two-year period, but if they did so a player became a free agent after the third rejection. Finally, the draft age was increased to nineteen from eighteen.

Overall, the contract constituted a victory for the owners and a mild defeat for the players. "Are we happy about the scars that have been created for the game of hockey?" Gartner asked. "Are we happy about losing millions of dollars? Are we happy about the relations between owners and players has been severely hindered? No, we're not happy about that. But we're happy that hockey is hopefully going to be played very soon." While there were grumblings by the players over the agreement, an overall majority of players and a majority of all players on every team ratified it. However, the NHLPA did not release the overall number, signifying that the ratification was far from unanimous. Likewise, not all owners were happy with the agreement. They ratified it by a margin of only nineteen to seven. The dissenting owners were not pleased that salaries were not linked to revenue.[25] While there was criticism of the NHLPA for agreeing to concessions in order to avoid a salary cap, that the players were able to avoid it for non-rookies while keeping limited free agency, salary arbitration, and guaranteed contracts proved very beneficial for them.

Salary Escalation and More Lockouts

Although its length was specified as six years, the 1995 collective bargaining agreement contained a clause that allowed either the owners or the NHLPA to reopen the contract following the 1997–98 season. However, in 1995 the two parties agreed to eliminate this clause. Indeed, both sides were relatively happy with the agreement, or at the very least did not want another crippling work stoppage, and it was extended twice. Even though the owners wanted to limit salaries and had locked out the players in 1994–95 to try to achieve this, they then went ahead and paid individual players massive amounts, and in the decade following the lockout, players' salaries escalated dramatically. Between 1994 and

2003, player salaries increased by an average of 12.3 percent per year; a total increase of 219.6 percent.

Faced with escalating salaries, the NHL was preparing for a lockout. In November 1998 the league alerted the teams to set aside $10 million for a lockout fund. Moreover, it asked the NHLPA to reopen the collective bargaining agreement in June 1999. Bettman wrote a letter to Goodenow stating, "If the current trend continues, I cannot predict what shape the league will be in in 2004. I can, however, tell you with certainty that the potential for conflict will be greater because we would, under this scenario, be likely to insist on significant retrenching (not just limiting increases) of player costs." Not surprisingly, given the escalating salaries, the NHLPA refused.

By 2002–03 the average player salary was $1.79 million, with the median over $1 million. Player salaries accounted for well over half of league revenue, with the owners losing somewhere between $123 million and $273 million. The lower figure was determined by an independent study by *Forbes*; the higher figure is the one arrived at in an NHL-commissioned report. The discrepancy between them is accounted for by competing definitions of what actually counts as revenue in the NHL. When the NHLPA was permitted to examine the books of two Canadian and two American teams, it found approximately $52 million in revenue not declared by the teams. Furthermore, the NHL had a lockout fund of $300 million; it was never determined when calculating how much the NHL lost whether the figure included money set aside for a potential lockout.

It didn't enhance the long-term profitability of the NHL when in 1998 it signed a five-year television deal worth $600 million with ABC and ESPN, because, following disappointing ratings and ABC's realization that it had massively overpaid for the rights, the NHL was able to secure a two-year renewal with the two networks for no more than $60 million a year. Furthermore, in the decade following the lockout, the NHL engaged in a dramatic expansion: the number of teams in the league was increased from twenty-one to thirty and there was a relocation from traditional Canadian NHL cities such as Winnipeg and Quebec, to non-hockey-identified regions in the American Sunbelt. As a result of the expansion, teams received lower revenue from the television deal than they had anticipated, as it was divided among more teams.

The NHL was losing money, and the players were, arguably, earning too much, although it was the owners who continued to dole out ever-increasing salaries. Indeed, while the 1995 collective bargaining agreement had introduced a rookie cap, a loophole was found by which the owners could give rookies bonuses. Not surprisingly, this led to gigantic bonuses being handed out.[26]

Nonetheless, the NHLPA was aware that the NHL was losing millions. The union indicated that it was willing to accept a 5 percent reduction in existing contracts, as well as reductions in rookie salaries and the implementation of a luxury tax for teams who spent more than $50 million, if it would relieve the financial pressure on the league. However, these concessions did not go far enough for the owners. Moreover, Bettman, seeking greater control over the negotiations, convinced the NHL to amend the bylaws to allow him to accept a collective bargaining agreement with the approval of a simple majority of the ownership, rather than the two-thirds previously required. Further, to reject any deal he required the assent of only eight owners.

Bettman was seeking what he called "cost certainty," that is, a true salary cap, and he proposed six different ways that "cost certainty" could be achieved. These ranged from imposing a hard, inflexible salary cap to permitting the league, rather than the teams to negotiate contracts with player agents. Moreover, he proposed that player salaries not exceed 50 percent of NHL revenue. In this, the league was attempting to reduce the average player's salary from approximately $1.83 million to $1.3 million.

Despite the number of ostensibly different proposals, NHL executive vice president Bill Daly admitted that they were not all that different from each other and the NHLPA rejected all them, claiming that five were traditional salary caps and the sixth a de facto salary cap. Toronto Maples Leafs player representative Bryan McCabe summed up the position of the NHLPA: "Bottom line, if they [the NHL] want a hard cap, we'll sit out the rest of our lives." One day after the previous collective bargaining agreement expired, and even though the players had vowed not to strike, the NHL imposed a lockout, on September 15, 2004.[27]

Overseas, hockey was thriving, and many players signed with European teams. At one point during the lockout, more than 350 NHL players were playing for teams in Europe. Once again trying to present a unified collective voice to the public, Bettman instructed the owners not to publicly speak about the negotiations or risk a fine. During the lockout, part owner of the Atlanta Thrashers Steve Belkin was fined $250,000 for suggesting that if the lockout continued the NHL would bring in replacement players.

Players were also not totally united. Canadiens fringe player Pierre Dagenais was quoted as saying, "Guys have started to talk in the last three weeks. . . . It could open Bob Goodenow's eyes. I'd be curious to see if they took a poll of the players on a salary cap. They may be surprised to see how many players in my situation would vote for a cap." Bettman attempted to portray the owners and the NHL as the people who loved the game while the players, and in particular Goodenow, were hell-bent on destroying it, greedy millionaires wanting more. He stated, "To use a hockey term, they [the NHLPA] are instigating a fight. . . . This union leadership negotiates by confrontation. We are hurting. We need help." He further claimed, "This union doesn't seem to care about the problems, the game or the fans."

For his part, Goodenow stated during the first few months of the lockout that the players were willing to make enormous sacrifices for the good of the NHL and the fans. In December, the NHLPA announced it was willing to accept a six-year contract with a 24 percent reduction in salaries, a reduction in rookie salaries, further restrictions on salary arbitration, a formula for revenue sharing, and a luxury tax beginning at $45 million, with teams spending more than $60 million particularly hard hit. The NHLPA estimated the savings to be $270 million in the first year and $528 million over the first three years of the agreement.

The size of the concessions shocked some player representatives, but they believed the membership would agree to them. Nonetheless, the players were far from happy, and they began to speak their minds. Minnesota Wild player Brian Rolston stated, "I think there was a lot of reaction from the players like, 'Twenty-four percent, this is ridiculous'. . . . It's something where we put a lot of faith in [Bob Goodenow] and we put a lot of faith in our executive committee to make these decisions for us. If you brought in every NHL player, there would probably be a lot of guys pretty [ticked] off about losing 24 percent. I know there are a lot of guys who didn't know that was going to be the case." Likewise Tampa Bay Lightning player representative Tim Taylor claimed, "What we are conceding is incredible. Twenty-four percent? When the executive committee told us that, we were all like, 'Are you kidding me?' We thought it might be 10 percent."

Even so, the owners rejected the offer almost immediately and countered by proposing that player salaries be 54 percent of NHL revenue, which would mean a salary cap between $34.6 million and $38.6 million. They also proposed the elimination of salary arbitration, and salary reductions for all players except those earning less than $800,000. Those players who earned between $800,000 and $4.99 million would have their salaries reduced by 24 percent and those earning over $5 million would receive a 35 percent reduction. In return, the age limit for free agency would be reduced to thirty, and the minimum salary would be increased from $185,000 to $300,000. The NHLPA rejected the offer. The issue was the salary cap; the owners wanted it and the NHLPA was adamantly opposed to it, and so the lockout continued into 2005.

A potential breakthrough appeared in February. Supposedly, Goodenow's Deputy Ted Saskin met secretly with Daly and agreed to a hard cap as long as there was no link between player salaries and revenue. It is uncertain whether or not Saskin did this with Goodenow's approval. The meeting led to the NHL agreeing that salaries could exceed 55 percent of revenue. The NHLPA accepted this and in a major concession agreed on a form of a salary cap. This angered some players and divided them. Buffalo Sabers player representative Jay McKee spoke out. "It's not so much I am angry that they offered a cap," he said. "I'm angry at 'why now'? Why not last June, last July?" Likewise, Chicago player Matthew Barnaby complained, "Something like that you think might have been able to get done in the summer. . . . Am I mad? No. I want to get back to work. But at the same time, I'm just a little disappointed that it went this far to play poker and to have someone call your bluff." However, despite the NHLPA accepting a cap, an agreement remained out of their grasp. The NHL proposed a cap of $42.5 million per team while the association pressed for a cap of $49 million, a difference of $195 million. Bettman wrote to Goodenow stating, "This offer is not an invitation to begin negotiations—it's too late for that. . . . This is our last effort to make a deal that's fair to the players and one that the clubs [hopefully] can afford. We have no more flexibility and there is no time for further negotiation." The two sides could not come to a compromise, and on February 16, 2005, Bettman and the owners cancelled the balance of the 2004–05 season.[28]

Despite numerous meetings during the "off-season" the two sides could move no closer to an agreement. As the lockout continued, cracks began to form in the players' unity. An increasing number of them indicated their willingness to accept a salary cap as long as it was not linked to NHL revenue. This, combined with Bettman's claim that the 2005–06 season would not occur either unless an agreement was in place (although at the same time he said he was committed to starting the season on time), eventually led the parties to hammer out an agreement. The compromise was helped to its conclusion by the further sidelining of Goodenow in mid-May. He wanted to stop negotiating with the NHL, but was overruled by the NHLPA's president Trevor Linden and the executive committee, and as a result Goodenow's deputy Ted Saskin took on a more leading role and the NHLPA as a whole had a much greater conciliatory stance.

The lockout was lifted on July 13, 2005, after 301 days. It was not a victory for the players. Under the terms of the six-year collective bargaining agreement there was a salary cap of $39 million, but teams only had to spend $21.5 million. Players' salaries were limited to 57 percent of hockey-related revenue and rookie salaries were capped at $850,000 per season. Players already under contract had their salaries reduced by 24 percent. Before the start of the new season, teams had the opportunity to fire players with the discharged player receiving two-thirds of the amount specified on his existing contract minus 24 percent. There was what amounted to an individual salary cap, as no player could earn more than 20 percent of a team's cap. The maximum amount a player could earn was $7.8 million.

While previously only players had the option to request arbitration of salary disputes, now the owners could also do so. Part of the each player's salary was put in escrow; if salaries exceeded the players' share of hockey-related revenue, the escrow money would be withdrawn and distributed to the owners, if it fell short, the same money would be returned to the players. In one of the few victories for the players, they were allowed to become unrestricted free agents for the 2006–07 season when they turned twenty-nine, and for 2007–08 when they turned twenty-seven. Players with seven years' service time also became unrestricted free agents.

Finally, the minimum salary was increased from $175,000 to $450,000 in 2005–06 and eventually to $500,000 in the final year of the agreement. Bettman claimed, "It's the type of agreement that we think a professional sports league like ours can thrive under for everybody's benefit because we are true economic partners, sharing fairly." In contrast, Goodenow somberly stated, "Clearly some of those issues were different than what we envisioned from the outset." Later that month, Goodenow resigned as NHLPA executive director. He was replaced by Ted Saskin.[29]

Who was to blame for the lockout that canceled the 2004–05 season? Did the union underestimate the need for financial reform? The NHL was losing millions of dollars, with players' salaries taking a large slice of league revenue. However, without the players there is no NHL, and they were willing to accept massive salary cuts to prevent a lockout. Was Goodenow to blame for taking such a hardline approach against the salary cap? If the players had accepted the NHL's offer before the season was cancelled they would have been in a better financial state, as they would not have lost a year's income. Or was it Bettman's fault? Dave Zirin argues that "Bettman took one look at this blue-collar league built on the backs of hardscrabble French Canadians, toothless grins, and rabid fans, and recoiled. He examined its base in northern de-industrializing cities and shook his head at the absence of revenue streams to suck dry. He saw the future of ice hockey and, unfathomably, saw Dixie. Bettman expanded the league to thirty teams, putting the sport in places like Nashville, Atlanta, Raleigh, Phoenix and Columbus. The NHL owners sat back and collected hundreds of millions of dollars in expansion fees, giving out fat contracts along the way, with no thought to the long-term consequences. Predictably, these new revenue streams were shockingly shallow. The big national TV contract Bettman promised never came and the NHL was left with unknowable new teams like the Hurricanes, Coyotes, and Predators playing in half-empty arenas."[30] In the end, all parties were at least partly to blame. However, the owners achieved what they had wanted all along: a salary cap and a massive reduction in player salaries. As for the fans, at least they could watch hockey again. The irony was that many of those fans did not care whether the players on their favorite team received equitable contracts, as they were in industries demanding massive concessions from their workers too. As for the players, well, at least they could play hockey again.

The 2012–13 Lockout

In the years following the 2004–05 lockout, the NHLPA experienced turmoil. Ted Saskin, who replaced Goodenow as executive director, was fired in 2007 for allegedly hacking into and reading players' e-mails. He was replaced by Paul Kelly. Kelly was previously a U.S. District Attorney who had prosecuted disgraced former NHLPA leader Alan Eagleson. However, less than two years after taking up the role, Kelly was fired, as the players believed he was too conciliatory to the owners and not "tough enough" to fight on their behalf in the forthcoming collective bargaining negotiations. Kelly was replaced by former MLBPA head Donald Fehr.

Despite the range of concessions agreed to by the players in the 2005 collective bargaining agreement, the NHL was still not in a robust state. NHL revenue increased from $2.2 billion in 2005 to $3.3 billion in 2011–12. In addition, the NHL signed a ten-year television deal with Versus and NBC worth $1.9 billion. However, while revenue was increasing, so were player salaries. The average salary of an NHL player rose to $2.17 million at the end of the 2010–11 season. The worth of an NHL team increased 18 percent compared to the previous year. However, the five most valuable teams' average worth was $605 million. The Toronto Maple Leafs were worth $1 billion, the New York Rangers were worth $750 million, the Montreal Canadiens $575 million, the Chicago Blackhawks $350 million, and the Boston Bruins were worth $348 million. In contrast, the five least valuable teams' average worth was "only" $145 million. The Carolina Hurricanes were worth $162 million, the New York Islanders $155 million, the Columbus Blue Jackets $145 million, the Phoenix Coyotes $134 million, and the St. Louis Blues $130 million. It is interesting to note that three out of the five least valuable franchises were either teams that had relocated or were expansion teams since 2000. In contrast, if one includes the Detroit Red Wings, the six most valuable teams were the "original six."

Forbes estimated that thirteen NHL teams lost money in the 2011–12 season, with five teams losing more than $5 million. The "original six" had healthy profits, as did a number of the established teams in the league, but the expansion sides were generally struggling, especially those in the American Sunbelt, which, if they did not go deep into the playoffs, were usually guaranteed to lose money. Despite the efforts of the NHL, not all cities can be hockey cities. As an example, in 2011 a consortium bought the money-losing Atlanta Jets for $170 million, which included a $60 million franchise fee to the NHL. The consortium relocated the team to Winnipeg, which had lost their previous NHL franchise to Phoenix in 2006 and were starved for big-time hockey. For the 2011–12 season, the Winnipeg Jets sold out every home game, turned a profit of $13.3 million, and the team's estimated worth increased to $200 million. A 2010 study found that Canadians outside of Quebec were forty times more likely to have watched the first week of the Stanley Cup playoffs than Americans. In Quebec, they were ninety times more likely.[31]

As in its initial proposal during the 2004–05 negotiations, the NHL wanted the players to accept a large reduction in salary. The NHL sought a ten-year contract with players' share of revenue reduced to 46 percent, down from the current 57 percent. This would amount to a 19 percent reduction in player salaries. The league also wanted salary arbitration to be eliminated, player contracts to only be five years in length with no bonuses and players receiving the same money every year, that is, no front-loaded or back-loaded contracts. Moreover, the NHL wanted to tighten free agency rules, proposing that the age players may achieve unlimited free agency be increased by three years, to thirty, as long as the player has at least ten years' service time. In disregard of the fact that the owners were about to ask for five-year contracts under which players would receive an unchanging amount for the life of the contract, a week before the NHL's proposal, the Minnesota Wild signed Ryan Sutter and Zach Parise to identical thirteen-year contracts worth $98 million each, with the majority of the money coming in the first nine years.

In response to the NHL's offer, the NHLPA indicated its willingness to lower somewhat the percentage of revenue that players receive as long as there was increased revenue sharing between teams and that current contracts were honored. The NHLPA proposed more than $250 million in revenue sharing, while the NHL offered $190 million. Under the previous agreement, revenue sharing had been $170 million. The NHLPA requested a three-year contract, with an option for a fourth year, with players receiving 53 percent of NHL revenue. The NHL countered by offering a six-year contract under which players would initially receive 49 percent of revenue, which would be reduced to 47 percent by the final year of the agreement.

History was repeating itself when the NHLPA offered to start the season without a collective bargaining agreement in place, but Bettman stated that if there was no contract the NHL would lock out the players. Fehr argued that the players were united. "The players are really pretty unified," he said. "If there was any doubt about their understanding of this negotiation that evaporated when we got the owners' proposal. Whatever lingering doubts there might have been that the players weren't on the same page has ceased to be there." Fehr did his best to unify the players. He traveled across America, Canada, and even went to Europe meeting the players and keeping them informed on what was happening. Moreover, the NHLPA formed a thirty-one-player negotiating committee and offered to pay for transport and accommodation for any player wishing to attend any negotiating session. Their solidarity was to be tested when agreement could not be reached and the owners locked out the players, on September 15, 2012.[32]

As the lockout got under way, the league initially cancelled all preseason games and then the first two weeks of the season. In the middle of October, there were signs of a possible breakthrough when the NHL proposed a six-year agreement with a fifty-fifty split of hockey-related revenue. Bettman claimed that existing contracts would be honored, but that there would be a deferral of some payments, and it was later revealed that the contracts would be "whole" for only the first two years of the agreement. Further, according to the proposal, the salary cap would be set at $59.9 million and teams would be required to spend at least $43.9 million. Revenue sharing would be $200 million.

Fehr responded by writing to the players: "Simply put, the owners' new proposal, while not quite as Draconian as their previous proposals, still represents enormous reductions in player salaries and individual contracting rights. As you will see, at the 5 percent industry growth rate the owners predict, the salary reduction over six years exceeds $1.6 billion." The NHL's proposal would have resulted in a 12 percent reduction in player salaries, with the league also wanting the players to accept a less generous definition of hockey-related revenue. Unable to come to a compromise, the NHL withdrew its offer; some owners now requested a majority share of hockey-related income, and the lockout dragged on. As far apart as they were, they agreed to mediation by the Federal Mediation and Conciliation Service, but after only two days the service's mediators admitted that, even though both sides had given some ground, they were too far apart for the mediation to continue. Bill Daly told the media, "After spending several hours with both sides over two days, the presiding mediators concluded that the parties remained far apart, and that no progress toward a resolution could be made through further mediation at this point in time."

While there was some dissent voiced by a few players during the lockout (and considering the size of the membership, total unity would have been impossible), it was relatively minor and a world away from the schism in the players' ranks during the previous lockout. Some of them found employment with overseas teams, and all of the players received $10,000 a month from the NHLPA's lockout/strike fund, which the association had built up over the years. In addition, on October 15, the players received escrow checks in the amounts deducted from their salaries during the previous season.

There were also cracks forming in the owners' unity. Pittsburgh Penguins owner Ron Burkle and representatives of the Los Angeles Kings, Montreal Canadiens, and Tampa Bay Lightning pressured Bettman to resume negotiations with the NHLPA after they broke down in the middle of December. Putting further pressure on Bettman, around the same time the NHLPA executive board authorized the membership to vote to decide whether the board should file a disclaimer of interest with the NLRB. This would dissolve the union and allow the players to file an antitrust lawsuit against the NHL, and the players overwhelmingly supported it, by a margin of 706–22. This strategy had been used successfully by the NBPA and the NFLPA in ending lockouts by their respective leagues, and it would prove to be productive for the NHLPA in bringing pressure on the league to end the lockout. Still, the lockout continued into 2013, with the NHL and the NHLPA proposing and counterproposing throughout December and into January. Little by little, the owners were yielding ground. The federal mediator was able to bring the two sides together again on January 4, and on January 6, 2013, agreement was reached. During the lockout, the owners had lost $2 billion in revenue and the players $800 million in salary.[33]

Under the terms of the ten-year agreement, which remains in effect as of this writing, players receive 50 percent of hockey-related income and will collect an additional $300 million to honor existing contracts. Teams have been permitted to buy out two existing contracts before the start of either the 2013–14 or the 2014–15 season; the buyouts do not count against the salary cap. The salary cap for the 2013–14 season was $64.3 million, the same as in the 2011–12 season. Teams must spend at least $44 million.

Player contracts are limited to seven years, or eight years if the team re-signs the player. Multiyear contracts may vary from year to year by no more than 35 percent, and the lowest annual salary may not amount to less than 50 percent of the highest. Revenue sharing was fixed at $200 million.

At the signing of the agreement, the minimum salary remained unchanged at $525,000, but by the end of the contract's life it will have increased to $750,000. In a victory for the players, there were no changes made to salary arbitration and free agency. However, there were major changes made in the pension system. Under the old system, the players deposited money into their retirement funds and the amount was matched by the NHL. Under the new system, players will receive a defined benefit pension plan, which means that they will be guaranteed a set monthly payment when they retire. While this is the norm in baseball, basketball, and football, it is becoming increasingly rare in non-sport industries.[34]

Overall, the agreement is undoubtedly good for the owners, as the players will receive lower salaries, with contract lengths limited, which promises a windfall for the owners estimated to be $231 million a year, or more than $2 billion over the length of the ten-year contract. If the

NHL grows during this time, the savings could amount to more than $3 billion. However, some owners were not happy with the agreement as they wanted larger concessions from the players.[35] As for the players, while the agreement was not beneficial to them it could have been a lot worse. The leadership of Fehr, and the fact that the players remained largely united through the lockout, helped their cause immensely. Agreeing to concessions is never characterized as a victory for a union or players' association, but as the 2004–05 lockout demonstrated, things could have been a lot worse, and in fact the deal the players ended up with was inherently better than the offer the NHL had put forth before the lockout began. However, not everything is about money.

Concussions in the NHL

Concussions in hockey are becoming a problem that has to be confronted and dealt with. While they have long been an issue of concern, in recent years people have realized how seriously getting hit repeatedly in the head can impact a player's long-term health. Like their brethren in the NFL, current and former NHL players increasingly acknowledge a range of post-concussion symptoms such as depression, anxiety, and suicidal thoughts, due to head trauma suffered playing the game that they love. The more concussions a player experiences in his career, the more severe those symptoms may be.

Following the 2013 settlement of the class action lawsuit regarding concussions that was brought against the NFL on behalf of former players, the NHL stands to be the next sports league to go to court to defend itself against charges of negligence. As of this writing, more than two hundred current and former NHL players are engaged in a series of suits that claim that the league could and should have done more to prevent head injuries to players.[36]

In response to pressure from both players and the public, the league has already begun to take steps to increase player protection. To make the playing arenas safer, seamless glass above the boards has been replaced by less-rigid Plexiglas and supporting posts have been more thickly padded. Moreover, in 2010–11 the NHL introduced Rule 48, which made body checking in which the head is the primary contact point illegal. In its first year of existence, only blindside hits to the head were banned, then, in 2011–12, all body checks involving the head, unless the player put himself in harm's way.

The introduction of Rule 48 was meant to reduce the number of concussions suffered by players, which in turn would mitigate any future health problems (and any potential litigation). However, in a comprehensive study it was determined that Rule 48 did not have any significant impact on the number of concussions suffered by players. Indeed, since its adoption the number of concussions has been increasing. In 2009–10, 3.58 verified concussions were suffered by players every one hundred games, a number that increases to 6.26 if you include suspected concussions. In 2010–11, the number increased to 5.28 concussions per one hundred games, 9.76 including suspected concussions. In 2011–12, despite the rule changes, the number of concussions per one hundred games increased further, to 6.83, and 10.24 including suspected concussions. It is possible that the numbers have increased due to better reporting and diagnosis.

In what is said to be a positive trend, the number of concussions suffered due to players being blindsided has been eliminated completely, but the fact is that they were not a major cause of concussions to begin with. The greatest cause of concussions is body checking, with or without head contact; it accounts for 64.2 percent. Secondary contact, such as happens when a player's head hits the ice or boards, causes 51.2 percent of concussions. Fighting caused only eleven concussions out of 123 in total over the course of three seasons. Another factor accounting for the increase in concussions is the increase in the number of deliberate collisions, or hits, inflicted and received during an NHL game. During the 2005–06 season, 29,305 hits were recorded, which amounts to thirty-two per game. By 2011–12, the number of hits was 55,445, forty-five per game. These were record amounts. During the lockout-shortened 2012–13 season, there were forty-seven hits per game; over a full season that would have added up to 57,810.[37]

Overall, then, the "easiest" way to eliminate concussions from the NHL would be to eliminate body checking and hits. This would turn hockey into a non-contact sport, and, as with football, this obviously is not going to happen. Nonetheless, something has to happen to reduce the number of concussions. Otherwise not only are the players receiving lower salaries, they are jeopardizing their long-term health. This would be a sad state of affairs for the players.

6

The Inevitability of Conflict?

Throughout the preceding chapters, there have been many examples where the labor struggles in baseball, basketball, football, and hockey were due to matters of principle. Like almost every employee, no matter the industry, professional athletes want a fair share of the economic pie. Moreover, in virtually every other industry, if you change jobs and go to a rival company your old employer is not entitled to compensation. Why should it not be the case in professional sports? The respective player associations have generally fought—although not always, in the case of the NHLPA—for their members' right to move to another team (i.e., company), as the majority of employees have the right to. In addition, the player associations have wanted their members to gain better financial rewards, as any union would. Sometimes the player associations have been successful, but quite often they have not. Labor struggles in basketball, football, and hockey, especially in recent years, have involved players trying to hold onto their hard-earned gains; the players have been happy with what they have gotten, they do not want more. It has been the owners who have been continually trying to gain a greater share of revenue while cutting costs in other areas. Only in baseball, thanks to the strength of the MLBPA, have the players been able to resist concessions while improving their financial well-being. This chapter provides a summary of all that has gone on before, as well as a glimpse into what the future may hold.

Baseball: From Labor Disharmony to Labor Peace

Baseball has a long, tumultuous history of labor unrest and attempts to end the exploitation of players. From the National Brotherhood of Baseball Players to the American Baseball Guild, various unions/player associations were formed to try to give the players their just rewards. However, while they led to the players achieving limited victories, they were generally short-lived. Continuing success for the players was finally achieved through the Major League Baseball Players Association; more specifically, this was achieved under the leadership of Marvin Miller and his successors as the heads of the association. It was inevitable that as we progressed through the twentieth and into the twenty-first century, assports became a multibillion-dollar industry, that players would receive increasing rewards for their labor. However, unlike their brethren in basketball, football, hockey, and in many other industries across the United States, it was never inevitable that the MLBPA would continue to deliver ever-enhanced benefits for its members without having to accept large-scale concessions. There are two reasons why major league baseball players have achieved and continue to achieve success in collective bargaining.

The first reason is Marvin Miller. From his previous experience as counsel for the steelworkers' union, he understood that both a strong, militant leadership and an equally strong and militant rank and file were necessary, *militant* being the crucial word. The steelworkers belonged to the Congress of Industrial Organizations (CIO) before its merger with the American Federation of Labor. The formation of the CIO was fundamental to labor's growth. The CIO utilized tactics that heavily involved the rank and file. As a *New York Times Magazine* report on the United Mine Workers stated: "Seizing plants by sit-down strikes regardless of their legality and massing thousands of pickets from other C.I.O. unions in other cities and States in front of the gates, it has defied the police and the courts to dislodge them and return the property to the owners until their demands are met."[1] This was what Miller brought to the MLBPA: the attitude that militancy matters, and that the rank and file must be united. This leads to the second reason the MLBPA was successful under Miller; solidarity.

Baseball players were willing to go out on strike not just for their own personal gain, but for future generations of players. Throughout repeated strikes and lockouts, the players were largely united. Only when their solidarity faltered, as in 1985, were the owners able to force the players to accept a somewhat substandard contract. In the end, after decades of exploitation, the MLBPA under Miller, which was militant and united, led to the rewards players enjoy today.

At the same time, the strength of the MLBPA led to the owners wanting to claw back what was lost, which led to the 1994–95 strike. Conversely, the unity of the players during the strike and its aftermath has led to labor peace, which would not have occurred, as seen in the other big three American sports, if the players were divided. In the end, baseball had to go through decades of industrial conflict to enjoy the relative harmony it enjoys today. At the conclusion of the 1985 strike, MLBPA leader Donald Fehr said, "Maybe some time down the road we can find a way to do this job in a way that does not result in a threat of a crisis or a crisis itself."[2] It does seem as though we have reached that point in time in baseball.

However, one potential future conflict could arise, due to players' share of revenue. The MLBPA has adamantly refused a salary cap; it has always pushed for the market to determine the wage of players, apart from the minimum salary. As I noted, this has led to escalating salaries for the players. Indeed, the average salary of players for the 2014 season is approximately $4 million; which is an 8 to 10 percent increase over the previous season. This is the largest increase since at least 2006. However, while the players are benefiting, so are the owners, to an even greater extent. The owners earned $8 billion in 2013 and are expected to make approximately $8.5 billion in 2014. This means that the players will be receiving less than 50 percent of revenue, the lowest amount since the owners colluded against the players in the 1980s. In contrast, players received 63 percent of revenue in 2003.[3] While the players are handsomely rewarded, the MLBPA is concerned that they are receiving a significantly lower portion of revenue than they did in the past. While it would not be in anyone's interest for there to be a strike or lockout in 2016, if players' share of revenue keeps declining there could be unrest. Indeed, if history has taught us anything, it is that the possibility of employer-employee conflict is a matter of when, not if.

Football: Fourth and Goal

The history of player strikes and lockouts in the NFL does not include any great successes for the players and the NFLPA. There has often been a lack, both of solidarity and of the planning that is necessary for any work stoppage to succeed. In almost every worker-management conflict in the NFL that has resulted in either a strike or a lockout the owners have generally been successful. This has meant that the players have not received adequate rewards for their labor. Considering the failure of the players in the majority of work stoppages, it is almost remarkable that they have been able to overturn decades of exploitation.

The NFLPA and the players have achieved their greatest successes through the court system and the battle for free agency. It was through obtaining a limited free agency that player salaries had a remarkable increase. Quite simply, if there had been different judges in the various free agency court cases it is entirely possible that the owners would still dominate, as they did until the early 1990s. However, through victory in the courts, there is now a more level playing field in the NFL. This was clearly evident in the 2011 lockout, where the players learned from the mistakes of the past. It was the first work stoppage in the NFL where the players remained united, and it was because of this new-found solidarity that the NFLPA and the players were largely able to resist granting the concessions demanded by the NFL and the owners. Without solidarity, the players would have had to accept larger wage reductions and a longer season. A longer season means a greater chance of physical injury and concussions.

With the signing of the ten-year collective bargaining agreement in 2011 and with no opt-out clause, there will be labor harmony until at least 2021. Considering the unrest in the 1970s and 1980s as well as the recent lockout, that there will be no threat of a work stoppage is to be welcomed. For NFL teams, this will mean increased wealth all around. Of the thirty-two clubs, only three had an operating loss as calculated by *Forbes* in September 2012. Operating revenue increased by 6 percent in 2011, with operating income an average of $41 million, an increase of $10 million from 2010. Moreover, the net worth of the teams continues to escalate. The Dallas Cowboys were worth an estimated $2.1 billion in 2011. Even the "least" valuable club, the Jacksonville Jaguars, was sold in January 2012 for $770 million. In 1993, the Jaguars had been worth $208 million.

The economic juggernaut continues unabated. The latest *Forbes* analysis of NFL finances has determined that the average NFL team is now worth $1.17 billion, an increase of 5 percent over the previous year. The Cowboys are now worth an estimated $2.3 billion. Average operating income increased by 7 percent to $44 million. Only the Detroit Lions posted a loss, and even then the team is worth $900 million. The Jaguars are now worth $840 million; a nice increase of value for their new owners. The Oakland Raiders are now the least valuable NFL side; they are "only" worth $825 million.[4]

Owning an NFL club means excellent returns and prestige for owners. Yet it is not enough and they want the schedule to increase so they can earn even more. While so far they have not been able to get the NFLPA to agree to an increase in the schedule, the owners are confident that they will be able to increase by two the number of teams that participate in the postseason, beginning with the 2015–16 season.[5] The owners believe that they will be able to make the increase without the NFLPA's approval; the NFLPA argues that any changes to the schedule need its approval. At the time of writing, the situation is still to be resolved.

But at what point do factors apart from money enter into consideration? The concussion issue will not go away; nor should it. Unfortunately, things are going to get worse before they will get better. More players will suffer from depression, dementia, mood swings, and other symptoms brought on by playing a game that they and hundreds of millions of people around the world love. More tragically, there will be a greater number of suicides from former players. Playing in the NFL has led to many players becoming millionaires, celebrities, and enjoying the so-called good life. Unfortunately, the price they pay to play in the NFL can be very high indeed. Considering the pain and suffering that many players go through, at the very least a positive is that NFL players are better rewarded for their labor than they were before the introduction of free agency. Nonetheless, it is important to remember that people are more important than profit.

Basketball: Labor Peace . . . for Now

Before the formation of the NBPA, the owners had the power. With the birth of the union, and more importantly the unity of the players and the realization that they were capable of militancy and could threaten strike action, under the strong leadership of Larry Fleisher the players began to wrest power from the owners. This state of affairs continued until 1995, when, following the failed decertification attempt by some star players, a new agreement was reached that included a clause allowing the owners to opt out of the agreement. In 1998, they did so, and when a new agreement could not be reached, the owners locked out the players. This led to a favorable contract for the owners.

Likewise, while there was no lockout in 2005, the owners threatened the players with one. This led to an agreement in which both sides received a fair deal; fair for the players meant that they did not have to make large concessions. This would not be the case in 2011. Once again, the owners locked out the players, and once again the union achieved a substandard contract. In the NBA, there is a salary cap, an individual salary cap, and a luxury tax. While the superstars can make up any shortfall through sponsorship and endorsements, for players earning minimum salary this is much harder to achieve. It was these players who were cruelly hit with a wage freeze in the 2011 collective bargaining agreement.

Players have to regain what was lost if they want to have any hope of recovering some of their power; they need to regain militancy and solidarity. In this regard, there is some hope for the future. Following racist comments by Los Angeles Clippers owner Donald Sterling, Golden State Warrior players announced that they would walk off the court in their playoff game against the Clippers following the opening jump ball if the NBA did not dish out the maximum punishment against Sterling. Warrior Stephen Curry stated, "It would have been our only chance to make a statement in front of the biggest audience that we weren't going to accept anything but the maximum punishment. . . . We would deal with the consequences later but we were not going to play." The Warrior players were hoping that Clipper players would join them in abandoning the game. While the proposed walkoff was rendered moot when the NBA slapped Sterling with a lifetime ban, it is this sort of militancy and solidarity that have to be undertaken if players want to resist concessions and achieve better collective bargaining agreements in the future.[6]

Overall, the state the NBPA and the players are in can be traced back to the failed decertification attempt in 1995. A few players pushed for too much; greedy millionaires wanted more. Their actions divided the union, undermined solidarity, and made the owners realize that the use of a lockout works wonders. For one dissident player in 1995 who wanted more, his dreams came true. Michael Jordan was a star player who earned hundreds of millions in his playing career. He is now worth approximately $650 million. Jordan "switched sides" once his playing career was over and now has an 80 percent stake in the Charlotte Bobcats. The 2011 lockout was good for Jordan; the Bobcats increased in value by 14 percent the following year. As for the players, especially those on minimum salary who saw their wages frozen for two years, well, not everyone can be like Mike.

Hockey: Labor Peace That Will Not Last

For many years, labor struggles in the NHL were nonexistent, as the NHLPA under Alan Eagleson was basically a company union. While there was often talk about going out on strike, Eagleson and whoever the NHL president was at the time came to a mutually satisfactory compromise. "Satisfactory" meant what was good for the NHL and Eagleson. As a result, while NHL wages had once been higher than those in baseball, basketball, and football, over time NHL players came to earn less than they deserved.

This changed under the leadership of Bob Goodenow. The NHLPA was militant and largely united, which led to a dramatic escalation of player salaries. Thus, one might easily assume that the NHLPA under Goodenow and Donald Fehr during the 2004–05 and 2012–13 collective bargaining negotiations respectively wanted even more and got greedy. As I have demonstrated, this view is mistaken. Before both lockouts began the NHLPA offered a raft of concessions, but Bettman and the owners wanted more. Thanks to Bettman as NHL commissioner and wielding his and the owners' hardline approach, players are earning a lower percentage of NHL revenue than they did throughout the 1990s and early 2000s, with their free agency options also being tightened. While it is easy to blame the players for the NHL's financial woes, under Bettman's rule two full seasons combined have been lost due to lockouts and the expansion of the league into the American Sunbelt has been a failure.

There are a number of healthy NHL teams, but as a general rule the recent expansion and relocation teams are struggling. As I noted in chapter 5, before the 2005–06 lockout, as Dave Zirin, correctly argues, "[t]he big national TV contract Bettman promised never came and the NHL was left with unknowable new teams like the Hurricanes, Coyotes, and Predators playing in half-empty arenas."[7] Bettman and the owners have blamed the players for the NHL's financial woes and the last three lockouts.

Now that the NHL has its relatively large television contract, with player salaries capped at 50 percent of hockey-related revenue and industrial peace assured for at least the next eight years, will the owners blame the players again if a certain number of teams are unprofitable? Or will they look at the man who adopted a hardline approach, whose expansion and relocation strategy has generally been a failure, and under whose watch more than two full seasons worth of games have been lost to industrial disputes? Since 1994, it has not been greedy millionaires wanting more, but the owners and the NHL wanting increasingly more.

The Future: Labor Peace or Labor Instability?

This book has highlighted labor struggles in MLB, the NBA, NFL, and NHL up to Fall 2014. What does the future hold? At the moment, labor relations in professional baseball, basketball, football, and hockey promise to be relatively stable for the next few years, or at least until 2016, when the current MLB-MLBPA collective bargaining agreement expires. The following year will bring the end of the NBA-NBPA agreement. After 2016, as the other leagues' collective bargaining agreements expire, the likelihood of work stoppages occurring depends largely on the owners. The last strike called by the players occurred in MLB during the 1994 season, more than nineteen years ago; since then, every work stoppage in professional sports in North America has taken place at the instigation of the league and its owners. If the owners continue to play hardball in negotiations there will be work stoppages; this has become an inevitable feature of the owner-player relationship as owners try to reverse gains made by the players. In the face of the owners' intransigence, it is almost impossible for the respective player associations to achieve a good contract for the players. At best, they might limit the number of concessions they accede to.

The owners in professional sports leagues are by far a wealthier class than the players and can absorb greater expenses for longer periods of time than their employees. Nonetheless, experience has shown that when the players have remained committed to their cause and not let their solidarity weaken, their chances of successfully negotiating for their cause have been enhanced. This has clearly been demonstrated by the MLBPA, which has consistently achieved its negotiating goals thanks to its strength and unity.

While there will be no work stoppages until at least 2016, this is not to claim that there will be no issues to be dealt with. In the NFL and the NHL, the most pressing questions concern how the respective leagues will deal with concussions and their aftereffects. In the recent settlement with former players, the NFL accepted no direct responsibility, which seems to indicate that it will make only limited changes to protect the players, while seemingly adopting a "hear no evil, see no evil" approach. It would seem that in order to focus the league's attention a former player or players will have to refuse its settlement offers and battle the NFL in court. Only then might it be determined whether and to what extent the NFL values profits over the health of its players.

Likewise, in the NHL the number of concussions incurred in games is on the rise. Disconcertingly, it appears that more of them are inflicted by hits to the body than to the head. While it is inconceivable that body checking in hockey will be outlawed, unless something is done, such as the adoption of greatly improved helmets, current players will continue to jeopardize their health and their futures.

In baseball, the use of performance-enhancing drugs (PEDs) currently attracts the greatest attention and publicity. It has become accepted as fact that players using PEDs are jeopardizing their own long-term health for the short-term benefits of being able to, for instance, recover more quickly from injury, be less fatigued over a long season, and hit the ball farther or pitch it faster. MLB, with the MLBPA's approval, has moved away from turning a blind eye to the use of PEDs and now cracks down on players suspected of using even if they have not failed any drug tests, as seen in the recent Biogenesis scandal.

These issues aside, the existence of labor peace until at least 2016 will be good for fans, owners, the respective leagues, and, for the most part, the players. Without crippling lockouts, players will not have to sacrifice some or all of their annual incomes because groups of billionaires want more. But when the respective collective bargaining agreements expire, the players will undoubtedly mobilize to regain what they think has been lost while the owners will attempt to browbeat the players' associations into engaging in concession bargaining. The fans should make a point of enjoying the uninterrupted seasons between now and 2016; then, if recent history is any guide, industrial conflict and work stoppages through strikes and lockouts brought about by billionaires will once again rear their ugly heads. In the end, unfortunately, labor conflict in professional sports is a matter of when, not if.

Notes

Chapter 1. Greedy Millionaires Wanting More?

1. Philip Dine, *State of the Unions* (New York: McGraw-Hill, 2008), xix.

2. Michael Schiavone, *Unions in Crisis? The Future of Organized Labor in America* (Westport, CT: Praeger, 2008), 2.

3. Howard Cosell, *What's Wrong with Sports* (New York: Simon and Schuster, 1991).

4. Robert C. Berry and William B. Gould, "A Long Deep Drive to Collective Bargaining: Of Players, Owners, Brawls, and Strikes," *Case Western Reserve Law* Review 31, no. 4, (Summer 1981): 708–10.

5. James Richard Hill and Jason E. Taylor, "Do Professional Sports Unions Fit the Standard Model of Traditional Unionism?" *Journal of Labor Research* 29 (2008): 60–66; See the following chapters for examples of sports unions fighting for higher wages and free agency, having seniority and accepting two-tier wage structures.

6. Rick Fantasia and Kim Voss, *Hard Work* (Berkley and Los Angeles: University of California Press, 2004), 65.

7. Darren Rovell, "New Owners' Tax Break Losing Value," *ESPN*, April 15, 2004. http://sports.espn.go.com/espn/sportsbusiness/news/story?id=1782953; Beeston, quoted in Dan Messeloff, "The NBA's Deal with the Devil: The Antitrust Implications of the 1999 NBA-NBPA Collective Bargaining Agreement," *Fordham Intellectual Property, Media & Entertainment Law Journal* 10, (2000): 566; Lance Taubin, "Welcome to the Real 2011 NBA Lockout: Where Owner-Friendly Tax Provisions and Non-Monetized Benefits Color the Lockout Landscape," *Cardozo Public Law Policy & Ethics Journal* 139 (2012): 154–55, 159–60, 172; Zimbalist, *In The Best Interests of Baseball?* (Lincoln and London: University of Nebraska Press, 2013), 9.

8. "Sarah Ahmed Quotes," *Goodreads*, n.d. http://www.goodreads.com/author/quotes/11036.Sara_Ahmed.

Chapter 2. Labor Relations in Baseball

1. Spalding quoted in Roger I. Abrams, "The Public Regulation of Baseball Labor Relations and the Public Interest," *Journal of Sports Economics* 4, no. 4 (2003): 297.

2. Ward quoted in Stuart Banner, *Baseball Trust* (Oxford and New York: Oxford University Press, 2013), 5.

3. Lee Lowenfish, *The Imperfect Diamond* (Lincoln and London: University of Nebraska Press, 2010), 34–36, 47–50, 59; Richard Peterson, *Extra Innings: Writings on Baseball* (Urbana and Chicago: University of Illinois Press, 2001), 43; David Q. Voigt, "Serfs versus Magnates: A Century of Labor Strife in Major League Baseball," in *The Business of Professional Sports*, ed. Paul D. Staudohar and James A. Mangan (Urbana and Chicago: University of Illinois Press, 1991), 101; James R. Devine, "Baseball's Labor Wars in Historical Context: The 1919 Chicago White Sox as a Case-Study in Owner-Player Relations," *Marquette Sports Law Journal* 5, issue 1 (1994). http://scholarship.law.marquette.edu/sportslaw/vol5/iss1/3.

4. Voigt, "Serfs versus Magnates," 106–107; Paul D. Staudohar, *Playing for Dollars* (Ithaca and London: Cornell University Press, 1996), 15; Ty Cobb, Al Stump, My *Life in Baseball: The True Record* (Nebraska: University of Nebraska Press, 1993), 108.

5. Lowenfish, *The Imperfect Diamond*, 76–78.

6. Jordan I. Kobritz and Jeffrey F. Levine, "Trying his Luck at Puck: Examining the MLBPA's History to Determine Don Fehr's Motivation for Agreeing to Lead the NHLPA and Predicting How He Will Fare," *University of Denver Sports and Entertainment Law Journal* 12 (2011): 7–8; Lowenfish, *The Imperfect Diamond*, 78–83, 87, 96–96; Staudohar, *Playing for Dollars*, 15–16, Voigt, "Serfs versus Magnates," 108–109. Andrew Zimbalist, *In the Best Interests of Baseball?* (Lincoln and London: University of Nebraska Press, 2013), 25, 26.

7. Devine, "Baseball's Labor Wars in Historical Context."

8. Banner, *The Baseball Trust*, 36, 85–88, 91.

9. For an overview of the Mexican League, the sanctions imposed by MLB, and Gardella's lawsuit, see Robert F. Burk, *Much More than a Game* (Chapel Hill and London: The University of North Carolina Press, 2001), 76, 85–86, 104–106; Banner, *Baseball Trust*, 95–103; Richard Goldstein, "Danny Gardella, 85, Dies; Challenged Reserve Clause," *The New York Times*, March 13, 2005, http://www.nytimes.com/2005/03/13/sports/baseball/13gardella.html?ex=1268370000&en=7ae29a51bacee15e&ei=5090&partner=rssuserland.

10. Burk, *Much More than a Game*, 88; Robert Weintraub, "Failed Baseball Union Helped Pave Way for Success," *The New York Times*, December 1, 2012, http://www.nytimes.com/2012/12/02/sports/baseball/failed-baseball-union-helped-pave-way-for-success.html?_r=0.

11. Burk, *Much More than a Game*, 88–91, 94; Charles P. Korr, *The End of Baseball as We Knew It*, (Urbana and Chicago: University of Illinois Press,

2005), 16–17; Voigt, "Serfs versus Magnates," 113; Lowenfish, *The Imperfect Diamond*, 145–46, 148–51; Weintraub, "Failed Baseball Union Helped Pave Way for Success"; Murphy quoted in Weintraub, "Failed Baseball Union Helped Pave Way for Success"; and Lowenfish, *The Imperfect Diamond*, 151.

12. Burk, *Much More than a Game*, 98–101; Derrick Goold, "On Jackie and the Cardinals." *St. Louis Post-Dispatch*, April 16, 2013, http://www.stltoday.com/sports/baseball/professional/birdland/goold-on-jackie-and-the-cardinals/article_0aecf971-2e97-569f-bc23-1f41a63ae27a.html.

13. For the formation of the MLBPA see Lowenfish, *The Imperfect Diamond*, 183–88; Burk, *Much More than a Game*, 120; Reynolds quoted in Charles B. Korr, "Marvin Miller and the New Unionism in Baseball," in *The Business of Professional Sports*, ed. Paul D. Staudohar and James A. Mangan (Urbana and Chicago: University of Illinois Press 1991), 116. Kiner quoted in Korr, *The End of Baseball as We Knew It*, 18, 20; Dean A. Sullivan, ed., *Late Innings: A Documentary History of Baseball, 1945–1972* (Lincoln and London: Bison Books, 2002), 82–84.

14. Burk, *Much More than a Game*, 121–22.

15. Cannon quoted in Korr, *The End of Baseball as We Knew It*, 23–24.

16. Burk, *Much More than a Game*, 123–124; Boros quoted in Korr, *The End of Baseball as We Knew It*, 27.

17. Marvin Miller, *A Whole Different Ballgame* (Chicago: Ivan R. Dee, 2004). Kindle edition.

18. Bisher quoted in Korr, *The End of Baseball as We Knew It*, 44; Lowenfish, *The Imperfect Diamond*, 200–201.

19. Korr, *The End of Baseball as We Knew It*, 54–55, 73–75; Miller, *A Whole Different Ballgame*.

20. Miller, *A Whole Different Ballgame*; Lowenfish, *The Imperfect Diamond*, 202–203, 211–12; Jon Wertheim, "Marvin Miller Changed Players' Union— and baseball—Forever," *Sports Illustrated*, November 27, 2012. http://www.si.com/more-sports/2012/11/27/marvin-miller-obituary.

21. Flood's letter to Kuhn reprinted at "Curt Flood's letter to Bowie Kuhn," *MLB.com*. http://mlb.mlb.com/news/article.jsp?ymd=20070315&content_id=1844945&vkey=news_mlb&c_id=mlb&fext=.jsp; Lowenfish, *The Imperfect Diamond*, 208–14; Kuhn quoted in Banner, *The Baseball Trust*, 213; Allen Barra, "How Curt Flood Changed Baseball and Killed His Career in the Process," *The Atlantic*, July 12, 2011, http://www.theatlantic.com/entertainment/archive/2011/07/how-curt-flood-changed-baseball-and-killed-his-career-in-the-process/241783/. For the best overview of Curt Flood and his challenging the reserve clause see Brad Snyder, *A Well-Paid Slave*, (London: Plume, 2007).

22. Banner, *The Baseball Trust*, 222–24; G. Michael Green and Roger D. Launius, *Charlie Finley: The Outrageous Story of Baseball's Super Showman* (New York: Walker, 2010), 208–15; Hal Bock, "Baseball's Emancipation: It Was Twenty Years Ago When Catfish Hunter, Sport's Best Pitcher, Was Declared a Free Agent," *Los Angeles Times*, December 11, 1994. http://articles.latimes.com/1994-12-11/sports/sp-7636_1_catfish-hunter.

23. For an overview of Messersmith and McNally seeking free agency, the arbitration ruling, and the Curt Flood Act see Banner, *The Baseball Trust,* 225–30, 246–47, 250; Seitz quoted in Korr, *The End of Baseball as We Knew It,* 156; Alex Belth, "Free Agency Turns 30," *Sports Illustrated,* December 23, 2005. http://sportsillustrated.cnn.com/2005/writers/alex_belth/12/23/messersmith. mcnally/; Messersmith quoted in Murray Chass, "Free-Agency Still A Battle," *Chicago Tribune,* December 25, 1985. http://articles.chicagotribune.com/1985-12-25/sports/8503290579_1_dave-mcnally-contract-cabrillo-community-college/2. For analysis of the link between *Brown v. Pro Football* and the Curt Flood Act see William B. Gould IV, "Labor Issues in Professional Sports: Reflections on Baseball, Labor, and Antitrust Law," *Stanford Law and Policy Review* 15, issue 1 (2004): 82.

24. Burk, *Much More than a Game,* 172–74; Reporter quoted in Lowenfish, *The Imperfect Diamond,* 216.

25. Mincher quoted in "Baseball Players to Strike Today Over Pension Issue: Baseball Players Vote to Start Strike Today Over Pension Fund Contributions," *The New York Times,* April 1, 1972, 1; Burk, *Much More than a Game,* 175–77; Lowenfish, *The Imperfect Diamond,* 215–18; Joseph Durso, "Baseball Strike Is Settled; Season to Open Tomorrow," *The New York Times,* April 14, 1972, 1.

26. Burk, *Much More than a Game,* 186–87.

27. Miller, *A Whole Different Ballgame;* Burk, *Much More than a Game,* 201–203; Murray Chass, "Baseball Owners Delay Spring Training Start," *The New York Times,* February 24, 1976, 55; Miller quoted in Murray Chass, "Training Slated to Start Today: Kuhn Orders Camps to Open," *The New York Times,* March 18, 1976, 64.

28. Miller, *A Whole Different Ballgame;* Burk, *Much More than a Game,* 205–206, 207–208.

29. Lowenfish, *The Imperfect Diamond,* 225–27; Simmons quoted in Lowenfish, *The Imperfect Diamond,* 227.

30. Ibid., 227–31; Murray quoted in Korr, *The End of Baseball as We Knew It,* 200; Burk, *Much More than a Game,* 224–27.

31. Pryor quoted in Lowenfish, *The Imperfect Diamond,* 243.

32. The analysis of the strike is from the following: Steinbrenner quoted in Burk, *Much More than a Game,* 228; Lowenfish, *The Imperfect Diamond,* 235—46; Burk, *Much More than a Game,* 228–34; Staudohar, *Playing for Dollars,* 30–31; Gould, "Labor Issues in Professional Sports," 70–71; "Chronology of the Baseball Strike," *The New York Times,* August 1, 1981, 18; Murray Chass, "Strike Over; Baseball Resumes Aug.9: 650 Players Affected 7-Week Baseball Strike Ends; All-Stars Will Reopen Season Mediator Not at Meeting," *The New York Times,* August 1, 1981, 1; Jane Gross, "Strike Losses Heavy and Widespread: Owners Aided by Insurance Financial Impact on cities Strike Created Heavy Losses Some Differences Among Owners," *The New York Times,* August 1, 1981,

17; Reinsdorf quoted in Korr, *The End of Baseball as We Knew It*, 223; Miller, *A Whole Different Ballgame*.

33. DeCinces quoted in "Chass, "Strike Over," 1.

34. The analysis of the 1985 strike is from: Staudohar, *Playing for Dollars*, 42–45; Gould, "Labor Issues in Professional Sports," 71–72; Zimbalist, *In the Best Interests of Baseball?*, 83; Mattingly quoted in Lowenfish, *The Imperfect Diamond*, 260; Miller, *A Whole Different Ballgame*.

35. Analysis of collusion is from: Staudohar, *Playing for Dollars*, 38–39; Lowenfish, *The Imperfect Diamond*, 263–64, 269–70; Burk, *Much More than a Game*, 251–52; 256, 260; Gould, *Bargaining with Baseball*, 90–91.

36. Overview of the lockout is from: Paul D. Staudohar, "Baseball Labor Relations: The Lockout of 1990," *Monthly Labor Review* (October 1990): 36; Lowenfish, *The Imperfect Diamond*, 275–76; Fehr quoted in Murray Chass, "Baseball's Labor Dispute Settled with Compromise on Arbitration," *The New York Times*, March 19, 1990, A23, A27; Zimbalist, *In the Best Interests of Baseball?*, 103–104.

37. Overview of the strike and its aftermath from: Andrew Zimbalist, *May the Best Team Win* (Brookings Institution Press, 2004), 87–88; Paul D. Staudohar, "The Baseball Strike of 1994–1995," *Monthly Labor Review* (March 1997): 24–26; Burk, *Much More than a Game*, 274; Gould, "Labor Issues in Professional Sports," 75–76; Gould, *Bargaining with Baseball*, 10, 103; Lowenfish, *The Imperfect Diamond*, 288–89; Zimbalist, *In the Best Interests of Baseball?*, 146–51; Harnish quoted in Korr, *The End of Baseball As We Knew It*, 260; Schott quoted in Lowenfish, *The Imperfect Diamond*, 292; Sotomayor quoted in Lowenfish, *The Imperfect Diamond*, 295.

38. Overview of the negotiations and agreement from: Zimbalist, *In the Best Interests of Baseball?*, 162–63; Zimbalist, *May the Best Team Win*, 95, 98–99, 111; Gould, "Labor Issues in Professional Sports," 93; Andrew Zimbalist, "Labor Relations in Major League Baseball," *Journal of Sports Economics* 4, no. 4 (2003): 339, 346–47; Paul D. Staudohar, "Baseball Negotiations: A New Agreement," *Monthly Labor Review* (December 2002): 21; Murray Chass, "Last Minute Deal in Baseball Talks Prevents a Strike," *The New York Times*, August 31, 2002, A1, D3. Fehr quoted in Chass, "Last Minute Deal in Baseball Talks Prevents a Strike," A1.

39. "MLB, Union Announce New Labor Deal," *MLB.com*, 2002. http://mlb. mlb.com/news/article.jsp?ymd=20061024&content_id=1722211&vkey=news_ mlb&fext=.jsp&c_id=mlb; "MLB players, owners announce five-year labor deal," http://sports.espn.go.com/mlb/news/story?id=2637615; Zimbalist, *In the Best Interests of Baseball?*, 220.

40. Anthony DiComo, "Key points of Collective Bargaining Agreement," *MLB.com*, 2011. http://mlb.mlb.com/news/article.jsp?ymd=20111122&content_ id=26026776; Selig and Weiner quoted in Paul White, "Done Deal: What's New in Baseball's Labor Agreement?" *USA Today*, November 23, 2011. http://

usatoday30.usatoday.com/sports/baseball/story/2011-11-22/mlb-collective-bargaining-agreement/51359552/1; "Baseball Announces Expanded Pension Benefits for Players Who Retired between 1947 and 1980," *NBC Sports*, April 21, 2011. http://hardballtalk.nbcsports.com/2011/04/21/baseball-announces-expanded-pension-benefits-for-players-who-retired-between-1947-and-1980/; "MLB and Union Agree to Pay Pre-1980 Players' Pensions," *Reuters*, April 21, 2011. http://www.reuters.com/article/2011/04/21/us-baseball-pensions-idUSTRE73K7 Q920110421; "Over 900 Players to Receive Money under MLB Pension Deal," *CBC Sports*, April 21, 2011. http://www.cbc.ca/sports/baseball/story/2011/04/21/ sp-mlb-pension.html; Jayson Stark, "How the New CBA Changes Baseball," *ESPN*, November 22, 2011. http://espn.go.com/mlb/story/_/id/7270203/ baseball-new-labor-deal-truly-historic-one.

41. "The Business of Baseball," *Forbes*, 2013. http://www.forbes.com/mlb-valuations/list/; "MLB Salaries," *CBS Sports*, 2013. http://www.cbssports.com/mlb/ salaries/avgsalaries; Mike Ozanian, "Baseball Team Valuations 2013: Yankees on Top At $2.3 Billion," *Forbes*, March 27, 2013. http://www.forbes.com/sites/mike ozanian/2013/03/27/baseball-team-valuations-2013-yankees-on-top-at-2-3-billion/; Mike Ozanian, "Baseball Team Values 2014 Led by New York Yankees at $2.5 Billion," *Forbes*, March 26, 2014, http://www.forbes.com/sites/mikeozanian/2014/03/26/ baseball-team-values-2014-led-by-new-york-yankees-at-2-5-billion/

42. For a good firsthand account of the use of amphetamines in baseball during the 1960s and 1970s see Jim Bouton, *Ball Four* (New York: Rosetta Books, 1980).

Chapter 3. The National Football League

1. Staudohar, *Playing for Dollars*, 56–57; Michael E. Lomax, "Conflict and Compromise: The Evolution of American Professional Football's Labour Relations 1957–1966," *Football Studies* 4, no. 1 (2001): 7.

2. See the baseball chapter for more details.

3. Kevin. G. Quinn, "Getting to the 2011–2020 National Football League Collective Bargaining Agreement," *International Journal of sports Finance* 7, no. 2 (2012): 142; Lomax, "Conflict and Compromise," 7–8.

4. Lomax, "Conflict and Compromise," 8.

5. Radovich quoted in Banner, *The Baseball Trust*, 134.

6. Banner, *The Baseball Trust*, 134–38; Radovich quoted in William C. Rhoden, "Sports of The Times; N.F.L.'s Labor Pioneer Remains Unknown," *The New York Times*, October 2, 1994. http://www.nytimes.com/1994/10/02/sports/ sports-of-the-times-nfl-s-labor-pioneer-remains-unknown.html?src=pm.

7. Jeffrey F. Levine and Bram A. Maravent "Fumbling Away the Season: Will the Expiration of the NFL-NFLPA CBA Result in the Loss of the 2011 Season?" *Fordham Intellectual Property, Media & Entertainment Law Journal* 1419, no. 4 (2010): 1430–31; NFLPA, "History," *NFLPlayers.com*, n.d. https://www.

nflplayers.com/About-us/History/; Lomax, "Conflict and Compromise," 13, 15; Miller quoted in NFLPA, "History."

8. Lomax, "Conflict and Compromise," 15–16; Sam Farmer, "Bill Radovich, 87; NFL Star Blacklisted after Court Case," *Los Angeles Times*, March 12, 2002, http://articles.latimes.com/2002/mar/12/local/me-radovich12; Radovich quoted in Banner, *The Baseball Trust*, 140; Radovich quoted in Rhoden, "Sports of The Times; N.F.L.'s Labor Pioneer Remains Unknown."

9. Staudohar, *Playing for Dollars*, 65; NFLPA, "History"; Lomax, "Conflict and Compromise," 18–21.

10. Lomax, "Conflict and Compromise," 22–23, 25; Staudohar, *Playing for Dollars*, 60.

11. Staudohar, *Playing for Dollars*, 79–80; Scott E. Backman, "NFL Players Fight for Their Freedom: The History of Free Agency in the NFL," *Sports Lawyers Journal* 9, no. 2, (2002): 9–10.

12. Jon Kendle, "Players boycott AFL All-Star Game," *Pro Football Hall of Fame*, February 18, 2010, http://www.profootballhof.com/history/2010/2/18/players-boycott-afl-all-star-game/; Blanks and Faison quoted in David Barron, "Protest of Race-Related Slights, Brought '65 Game Here," *Houston Chronicle*, January 16, 2005, http://www.chron.com/sports/texans/article/Protest-of-race-related-slights-brought-65-game-1940910.php.

13. Lomax, "Conflict and Compromise," 26–29; NFLPA, "History."

14. Overview of the lockout and strike from: NFLPA, "History"; "Players Reject NFL Offer, Talks Falter," *Boston Globe*, July 9, 1968, 21; William N. Wallace, "Sports of The Times; The Players Won," *The New York Times*, July 17, 1968, 48; "NFL Negotiators Attain Settlement," *The Washington Post*, July 15, 1968, D5; Gordy quoted in Bud Shrake, "Let's Get Back to Playing Football," *Sports Illustrated*, July 22, 1968, http://sportsillustrated.cnn.com/vault/article/magazine/MAG1081412/1/index.htm.

15. Overview of the lockout and strike from: NFLPA, "History"; Bob Oates, "It's Official: NFL Players on Strike," *Los Angeles Times*, July 31, 1970, C2; "NFL Opens Up Camps to Veterans," *The Washington Post*, July 30, 1970, G1; Bob Oates, "Rozelle Counters NFL Strike Threat by Delaying Camps," *Los Angeles Times*, July 8, 1970, D3; "NFL Negotiators $1 Million Apart," *The Washington Post*, August 2, 1970, C1; "Pro Football Players End Strike Of Clubs." *The Sun*, August 4, 1970, A1; Dave Brady, "Players Settled For a Field Goal," *The Washington Post*, August 9, 1970, C4.

16. Overview of the strike from: NFLPA, "History"; Halas quoted in "NFL Picket Crossing Due to Begin Today," *The Washington Post*, July 3, 1974, D1; Tannen quoted in "NFL players not fully behind strike," *Boston Globe*, July 14, 1974, 94; Korr, *The End of Baseball As We Knew It*, 171–72; "NFL Strike: Fans Will Pay," *Boston Globe*, August 6, 1974, 22; Garvey quoted in Korr, *The End of Baseball As We Knew It*, 171.

17. Eighth Circuit Court of Appeals quoted in Peter C. Goplerud, III "Collective Bargaining in the National Football League: A Historical and

Comparative Analysis," *Jeffrey S. Moorad Sports Law Journal* 4, no. 1, Article 2, http://digitalcommons.law.villanova.edu/mslj/vol4/iss1/2; Richard Goldstein, "John Mackey Dies at 69," *The New York Times*, July 7, 2011, http://www.nytimes.com/2011/07/08/sports/football/john-mackey-dies-at-69-helped-revolutionize-nfl.html?_r=0; Quinn, "Getting to the 2011–2020 National Football League Collective Bargaining Agreement," 142–43.

18. Bruce H. Singman, "Free Agency and the National Football League," *Loyola L.A. Entertainment Law Revue* 259 (1988), http://digitalcommons.lmu.edu/elr/vol8/iss2/2; Jonathan S. Shapiro, "Warming the Bench: The Nonstatutory Labor Exemption in the National Football League," *Fordham Law Revue* 61 (1993), http://ir.lawnet.fordham.edu/flr/vol61/iss5/9; Backman, "NFL Players Fight for Their Freedom," 17–18; Staudohar, *Playing for Dollars*, 60, 77; "Average N.F.L. Salary Is $90,102, Survey Says," *The New York Times*, January 29, 1982, http://www.nytimes.com/1982/01/29/sports/average-nfl-salary-is-90102-survey-says.html; Mackey quoted in Goldstein, "John Mackey Dies at 69."

19. Overview of the 1982 strike and agreement from: NFLPA, "History"; Goplerud, III "Collective Bargaining in the National Football League"; Staudohar, *Playing for Dollars*, 71–73; Jeter quoted Gene Wojciechowski, "NFL STRIKE: 1982: A History Lesson Not Learned," *Los Angeles Times*, September 23, 1987, http://articles.latimes.com/1987-09-23/sports/sp-6303_1_nfl-strike; Allen quoted in Wojciechowski, "NFL STRIKE: 1982: A History Lesson Not Learned."

20. Quinn, "Getting to the 2011–2020 National Football League Collective Bargaining Agreement," 144; Paul D. Staudohar, "The Football Strike of 1987: The Question of Free Agency," *Monthly Labor Review* (August 1988): 26; NFLPA, "History."

21. NFLPA, "History"; Staudohar, *Playing for Dollars*, 73–76; Staudohar, "The Football Strike of 1987," 27; Quinn, "Getting to the 2011–2020 National Football League Collective Bargaining Agreement," 145; Levine and Maravent, "Fumbling Away the Season," 1440–41; Lynn quoted in Mark Craig, "The 1987 NFL Strike: Picking at an old Scab," *Star Tribune*, June 28, 2011, http://www.startribune.com/sports/vikings/124627618.html; Irwin quoted in Larry Weisman, "NFL Reflects on Changes at Anniversary of Strikes," *USA Today*, October 11, 2007, http://usatoday30.usatoday.com/sports/football/nfl/2007-10-06-sw-labor-anniversary_N.htm.

22. Overview of Plan B and *Powell v. NFL* from: NFLPA, "History"; Eighth Circuit Court of Appeals quoted in Goplerud, III "Collective Bargaining in the National Football League"; NFLPA report quoted in Ian Craig Pulver, "A Face Off between the National Hockey League and the National Hockey League Players' Association: The Goal a More Competitively Balanced League," *Marquette Sports Law Review* 39 (1991), http://scholarship.law.marquette.edu/sportslaw/vol2/iss1/4; Carol T. Rieger and Charles J. Lloyd, "The Effect of *McNeil v. NFL* on Contract Negotiation in the NFL—That Was Then, This Is Now," *Marquette Sports Law Review* 45 (1992), http://scholarship.law.marquette.edu/sportslaw/vol3/iss1/6; Weisman, "NFL Reflects on Changes at Anniversary of

Strikes"; Robert A. McCormick, "Interference on Both Sides: The Case against the NFL-NFLPA Contract," *Washington & Lee Law Review* 397 (1996): 415–16.

23. Chris Deubert, Glenn M. Wong, John Howe, "All Four Quarters: A Retrospective and Analysis of the 2011 Collective Bargaining Process and Agreement in the National Football League," *UCLA Entertainment Law Review* 19, no. 1, (2012): 3, 12–13; Gould, "Labor Issues in Professional Sports," 80–82.

24. Staudohar, *Playing for Dollars*, 60; NFLPA, "History"; Court quoted in Backman, "NFL Players Fight for Their Freedom," 32.

25. Bowlen quoted in Carol T. Rieger and Charles J. Lloyd, "The Effect of *McNeil v. NFL* on Contract Negotiation in the NFL"; Backman, "NFL Players Fight for Their Freedom," 37–42.

26. NFLPA, "History"; Backman, "NFL Players Fight for Their Freedom," 42–43, note 266.

27. Staudohar, *Playing for Dollars*, 60, 88–89; Backman, "NFL Players Fight for Their Freedom," 43–47, 51–52; Weisman, "NFL Reflects on Changes at Anniversary of Strikes"; NFLPA, "History."

28. Tagliabue and Upshaw quoted in Backman, "NFL Players Fight for Their Freedom," 54, 55; Quinn, "Getting to the 2011–2020 National Football League Collective Bargaining Agreement," 146; Miller interviewed in Jon Wertheim, "Marvin Miller on Barry Bonds, Drug Testing, and the NFL Labor Situation," *Sports Illustrated*, April 12, 2011, http://sportsillustrated.cnn.com/2011/writers/jon_wertheim/04/12/marvin.miller/index.html#ixzz2bAQHj851; Weisman, "NFL Reflects on Changes at Anniversary of Strikes."

29. "NFL Owners Approve Six-Year CBA Extension," *ESPN*, March 9, 2006, http://sports.espn.go.com/nfl/news/story?id=2360258; John Clayton, "Owners Finally Come to Resolution on Revenue Sharing," *ESPN*, March 8, 2006, http://sports.espn.go.com/nfl/columns/story?columnist=clayton_john&id=2360296.

30. Quinn, "Getting to the 2011–2020 National Football League Collective Bargaining Agreement," 147–48; "NFL Team Valuations," *Forbes*, September 2, 2009, http://www.forbes.com/lists/2009/30/football-values-09_NFL-Team-Valuations_Revenue.html; John Vrooman, "The Economic Structure of the NFL," *Sports Economics, Management and Policy* 2 (2012): 12; Paul D. Staudohar, "The Football Lockout of 2011," *Monthly Labor Review* (August 2012): 30.

31. Kevin W. Wells, "Labor Relations in the National Football League: A Historical and Legal Perspective," *Sports lawyers Journal* 18 (2011): 102; Staudohar, "The Football Lockout of 2011," 31–32.

32. Vrooman, "The Economic Structure of the NFL," 30.

33. Overview of the lockout from: Deubert, Wong, Howe, "All Four Quarters," 3, 22–27; NFL quoted in Nate Davis "Official Statement from NFL Following Union Decertification," *USA Today*, May 11, 2011, http://content.usatoday.com/communities/thehuddle/post/2011/03/official-statement-from-nfl-following-union-decertification/1#.Ufhtf22SAno; Staudohar, "The Football Lockout of 2011," 31–32; Polamalu quoted in David Meggyesy and Dave Zirin, "How Players Won the NFL Lockout," *The Nation*, July 27, 2011, http://www.thenation.

com/article/162397/how-players-won-nfl-lockout?page=full; Jim Trotter, "Players' Secret Lockout Insurance Could Have Sparked Talks," *Sports Illustrated*, July 15, 2011, http://sportsillustrated.cnn.com/2011/writers/jim_trotter/07/15/secret-lock-out-fund/index.html#ixzz2hDALHKJ8; http://sportsillustrated.cnn.com/2011/writers/jim_trotter/07/15/secret-lockout-fund/index.html#ixzz2hD8lVnkB.

34. Overview of the agreement from: Staudohar, "The Football Lockout of 2011," 33; Quinn, "Getting to the 2011–2020 National Football League Collective Bargaining Agreement," 151, 153; Deubert, Wong, Howe, "All Four Quarters," 60–61, 62–63, 70; Sean Leahy, "Rams Agree with No. 1 Overall Pick Sam Bradford on Record Contract with $50 Million Guaranteed," *USA Today*, July 30, 2010, http://content.usatoday.com/communities/thehuddle/post/2010/07/rams-agree-with-no-1-overall-pick-sam-bradford-on-record-contract-with-50-million-guaranteed/1#.UfioXW2SAno.

35. "Brain Injuries Haunt Football Players Years Later," *NPR*, January 20, 2011, http://www.npr.org/2011/01/20/133053436/brain-injuries-haunt-football-players-years-later; Daniel S. Goldberg, "Concussions, Professional Sports, and Conflicts of Interest: Why the National Football League's Current Policies are Bad for Its (Players') Health," *HEC Forum* 20, issue 4 (2009): 337; Tim Keown, "After the NFL," *ESPN Magazine*, June 26, 2013, http://espn.go.com/nfl/story/_/id/9417902/steve-hendrickson-nfl-concussions-taking-their-toll-espn-magazine; Alexander C. Hart, "NFL head injuries a hot topic in Congress," *Los Angeles Times*, October 29, 2009, http://articles.latimes.com/2009/oct/29/sports/sp-football-congress29; Mike Tierney, "THE FIFTH DOWN; Study Finds Risk of Brain Disease for N.F.L. Players," *The New York Times*, September 6, 2012, http://query.nytimes.com/gst/fullpage.html?res=9C02E3DB143FF935A3575AC0A9649D8B63; Dustin Fink, "What Is CTE?," *The Concussion Blog*, n.d. http://theconcussionblog.com/what-is-cte/.

36. Nowinski quoted in "Brain Injuries Haunt Football Players Years Later"; Staudohar, "The Football Lockout of 2011," 33; Dustin Fisk, "In Case You Missed It, the NFL/NFLPA Agree on Neuro Benefits," *The Concussion Blog*, December 11, 1012, http://theconcussionblog.com/2012/12/11/in-case-you-missed-it-the-nflnflpa-agree-on-neuro-benefits/; Deubert, Wong, and Howe, "All Four Quarters," 70; Chris Mortensen, "NFLPA Sends Email to 2,000 Players," *ESPN*, September 10, 2013, http://espn.go.com/nfl/story/_/id/9650364/nflpa-reminds-players-concussion-rules; Gary Mihoces, "Judge Orders Mediation on NFL Concussion Suits," *USA Today*, July 11, 2013, http://www.usatoday.com/story/sports/nfl/2013/07/11/nfl-players-concussions-lawsuits/2510275/.

37. Mary Claire Dale, "NFL Concussion Settlement: League, Players Reach Tentative $765M Deal In Concussion-Related Lawsuits," *Huffington Post*, August 29, 2013, http://www.huffingtonpost.com/2013/08/29/nfl-concussion-settlement-lawsuits_n_3837474.html; Hunter Felt, "Concussions Lawsuit Settlement Lets NFL off the Hook," *The Guardian*, August 30, 2013, http://www.theguardian.com/sport/2013/aug/30/nfl-concussion-lawsuit-settlement-off-the-hook; Mike Florio, "NFLPA Issues Brief Statement on Settlement of Con-

cussion Lawsuits," *NBC Sports*, August 29, 2013, http://profootballtalk.nbcsports.
com/2013/08/29/nflpa-issues-brief-statement-on-settlement-of-concussion-law-
suits/; Kevin Mawae, "Cost of the Concussion Settlement," *Sportsblog*, August
30, 2013, http://kevinmawae.sportsblog.com/post/190840/cost_of_the_concus-
sion_settlement.html; James Andrew Miller, "N.F.L. Pressure Said to Lead
ESPN to Quit Film Project," *The New York Times*, August 23, 2013, http://
www.nytimes.com/2013/08/24/sports/football/nfl-pressure-said-to-prompt-espn-
to-quit-film-project.html?hp&_r=1&.

Chapter 4. NBA

1. Beginning in the 1990s, there has been a backlash against globalization and Americanization. However, this has not been the case for the NBA
whose popularity is increasing across the globe. For an analysis of the so-called
spread of anti-Americanism see, Martin Griffiths and Michael Schiavone,
"Anti-Americanism and Anti-Globalisation," in *The History of Anti-Americanism*, ed. Brendon O'Connor (Oxford: Greenwood, 2007).

2. Frank Elkins, "Rival Basketball Circuits Merge into One Loop of Eighteen Clubs," *The New York Times*, August 4, 1949, 29; Robert Bradley, "Labor
Pains Nothing New to the NBA," http://www.apbr.org/labor.html.

3. Staudohar, *Playing for Dollars*, 100; NBPA, "About the NBPA," *NBPA
website*, http://www.nbpa.com/about-nbpa.

4. Bradley, "Labor Pains Nothing New to the NBA"; Michael D. McClellan, "Captain Fantastic: The Bob Cousy Interview," *Celtic Nation*, February 9,
2004, http://www.celtic-nation.com/interviews/bob_cousy/bob_cousy_page7.htm.

5. Bradley, "Labor Pains Nothing New to the NBA"; Staudohar, *Play-
ing for Dollars*, 105; McClellan, "Captain Fantastic: The Bob Cousy Interview";
"NBA Okays Player Union," *The Sun*, April 19, 1957, 22; Jack Barry, "NBA
Players May Sign, With AFL-CIO," *Boston Globe*, January 12, 1957, 6; "NBA
Approves Players' Association, Arbitration," *The Washington Post and Times Her-
ald*, April 19, 1957, D3.

6. Chris Tommason, "Hall of Famers Split, Agree Lockout Hurts NBA,"
Fox Sports Florida, October 11, 2011, http://www.foxsportsflorida.com/pages/lan
ding?blockID=580008&tagID=124597; Cousy quoted in Phil Elderkin, "Bob
Cousy Eyes NBA Coaching Career after Playing Days Completed," *The Christian Science Monitor*, February 17, 1959, 11; David George Surdam, *The Rise of
the National Basketball Association* (Urbana and Chicago: University of Illinois
Press), 142.

7. "Pension Plan Started by NBA Players," *The Washington Post*, January
10, 1961, A19; Staudohar, *Playing for Dollars*, 105; Unnamed player quoted in
Dan Hafner, "East Wins All-Star Classic Delayed By Player Revolt," *The Los
Angeles Times*, January 15, 1964, 1–2; Jack Leone, "Labor Relations in a Locker
Room," *Newsday*, January 15, 1964, 32C; "Heinsohn, Boss in Pension Feud,"

Newsday, January 18, 1964, 47; "NBA Okays Pension Plan," *Boston Globe*, May 27, 1964, 58.

8. Phil Elderkin, "Strike Threat Bubbles in Pro Court Caldron," *The Christian Science Monitor*, January 28, 1967, 13; Staudohar, *Playing for Dollars*, 106–107; Deane McGowen, "N.B.A. Players Threaten to Strike Playoffs If Pension Demands Are Not Met," *The New York Times*, March 1, 1967, 34; "NBA Players Threaten to Strike in Playoffs," *Los Angeles Times*, March 1, 1967, C1-C2; Fleischer quoted in "NBA Players Threaten Pension Plan Strike," *Chicago Daily Defender*, March 6, 1967, 27; Robertson quoted in "Noon Today Is Deadline in NBA Row," *The Washington Post and Times Herald*, March 14, 1967, D1; Phil Elderkin, "NBA Pension: Pro Basketball's Races Are Over but the Playoffs May Not Start," *The Christian Science Monitor*, March 8, 1967, 11; "Oscar Robertson Headed NBA Players' Pension Fund Fight," *Philadelphia Tribune*, June 13, 1967, 14; Fleisher quoted in "NBA Promises Pensions, Players End Strike Threat," *Boston Globe*, March 15, 1967, 55; Robertson quoted in "Players, Owners Settle Dispute," *Los Angeles Times*, March 15, 1967, 1, 6.

9. "NBA to Increase Rookies Salaries," *The New York Times*, August 21, 1968, 55; "NBA Boosts Pay," *Chicago Daily Defender*, August 22, 1968, 38.

10. "NBA, Players Announce Terms," *Atlanta Daily World*, October 22, 1970, 9; "NBA Raises Cage Salary," *Chicago Daily Defender*, October 12, 1970, 29.

11. Staudohar, *Playing for Dollars*, 101–103; Al Harvin, "A.B.A. Owners Agree to Pay $11-Million Merger Indemnity," *The New York Times*, April 15, 1970, 75; Jane Gross, "NBA Absorbs Four ABA Teams for $3.2 Million Each," *Newsday*, June 18, 1976, 117, 120.

12. Robert Bradley, "Pro Basketball Legal Cases 1946–69," *Robert Bradley's Pro Basketball History Revisited*, 2010, http://apbrbasketball.blogspot.com/2010/12/pro-basketball-legal-cases-1946-69.html; Staudohar, *Playing for Dollars*, 109–10.

13. Staudohar, *Playing for Dollars*, 110–11; Bradley, "Pro Basketball Legal Cases 1946–69"; Michela Lava, "The Battle of Superstars: Player Restraints in Professional Teams Sports," *University of Florida Law Review* 32, no. 4 (Spring 1980): 682–83; Drewes quoted in "Judge Rules Barry Stays," *The Spokesman-Review*, August 9, 1967, 15.

14. Lava, "The Battle of Superstars," 683–84; Seymour Smith, "NBA Owners to Drop the Reserve Clause," *The Sun*, September 22, 1971, C4; Sam Goldaper, "N.B.A. Players Spurn Offer by Owners as Senate Hearings on Merger Near," *The New York Times*, September 19, 1971, S2.

15. "N.B.A. and Players Sign a Basic Pact," *The New York Times*, March 6, 1973, 51; "Accord Reached in NBA," *The Washington Post and Times Herald*, March 6, 1973, D5; Fleisher quoted in Seymour Smith, "Fleisher Big Figure in NBA Labor Moves," *The Sun*, March 7, 1973, C5.

16. Staudohar, *Playing for Dollars*, 107–108.

17. *Robertson v. National Basketball Association*, 1975, reprinted at http://www.leagle.com/decision/19751256389FSupp867_11127; Fleisher quoted in Charles

Maher, "Pro Basketball: Suit Threatens Life of NBA," *Los Angeles Times*, October 30, 1975, 1, 11–12; Lava, "The Battle of Superstars," 685; Staudohar, *Playing for Dollars*, 114.

18. Staudohar, *Playing for Dollars*, 108, 114–15; Bob Logan, "Owners, Players Make Peace in NBA," *Chicago Tribune*, February 4, 1976, C1; David Dupree, "NBA Drops Option Rule, Settles Suit," *The Washington Post*, February 4, 1976, D1; Fleisher and Silas quoted in Sam Goldaper, "N.B.A. Obtains Labor Peace and Plans Talks with A.B.A," *The New York Times*, April 13, 1976, 41, 44; "Players, NBA Sign New Pact," *The Sun*, April 13, 1976, C7, C9; Obrien quoted in Fred Rothenberg, "NBA Didn't Surrender to Players—O'Brien," *Boston Globe*, February 22, 1976, 72.

19. O'Brien quoted in Bob Logan, "NBA Players Ready to Strike over Pay Limits," *Chicago Tribune*, February 2, 1980, A3; Bob Logan, "NBA Approves Pact with Players, Expansion to Dallas," *Chicago Tribune*, February 3, 1980, C2; David DuPree, "NBA, Union Agree; Expansion to Dallas Is Voted," *The Washington Post*, February 3, 1980, D5; Staudohar, *Playing for Dollars*, 108.

20. "NBA Owners and Players Talking," *Newsday*, October 5, 1982, 94; Fleisher quoted in Steve Hershey, "NBA Owners Meet Today On Union Negotiations," *The Washington Post*, October 20, 1982, D5; Sam Goldaper, "N.B.A. Owners Will Be Briefed on Talks," *The New York Times*, October 20, 1982, B15; Fred Mitchell, "Pro Basketball: Owners Seek New Salary Plan," *Chicago Tribune*, October 21, 1982, C2; Phil Elderkin, "Larry O'Brien Trying to Steer NBA toward Black Ink," *The Christian Science Monitor*, November 4, 1982, 15.

21. Staudohar, *Playing for Dollars*, 118–19; Sam Goldaper, "N.B.A. and Players Schedule New Talks," *The New York Times*, February 25, 1983, A26; Bridgeman quoted in Bryan Burwell, "NBA Threatened with Walkout," *Newsday*, February 18, 1983, 119, 124; David DuPree, "Strike Date of April 2 Set by NBA Players," *The Washington Post*, February 18, 1983, D5; Fleisher quoted in Bryan Burwell, "Fleisher Ready to Bargain as NBA's Deadline Looms," *Newsday*, February 22, 1983, 71, 76; Derrick Jackson, "Fleisher Anticipates Strike," *Newsday*, March 25, 1983, 125.

22. O'Brien quoted in David Dupree, "Strike Is Averted as NBA, Players Agree in Principle," *The Washington Post*, April 1, 1983, C1, C6. Fleisher quoted in "NBA Averts Strike with Salary Cap," *Los Angeles Times*, April 1, 1983, 1, 10; Lanier quoted in Sam Goldaper, "Revenue Sharing Instituted: N.B.A. Strike Averted with 4-Year Pact," *The New York Times*, April 1, 1983, A19, A23.

23. Staudohar, *Playing for Dollars*, 108; "NBA, Players' Association Agree No New Signings after June 17," *The Sun*, June 10, 1987, 4H; Stern quoted in Michael Wilbon, "NBA, Players Set Signing Moratorium," *The Washington Post*, June 10, 1987, B2; Paxon quoted in Bob Sakamoto, "NBA Union Takes League to Court, but at Least Averts a Strike," *Chicago Tribune*, October 2, 1987, C6; Sam Goldaper, "N.B.A. Target of Players' Antitrust Suit," *The New York Times*, October 2, 1987, B13–B14; "Judge Rules against Players in Antitrust Charge on Owners," *The Sun*, December 18, 1987, 2C; "NBA Union, Management Both

Loose," *The Washington Post*, December 18, 1987, D4; "Players Reject Offer," *The Washington Post*, December 30, 1987, E2.

24. Bob Sakamoto, "NBA Player Reps Vote to Dump Union," *Chicago Tribune*, February 6, 1988, A1; Anthony Cotton, "Players Aren't Sure About Union Ploy," *The Washington Post*, February 7, 1988, D6; Anthony Cotton, "No Fast Break on Union Front," *The Washington Post*, February 29, 1988, D4.

25. Sam Smith and Bob Sakamoto, "NBA Players, Owners Settle on 6-Year Deal," *Chicago Tribune*, April 27, 1988, 1, 9; "The NBA and Players' Union Reach Agreement on a 6-Year Contract," *Los Angeles Times*, April 27, 1988, D4; Fleisher quoted in Smith and Sakamoto, "NBA Players, Owners Settle on 6-Year Deal," 9; Unnamed Eastern Coach and Stern's reply quoted in Anthony Cotton, "New Collective Bargaining Pact Leaves Prospects, Questions," *The Washington Post*, May 17, 1988, E3.

26. Richard Justice, "Stern, Players Tell Court What They're Made Of," *The Washington Post*, July 13, 1994, F9.

27. Staudohar, *Playing for Dollars*, 123–24; "NBA Files Suit to Keep Agreement Intact," *The Washington Post*, June 21, 1994, C8; Richard Justice, "Judge: NBA Draft, Salary Cap Are Legal," *The Washington Post*, July 19, 1994, 2; Sam Smith, "NBA Plan: Exploit Union Cracks for Deal or Call Lockout," *Chicago Tribune*, September 23, 1994, 1; Sam Smith, "NBA Keeps Eye on the Ball, Avoids Strike 3 Players, Owners Announce They'll Play Full Season," *Chicago Tribune*, October 28, 1994, 1; Richard Justice, "NBA Union Chief Resigns," *The Washington Post*, April 15, 1995, C1.

28. Justice, "NBA Union Chief Resigns," C1; Phil Taylor, "The NBA," *Sports Illustrated*, April 24, 1995, http://sportsillustrated.cnn.com/vault/article/magazine/MAG1006502/index.htm.

29. Richard Justice, "Bargaining Secrecy Raises Agents' Ire," *The Washington Post*, June 19, 1995, C3; Sam Smith, "Top NBA Players Hope to Decertify Their Union," *Chicago Tribune*, June 20, 1995, 2.

30. Mark Asher, "NBA, Union Reach Six-Year Agreement," *The Washington Post*, June 22, 1995, D1, D3; John Helyar, "Civil War Pits NBA's Players against Players," *Wall Street Journal*, June 23, 1995, B1; Murray Chass, "NBA Locks Out Its Players as Labor Battle Continues," *Chicago Tribune*, July 1, 1995, 1.

31. Gourdine quoted in Chass, "NBA Locks Out Its Players as Labor Battle Continues," 1; Jordan quoted in "Michael Jordan Convinced . . . Players Association Should Go," *New York Beacon*, August 9, 1995, 48; Mark Asher, "Jordan, Ewing Join Class-Action Lawsuit," *The Washington Post*, June 29, 1995, B6; Terry Armour, "Stern Says No Agreement, No Season," *Chicago Tribune*, August 16, 1995, 1; Terry Armour, "New NBA Deal Means Little NBA Players Still At Odds," *Chicago Tribune*, August 9, 1995, 1; Phil Taylor, "Wanna Be Like Mike . . ." *Sports Illustrated*, September 4, 1995, http://sportsillustrated. cnn.com/vault/article/magazine/MAG1007044/1/index.htm; John Helyar, "NBA Players Reject Bid to Scrap Union As Faction Led by Jordan Is Defeated," *The Wall Street Journal*, September 13, 1995, A4; Richard Justice, "NBA Players

Retain Union," *The Washington Post*, September 13, 1995, A1; Richard Justice, Mark Asher, "Owners Approve Agreement," *The Washington Post*, September 16, 1995, H8; Smith quoted in Fred Mitchell, "For NBA Teammates, Split Decisions," *Chicago Tribune*, September 14, 1995, 2. For explanation on the difference between defined gross revenue and basketball-related income see Andrew S. Zimbalist, "Economic Issues in the 1998–1999 NBA Lockout and the Problem of Competitive Balance in Professional Sports," in *The Economics of Sports*, ed. William S. Kern (Kalamazoo: W. E. Upjohn Institute for Employment Research, 2000): 94, 97–98.

32. Sam Smith, "What Lockout? Free-Agent Clock Is Reset," *Chicago Tribune*, July 10, 1996, 3; Mark Asher, "NBA, Players Agree on Labor Deal," *The Washington Post*, June 29, 1996, C1, C8.

33. Paul D. Staudohar, "Labor Relations in Basketball: The Lockout of 1998–99," *Monthly Labor Review* (April 1999): 4–5; Stern quoted in Sam Smith, "NBA Owner's Actions Could Lead to Lockout," *Chicago Tribune*, March 28, 1998, 5; Hunter quoted in Stefan Fatsis, "NBA Owners Vote to Reopen Labor Pact, Risking Possibility of Strike-Hit Season," *Wall Street Journal*, March 24, 1988, B9; Michael K. Ozanian, "Selective Accounting," *Forbes*, December 14, 1988, http://www.forbes.com/forbes/1998/1214/6213124a.html.

34. Overview of the lockout from: Staudohar, "Labor Relations in Basketball: The Lockout of 1998–99," 7–8; Chris Sheridan, "NBA Union Gets Money, Files Grievance," *New Pittsburgh Courier*, July 18, 1988, 7; Hunter quoted in Stephen Nidetz, "NBA Union Won't Budge on 'Soft Cap,'" *Chicago Tribune*, August 15, 1988, 2; Terry Armour, "Players: No Settlement in Sight," *Chicago Tribune*, October 15, 1988, 7; Sam Smith, "Stern Now Blames Agents for Lack of Labor Deal," *Chicago Tribune*, November 5, 1988, 5; Williams quoted in Selena Roberts, "Key Players' Group Defends Its Negotiating Stance," *The New York Times*, December 30, 1998, http://www.nytimes.com/1998/12/30/sports/basketball-key-players-group-defends-its-negotiating-stance.html; MacDonald quoted in Mike Wise, "Is Falk Calling the Shots For Players in N.B.A. Talks?" *The New York Times*, December 28, 1998, http://www.nytimes.com/1998/12/28/sports/pro-basketball-is-falk-calling-the-shots-for-players-in-nba-talks.html; Sam Smith, "Stern Bypasses the Union Commissioner's Letter to Players is Rebutted," *Chicago Tribune*, December 18, 1988, 1; Willis quoted in "Raptors' Willis Questions His Union's Stand in NBA Lockout," *Amarillo Globe-News*, December 23, 1998, http://amarillo.com/stories/122398/spo_willis.shtml; Thomas quoted in Stephen A. Smith, "Group Of NBA Players Asks Former Star's Help The Players Want Isiah Thomas to Intervene for Them with the Union," *Philly.com*, January 2, 1999, http://articles.philly.com/1999-01-02/sports/25491332_1_voting-system-thomas-and-two-nbpa.

35. Staudohar, "Labor Relations in Basketball: The Lockout of 1998–99," 8; Stefan Fatsis, "NBA, Players Reach Accord, Saving Season," *Wall Street Journal*, January 7, 1999, A3; For a full list of the various salary cap exemptions, see J. Richard Hill, and Peter. A. Groothuis, "The New NBA Collective Bargaining

Agreement, The Median Voter Model and a Robin-Hood Rent Redistribution," *Journal of Sports Economics* 2, no. 2 (May 2001). Discussion of the luxury tax from Elizabeth Gustafson, "The Luxury Tax in Professional Sports," in *Handbook on the Economics of Sport*, ed. Wladamir Andreff and Stefan Szymansk (Massachusetts: Edward Elgar Publishing, 2009): 652–60.

36. Hill and Groothuis, "The New NBA Collective Bargaining Agreement," 139–40.

37. "NBA Team Valuations," *Forbes*, December 22, 2005, http://www.forbes.com/lists/2005/32/Rank_1.html; Jack Gage and Michael K. Ozanian, "Inside the Forbes NBA Valuation List," *Forbes*, December 22, 2005, http://www.forbes.com/2005/12/22/nba-team-valuations_cz_mo_1222nbaintro.html; "NBA Lockout Looming," *Chicago Tribune*, February 11, 2005, 22; Stern and Hunter quoted in Sam Smith, "NBA Commissioner, Union Leader Promise Contract Accord," *Knight Ridder Tribune News Service*, February 19, 2005, 1; David Aldridge, "Talks Stall between NBA, Players Union," *Knight Ridder Tribune News Service*, May 18, 2005, 1; Michael O'Keeffe, "Stern: Lockout Is Coming," *New York Daily News*, May 20, 2005, 88.

38. "CBA Principal Deal Points," *NBA.com*, August 4, 2005, http://www.nba.com/news/cba_summary_050804.html; Peter May, "NBA and Union Reach Agreement on 6-Year Contract," *Boston Globe*, June 22, 2005, E1; Larry Coon, "Breaking Down Changes in New CBA," *ESPN*, November 28, 2011, http://espn.go.com/nba/story/_/page/CBA-111128/how-new-nba-deal-compares-last-one; "NBA Minimum Salary," *Inside Hoops*, August 10, 2005, http://www.insidehoops.com/minimum-nba-salary.shtml; Stern quoted in Sam Smith, "NBA, Players Reach Deal on Collective Bargaining Agreement," *Knight Ridder Tribune News Service*, June 21, 2005, 1; Hunter quoted in David Moore, "NBA Avoids Potential Work Stoppage with Fresh Labor Deal," *Knight Ridder Tribune News Service*, June 21, 2005, 1.

39. Michael R. Wilson, "Why So Stern? The Growing Power of the NBA Commissioner," *DePaul Journal Sports Labor & Contemporary Problems* 45 (2010): 48–49, 54–56; NBA, "NBA Player Dress Code," *NBA.com*, 2005, http://www.nba.com/news/player_dress_code_051017.html.

40. Wilson, "Why So Stern?" 57–60.

41. Chris Mannix, "Money Ball," *Sports Illustrated*, December 20, 2010, http://sportsillustrated.cnn.com/vault/article/magazine/MAG1179930/index.htm; Paul D. Staudohar, "The Basketball Lockout of 2011," *Monthly Labor Review* (December 2012): 29–30; Mike Ozanian, "The NBA's Most Valuable Teams," *Forbes*, January 26, 2011, http://www.forbes.com/sites/mikeozanian/2011/01/26/the-nbas-most-valuable-teams-2/; Lacob quoted in David J. Berri, "Did the Players Give Up Money to Make the NBA Better? Exploring the 2011 Collective Bargaining Agreement in the National Basketball Association," *International Journal of Sport Finance* 7, no. 2 (2012): 160.

42. "Wizards Owner's Words Draw Fine," *Philadelphia Daily News*, September 30, 2010, 50.

43. See below for details on fines during the lockout. In regard to revenue sharing see Kristi Dosh, "Want to Repair the NBA? Start with Revenue Sharing," *Forbes*, August 9, 2011, http://www.forbes.com/sites/sportsmoney/2011/08/09/want-to-repair-the-nba-start-with-revenue-sharing/.

44. William B. Gould IV, "The 2011 Basketball Lockout: The Union Lives to Fight Another Day—Barely," *Stanford Law Review Online* 64, no. 51 (2012): 54; Lance Pugmire, "Players' Union Head Rejects Contract Offer," *Orlando Sentinel*, May 11, 2011, C2; Gary Washburn, "NBA Owners Now Offering Players 'Flex Cap,'" *Boston Globe*, June 22, 2011, C6; Brian Mahoney, "Flex Cap A Small Mark of Progress Still Far from Deal as Deadline Nears," *Pittsburgh Post-Gazette*, June 22, 2011, D2; Staudohar, "The Basketball Lockout of 2011," 30; Howard Beck, "Sides Remain Far Apart in N.B.A. Labor Talks," *The New York Times*, June 21, 2011, http://www.nytimes.com/2011/06/22/sports/basketball/nba-and-players-union-remain-far-apart-in-labor-talks.html?_r=0; Howard Beck, "As Lockout Approaches, N.B.A. Players Wear Unity on Their Shirts," *The New York Times*, June 24, 2011, http://www.nytimes.com/2011/06/25/sports/basketball/as-an-nba-lockout-looms-t-shirts-proclaim-players-solidarity.html.

45. Staudohar, "The Basketball Lockout of 2011," 30, 31; Chris Broussard, "Sources: Michael Jordan fined $100K," *ESPN*, September 12, 2011, http://espn.go.com/nba/story/_/id/6961508/michael-jordan-charlotte-bobcats-fined-100k-talking-lockout-sources-say; Brian Windhorst, "NBA Fines Heat Owner Micky Arison," *ESPN*, November 2, 2011, http://espn.go.com/nba/truehoop/miamiheat/story/_/id/7175679/nba-lockout-miami-heat-owner-micky-arison-fined-500000-twitter-comments-labor-talks-sources-say; Jason Whitlock, "Is Fisher in Stern's Back Pocket?," *Fox Sports*, October 29, 2011, http://msn.foxsports.com/nba/story/Whitlock-NBA-lockout-David-Stern-has-Derek-Fisher-in-back-pocket-Billy-Hunter-players-union-not-pleased-102811; Adrian Wojnarowski, "Hunter's Actions in NBA Labor Talks Weaken Union," *Yahoo! Sports*, November 1, 2011, http://sports.yahoo.com/nba/news;_ylt=AtACK8MQYNrL8lI41qbg4SY5nYcB?slug=aw-wojnarowski_nba_lockout_billy_hunter_110111; Howard Beck, "High-Tension N.B.A. Talks Resume, but They're between Union Officials," *The New York Times*, November 2, 2011, http://www.nytimes.com/2011/11/03/sports/basketball/nba-talks-resume-between-union-officials.html?_r=0.

46. Staudohar, "The Basketball Lockout of 2011," 31; Howard Beck, "In Attempt to Force Talks, N.B.A. Players File Antitrust Suit," *The New York Times*, November 15, 2011, http://www.nytimes.com/2011/11/16/sports/basketball/nba-players-file-antitrust-suit-against-the-league.html; "Players File Pair of Antitrust Lawsuits against NBA," *NBA.com*, November 16, 2011, http://www.nba.com/2011/news/11/15/tuesday-labor.ap/index.html.

47. Davis quoted in Mark Murphy, "Big Baby: Everyone Has to Stop 'Sticking Their Chests Out,'" *Boston Herald*, November 14, 2011, http://bostonherald.com/sports/celtics_nba/celtics_insider/2011/11/big_baby_everyone_has_stop_sticking_their_chests_out; Cousins quoted in Ariel Sandler, "Several NBA Players Are Already Speaking Out Against the Decision to Disband the

Union," *Business Insider*, November 15, 2011, http://www.businessinsider.com/nba-lockout-nba-players-against-disbanding-the-union-2011-11; Samuels quoted in Jason Lloyd, "Cavs' Samuels Would Have Accepted Deal but NBA Players Union Rejects Owners' Offer; Season in Jeopardy," *Ohio.com*, November 14, 2011, http://www.ohio.com/sports/cavs-samuels-would-have-accepted-deal-but-nba-players-union-rejects-owners-offer-season-in-jeopardy-1.245552.

48. Coon, "Breaking Down Changes in New CBA"; "NBA Minimum Salaries," *Hoops World*, 2011, http://www.hoopsworld.com/nba-minimum-salaries; Fisher quoted in Howard Beck, "N.B.A. Reaches a Tentative Deal to Save the Season," *The New York Times*, November 26, 2011, http://www.nytimes.com/2011/11/27/sports/basketball/nba-and-basketball-players-reach-deal-to-end-lockout.html?pagewanted=all&_r=0; Gould, "The 2011 Basketball Lockout," 56; See John Lombardo, "Inside NBA's Revenue Sharing," *Sports Business Journal*, January 23, 2012, http://www.sportsbusinessdaily.com/Journal/Issues/2012/01/23/Leagues-and-Governing-Bodies/NBA-revenue.aspx; For the full calculations on how revenue sharing is determined see Larry Coon, *NBA Salary Cap FAQ*, http://www.cbafaq.com/salarycap.htm#Q24; For an overview on what is included as basketball related income see Larry Coon, *NBA Salary Cap FAQ*, http://www.cbafaq.com/salarycap.htm#Q12.

49. Kurt Badenhausen, "Billion-Dollar Knicks and Lakers Top List Of NBA's Most Valuable Teams," *Forbes*, January 23, 2013, http://www.forbes.com/sites/kurtbadenhausen/2013/01/23/billion-dollar-knicks-and-lakers-top-list-of-nbas-most-valuable-teams/; "NBA Team Values," *Forbes*, January 23, 2013, http://www.forbes.com/nba-valuations/list/; Kurt Bandenhausen, "As Stern Says Goodbye, Knicks, Lakers Set Records as NBA's Most Valuable Teams," *Forbes*, January 22, 2014, http://www.forbes.com/sites/kurtbadenhausen/2014/01/22/as-stern-says-goodbye-knicks-lakers-set-records-as-nbas-most-valuable-teams/; Kelly Dwyer, "LeBron James and Deron Williams Warn NBA Owners that Cries of Lockout Losses 'Will not Fly with Us This Time,'" *Yahoo! Sports*, October 6, 2014. http://sports.yahoo.com/blogs/nba-ball-dont-lie/lebron-james-and-deron-williams-warn-nba-owners-that-cries-of-lockout-losses--will-not-fly-with-us-this-time-205656424.html.

50. Ken Berger, "NBPA Votes 24–0 to Oust Billy Hunter as Director," *CBS Sports*, February 16, 2013, http://www.cbssports.com/nba/writer/ken-berger/21716401/nbpa-votes-24-0-to-oust-billy-hunter-as-director.

51. Berri, "Did the Players Give Up Money to Make the NBA Better?" 168.

Chapter 5. Labor Struggles in the NHL

1. Leo H. Kahane, "The Economics of the National Hockey League: The 2004–05 Lockout and the Beginning of a New Era," in *Sports Economics After Fifty Years: Essays in Honour of Simon Rottenberg*, edited by Placido Rodriguez,

Stefan Kesenne, and Jaume Garcia (Oviedo: University of Oviedo Press, 2006), 108; Staudohar, *Playing for Dollars*, 133–34; "Lord Stanley," *Hockey Hall of Fame*, n.d. http://www.legendsofhockey.net/LegendsOfHockey/jsp/LegendsMember.jsp? mem=b194502&type=Builder&page=bio&list=ByName.

2. "Setting the Foundation," *Hockey Central*, n.d., http://www.hockeycentral.co.uk/nhl/history/nhl-setfound.php; "Inside the NHL S-Z," *Hockey Central*, n.d., http://www.hockeycentral.co.uk/nhl/insidenhl/Inside-the-NHL-S-Z.php; Joe Pelletier, "Those Were the Days: Salary Cap," *Greatest Hockey Legends*, February 9, 2011, http://www.greatesthockeylegends.com/2011/02/those-were-days-salary-cap.html; D'Arcy Jenish, *The NHL: 100 Years of On-Ice Action and Boardroom Battles* (Canada: Doubleday, 2013) Kindle Edition.

3. Jenish, *The NHL*.

4. Adams and Tobin quoted in "Pension Plan for Hockey Players Gains Momentum: Must Be Voluntary Equal Contribution," *The Christian Science Monitor*, January 17, 1947, 13; "Players' Pension, Savings Plan Approved by Hockey Governors," *The New York Times*, September 5, 1947, 27; "Pension Plan Approved for Hockey Stars," *The Christian Science Monitor*, September 5, 1947, 16.

5. J. Andrew Ross, "Trust and Antitrust: The Failure of the First National Hockey League Players' Association, 1957–1958," *Business and Economic History* 8 (2010): 3–5; Harold Kaese, "Hockey Players Seeking Better Pension," *Daily Boston Globe*, February 13, 1957, 18; Lindsay quoted in "Hockey Players Form Association," *Chicago Daily Tribune*, February 12, 1957, 1–2; "Pro Hockey Players Organize," *Daily Boston Globe*, February 12, 1957, 8; Campbell quoted in "New 'Union' Formed By Hockey Players, Boss Wonders Why," *Newsday*, February 12, 1957, 15C. Campbell quoted in Jenish, *The NHL*.

6. Campbell quoted in Jenish, *The NHL*; Harvey quoted in "Harvey Calls N.H.L. Suit Regrettable," *New York Herald Tribune*, October 12, 1957, B3; "Hockey Clubs Hit in Antitrust Suit," *The New York Times*, October 11, 1957, 38; "Red Wings' Squad Quits Association," *The New York Times*, November 13, 1957, 45; Ross, "Trust and Antitrust," 10–11; Charles Bartlett, "Lindsay, Two Other Hawks Meet with Hockey Owners," *Chicago Daily Tribune*, January 29, 1958, B4; "Hockey Players Plan Peace Moves," *The New York Times*, February 1, 1958, 15.

7. "NHL Players Lose Bid, but Make Gains," *Chicago Daily Tribune*, February 5, 1958, c1; Ross, "Trust and Antitrust," 12–13; Lindsay quoted in "Hockey Group Survives," *The New York Times*, February 7, 1958, 24.

8. Jim Baillie, *An Investigation into the Collective Bargaining Relationship between the NHL and the NHLPA, 1994–2005*, Industrial Relations Centre, Queen's University, 2005, 16–17; "Teamsters Union Plans to Organize Pro Athletes," *The Sun*, February 5, 1966, B1; Jordan I. Kobritz and Jeffrey F. Levine, "Don Fehr Leads the NHLPA: Does the NHL Have Anything to Fear?" *Virginia Sports & Entertainment Law Journal* (Fall 2011): 2–3; Campbell quoted in Baillie, *An Investigation into the Collective Bargaining Relationship*, 16; Eagleson quoted in "Hockey Players Organize, Too," *Newsday*, June 8, 1967, 33A.

9. "Progress Made in Salary Talks," *The Sun*, June 24, 1967, B4; "Owners to Assume Full Pension Costs of N.H.L. Players," *The New York Times*, August 23, 1969, 21.

10. Jenish, *The NHL*; Staudohar, *Playing for Dollars*, 158; James Quirk and Rodney D. Fort, *Pay Dirt: The Business of Professional Team Sports* (Princeton: Princeton University Press 1997), 330; Jonathan Gatehouse, *The Instigator: How Gary Bettman Remade the NHL and Changed the Game Forever* (Chicago: Triumph Books, 2012), Kindle Edition.

11. Quirk and Fort, *Pay Dirt*, 206–207; Higgenbotham quoted in Jenish, *The NHL* and Ian Craig Pulver, "A Face Off Between the National Hockey League and the National Hockey League Players' Association: The Goal a More Competitively Balanced League," *Marquette Sports Law Review* 2, no. 1 (1991): 44.

12. Parton Keese, "Compensation Rule Key to N.H.L. Pact Free-Agent Clause Key to N.H.L. Pact," *The New York Times*, October 7, 1975, 27; Jane Gross, "NHL's Players Accept a 'Rozelle Rule' Contract," *Newsday*, October 7, 1975, 3; Ziegler quoted in Jenish, *The NHL*; Wirtz quoted in "Players' Group Certifies NHL Option Compensation," *The Washington Post*, October 7, 1975, 13; Staudohar, *Playing for Dollars*, 155; Jenish, *The NHL*.

13. Stein quoted in Bruce Dowbiggin, *Money Players: How Hockey's Greatest Stars Beat the NHL at Its Own Game* (Toronto: McClelland and Stewart, 2003), 3; and Gatehouse, *The Instigator*.

14. Staudohar, *Playing for Dollars*, 159–60; Judy Handle, "NHL Players Assn. to Seek $12 Million in WHA Merger," *Boston Globe*, March 16, 1979, 58; "Players Agree to Merger," *The Washington Post*, June 7, 1979, F6; "N.H.L. Players' Group Consents to Merger," *The New York Times*, June 7, 1979, D21; Eagleson quoted in Jenish, *The NHL*.

15. Staudohar, *Playing for Dollars*, 159; Alex Yannis, "Free Agency Is Hockey Topic," *The New York Times*, February 10, 1981, B13; "Progress Is Reported in Talks on N.H.L. Pact," *The New York Times*, July 10, 1981, 18; Tim Moriarty, "NHL Players Surveying Strike Insurance," *Newsday*, October 23, 1981, 134.

16. Staudohar, *Playing for Dollars*, 155–56; "Agreement Is Reached on a New NHL Pact," *Newsday*, August 18, 1982, 84; Eagleson quoted in "The New Deal," *Chicago Tribune*, August 23, 1982, d8.

17. Staudohar, *Playing for Dollars*, 137, 140.

18. Ibid., 156–57; "New NHL Agreement Includes Best-of-7 Series in All Playoffs," *The Sun*, July 26, 1986, 11B; Ker quoted in Al Morganti, "In the NHL, 'Free' Agents Don't Exist," *Philly.com*, August 22, 1986, http://articles. philly.com/1986-08-22/sports/26063167_1_free-agent-first-refusal-premier.

19. Staudohar, *Playing for Dollars*, 141, 149; Stevie Cameron, "Fall of the Eagle," *Maclean's*, March 14, 1994, 14–15; Jenish, *The NHL*; Gatehouse, *The Instigator*; Jane O'Hara, "In the Name of Greed: As Many Former Players Cheer, Alan Eagleson Goes to Jail," *Maclean's*, January 19, 1988, 22; Adam Proteau, "No Room for Alan Eagleson at Summit Series Celebrations," *The Hockey News*,

June 9, 2012, http://www.thehockeynews.com/articles/48355-No-room-for-Alan-Eagleson-at-Summit-Series-celebrations.html. For the best overview of the fall of Eagleson see Russ Conway, *Game Misconduct: Alan Eagleson and the Corruption of Hockey* (Toronto: Macfarlane Walter, and Ross, 1995).

20. Overview of the leadup to the strike from Baillie, *An Investigation into the Collective Bargaining Relationship*, 21–23; Unnamed player quoted in Mike Kiley, "Money's the Key Issue in NHL-Union Dispute," *Chicago Tribune*, August 25, 1981, 8; "Players Hope Cooler Heads Prevail," *Chicago Tribune*, March 8, 1992, 4; Mike Kiley, "Hawks Testing the Ice as Strike Replacements," *Chicago Tribune*, March 14, 1992, 5; Dave Sell, "NHL, Players Association Face Off," *The Washington Post*, March 9, 1992, C6; Dave Sell, "Ziegler Says Players Not Getting Big Picture," *The Washington Post*, March 22, 1992, D6; Dave Sell, "NHL Profits and Losses Are Argued Union, Owners Report Little Overall Progress in Bargaining," *The Washington Post*, March 27, 1992, D4; McMullen quoted in Joe Lapointe, "N.H.L. Owners Drop the Gloves," *The New York Times*, March 27, 1992, B10; Liut quoted in Jenish, *The NHL*.

21. Brown quoted in Mike Kiley, "NHL Strike One Huge Power Play," *Chicago Tribune*, April 2, 1992, 1; Ziegler quoted in Flip Bondy, "N.H.L. Players Reject 'Final' Offer," *The New York Times*, April 8, 1992, B7, B11; Jenish, *The NHL*.

22. Staudohar, *Playing for Dollars*, 151, 157; Dave Sell, "Vote to Approve Agreement Is 409–61," *The Washington Post*, April 12, 1992, D1; Joe Lapointe, "Play Hockey! Settlement Ends 10-Day Strike," *The New York Times*, April 11, 1992, 35, 39; Aubut quoted in James Deacon, "Settlement on Ice," *Maclean's*, April 20, 1992, 42.

23. Overview of the leadup to the lockout from: Jenish, *The NHL*; Mike Kiley, "NHL's Silent Treatment League Toils Quietly on New Player's Deal," *Chicago Tribune*, September 5, 1993, 8; Liut quoted in Jenish, *The NHL*; Paul D. Staudohar, "The Hockey Lockout of 2004–2005," *Monthly Labor Review* (December 2005): 24; Dave Sell, "NHL on the Rise, but How High Can It Go?," *The Washington Post*, January 23, 1994, D14; Robert McG. Thomas Jr, "Shades of Baseball: N.H.L. Labor Impasse," *The New York Times*, August 9, 1994, B17; Leonard Hochberg, "Players, NHL Begin Bargaining," *The Washington Post*, August 19, 1994, D7; Gartner quoted in "Will the NHL Be Next? Players Union president Calls Proposal 'Warfare.'" *Chicago Tribune*, August 9, 1994, 2; "Players Turn Down Latest NHL Proposal Friday Deadline Means Season Start Likely to be Delayed," *Chicago Tribune*, September 29, 1994, 4; Ranford quoted in "NHL Players Prepare for Lockout," *Chicago Tribune*, August 26, 1994, 2; Bettman quoted in Joe Lapointe, "N.H.L. Warning: No Deal, No Season," *The New York Times*, September 23, 1994, B9; Mark Asher, "NHL Players Make Late Offer, but Owners Reject It," *The Washington Post*, September 30, 1994, C1; Bettman quoted in Gatehouse, *The Instigator*.

24. Len Hochberg, "Players Offer to Cap Rookies' Salaries, But League Says No," *The Washington Post*, November 11, 1994, F9; Joe Lapointe, "Hockey Negotiators Stop Talks, For Now," *The New York Times*, December 3, 1994, 35; "50-Game Season or Bust? Bettman," *Chicago Tribune*, November 16, 1994, 2;

Joe Lapointe, "Playing the Numbers Game, Ownership Style," *The New York Times*, November 17, 1994, B21; Gatehouse, *The Instigator*; Joe Lapointe, "Owners Offer Players a Deal That Will Exclude a Payroll Tax," *The New York Times*, December 21, 1994, B23.

25. Joe Lapointe, "Pact Reached For Salvaging Hockey Season," *The New York Times*, January 12, 1995, A1; Len Hochberg, "Last-Minute Deal Saves NHL Season," *The Washington Post*, January 12, 1995, A1; Gartner quoted in "Hockey Union Offer Ratification by NHL's 700 Players Would Salvage 48-Game Season," *Chicago Tribune*, January 11, 1995, 1; Richard Sandomir, "The Players Approve Agreement With N.H.L." *The New York Times*, January 14, 1995, 35; Len Hochberg, "NHL Players Union Ratifies Labor Deal," *The Washington Post*, January 14, 1995, H1, H5.

26. Staudohar, "The Hockey Lockout of 2004–2005," 24–25; Bettman quoted in Gatehouse, *The Instigator*; Baillie, *An Investigation into the Collective Bargaining Relationship*, 26–27.

27. Jenish, *The NHL*; Charlie Gills, "Game Over?" *Maclean's*, November 3, 2003, 38; Staudohar, "The Hockey Lockout of 2004–2005," 25–26; McCabe quoted in Adrian Dater, "NHL Lockout 2012 Compared to 2004–05," *Sports Illustrated*, February 14, 2013, http://m.si.com/1559999/nhl-lockout-timeline-comparing-2004-05-to-2012-13-2/; Richard Sandomir, "N.H.L. Offers Six Proposals to Cut Costs to the Union," *The New York Times*, July 22, 2004, D2; "N.H.L. Makes Proposals," *The New York Times*, August 5, 2004, D4.

28. Overview of the lockout from: Gatehouse, *The Instigator*; Dagenais quoted in Jenish, *The NHL*; Joe Lapointe, "Owner Is Criticized for Comments," *The New York Times*, October 13, 2004, D5; Bettman quoted in Joe Lapointe, "Lockout Is First Shot in Hockey's Labor War," *The New York Times*, September 16, 2004, D1, D3; Joe Lapointe, "Players Offer 24% Solution To the N.H.L.," *The New York Times*, December 10, 2004, D1, D8; Rolston and Taylor quoted in Jonathan Willis, "NHL Lockout: Donald Fehr Has Avoided the Mistakes of Former NHLPA Head Bob Goodenow," *Edmonton Journal*, November 24, 2012, http://blogs.edmontonjournal.com/2012/11/24/nhl-lockout-donald-fehr-has-avoided-the-mistakes-of-former-nhlpa-head-bob-goodenow/; Staudohar, "The Hockey Lockout of 2004–2005," 26; Barnaby and McKee quoted in John Wawrow, "Players Wonder What Took So Long for NHLPA to Accept Cap," *USA Today*, February 15, 2005, http://usatoday30.usatoday.com/sports/hockey/nhl/2005-02-15-lockout-players_x.htm; Bettman quoted in Bob Foltman, "Proposals, No 'I Dos'; NHL, Union Agree to Salary Cap, but not Dollar Amount," *Chicago Tribune*, February 16, 2005, 1, 4.

29. Staudohar, "The Hockey Lockout of 2004 . . . 2005," 27; Rick Westhead, "Ice in July Sounds Good to N.H.L. Players," *The New York Times*, July 21, 2005, D7; Dave Caldwell, "N.H.L. and Players Reach Agreement," *The New York Times*, July 14, 2005, D1, D7; Bettman and Goodenow quoted in Bob Foltman, "The Year of No NHL Almost Reaches End; Players Accept Deal; Governors'

Turn Next," *Chicago Tribune*, July 22, 2005, 4, 8; Bob Foltman, "NHL's Union Chief Resigns," *Chicago Tribune*, July 29, 2005, 4, 7.

30. Dave Zirin, "CSI: Hockey—How Owners Destroyed the NHL," *Edge of Sports*, February 24, 2005, http://www.edgeofsports.com/2005-02-24-118/.

31. Paul D. Staudohar, "The Hockey Lockout of 2012–2013," *Monthly Labor Review* (July 2013), http://www.bls.gov/opub/mlr/2013/article/the-hockey-lockout-of-2012.htm; Mike Ozanian, "NHL Team Values 2012: Toronto Maple Leafs Are First Hockey Team Worth $1 Billion," *Forbes*, November 28, 2012, http://www.forbes.com/sites/mikeozanian/2012/11/28/nhl-team-values-2012-maple-leafs-first-hockey-team-worth-1-billion/; Gatehouse, *The Instigator*.

32. Overview of the leadup to the lockout from Staudohar, "The Hockey Lockout of 2012–2013"; Dater, "NHL Lockout 2012 Compared to 2004–05"; Chris Kuc, "Walking Down Familiar Road," *Chicago Tribune*, August 5, 2012, 3.10; Michael Russo, "NHL Players' Proposal Could Serve as Olive Branch," *McClatchy-Tribune Business News*, August 15, 2012; Fehr quoted in Chris Kuc, "Fehr: NHL Lockout Would Be 'Real shame,'" *McClatchy-Tribune Business News*, August 17, 2012; Chris Kuc, "Talks Go Nowhere: Union Proposal 'Not Much Different' According to Bettman," *Chicago Tribune*, September 13, 2012, 3.13; Willis, "NHL Lockout."

33. Overview of the lockout from: Staudohar, "The Hockey Lockout of 2012–2013"; Chris Kuc, "50-50: League Offers to Split Hockey Revenue in Bid to Save Full Season," *Chicago Tribune*, October 17, 2012, 3.8; Fehr quoted in Sam Carchidi, "Fehr Questions NHL's Latest Offer to Players," *McClatchy-Tribune Business News*, October 18, 2012; Jeremy Rutherford, "NHL Owners Reject Players' Counter-Offers Quickly," *McClatchy-Tribune Business News*, October 19, 2012; Daly quoted in Steve Conroy, "Mediation Fails in NHL," *McClatchy-Tribune Business News*, November 29, 2012; "NHL, Players Make Peace: Framework in Place for 10-Year Deal after 16-Hour Bargaining Session Ends Lockout," *Chicago Tribune*, January 7, 2013, 7; Ira Podell, "NHL Lockout 2012: Mediator Gets League, Union Back Together," *The Washington Times*, January 5, 2013, http://www.washingtontimes.com/news/2013/jan/5/nhl-lockout-2012-mediator-gets-league-union-back-t/?page=all.

34. Staudohar, "The hockey lockout of 2012–2013"; "NHL, players make peace," 7; Mike Sielski, "NHL Races Back to Business," *Wall Street Journal*, January 7, 2013, B1; Schuyler Velasco, "NHL lockout: CBA gives players defined pension plans. How rare is that?," *The Christian Science Monitor*, January 14, 2013, http://www.csmonitor.com/Business/2013/0114/NHL-lockout-CBA-gives-players-defined-pension-plans.-How-rare-is-that.

35. Greg Wyshynski, "Winners and Losers of the NHL Lockout," *Yahoo! Sports*, January 7, 2013, http://sports.yahoo.com/blogs/nhl-puck-daddy/winners-losers-nhl-lockout-233434771--nhl.html; Kevin Allen, "Winners and Losers of the NHL Lockout," *USA Today*, January 6, 2013, http://www.usatoday.com/story/sports/nhl/2013/01/06/nhl-lockout-winners-losers/1812017/.

36. "Ex-Players Sue NHL over Concussions," *ESPN.com*, November 25, 2013, http://espn.go.com/nhl/story/_/id/10036795/former-players-sue-nhl-concussions; Sean Gentille, "NHL Concussion Lawsuit: What Are the Players Claiming?" *Sporting News*, November 25, 2013, http://www.sportingnews.com/nhl/story/2013-11-25/nhl-concussion-lawsuit-what-are-the-players-claiming.

37. Laura Donaldson, Mark Asbridge, Michael D. Cusimano, "Bodychecking Rules and Concussion in Elite Hockey," *PLS One*, 2013, http://www.plosone.org/article/info:doi/10.1371/journal.pone.0069122; Jeffrey G. Caron, Gordon A. Bloom, Karen M. Johnston, and Catherine M. Sabiston, "Effects of Multiple Concussions on Retired National Hockey League Players," *Journal of Sport & Exercise Psychology* 35 (2013): 168–79; Stu Hackel, "Study Shows Where NHL Can Improve Concussion Prevention," *Sports Illustrated*, July 19, 2013, http://sportsillustrated.cnn.com/nhl/news/20130719/nhl-concussions-hits-to-head-study/#all.

Chapter 6. The Inevitability of Conflict?

1. Russell B. Porter, "The C.I.O.," in *American Labor since the New Deal*, ed. Melvyn Dubofsky (Chicago: Quadrangle Books, 1971), 99. Throughout U.S. history, militancy in collective bargaining has led to better contracts for workers; see, for example Michael Schiavone, "Social Movement Unionism and the UE," *The Flinders Journal of History and Politics* 23 (2006) and "Rank-and-File Militancy and Power: Revisiting the Teamster Struggle with the United Parcel Service Ten Years Later," *WorkingUSA* 10 (June 2007).

2. Fehr quoted in Murray Chass, "Baseball Strike Is Settled; Games to Resume Today," *The New York Times*, August 8, 1985, http://www.nytimes.com/1985/08/08/sports/baseball-strike-is-settled-games-to-resume-today.html.

3. Ronald Blum, "Dodgers Top Spender, Ending Yanks' 15-Year Streak," *Yahoo! Sports*, March 26, 2014, http://sports.yahoo.com/news/dodgers-top-spender-ending-yanks-211228074--mlb.html; David Brown, "Players Get Smaller Slice of MLB Economic Pie in 2014," *Yahoo! Sports*, March 26, 2014, http://sports.yahoo.com/blogs/mlb-big-league-stew/players-get-smaller-slice-of-mlb-economic-pie-in-2014-172418924.html; Ken Rosenthal, "Archer's Contract Another Sign of Baseball's Economic Health," *Fox Sports*, April 3, 2014, http://msn.foxsports.com/mlb/story/archer-s-contract-another-sign-of-baseball-s-economic-health-040214?cmpid=tsmtw:fscom:mlbonfox.

4. Mike Ozanian, "Dallas Cowboys Lead NFL With $2.1 Billion Valuation," *Forbes*, September 5, 2012, http://www.forbes.com/sites/mikeozanian/2012/09/05/dallas-cowboys-lead-nfl-with-2-1-billion-valuation/; Mike Ozanian, "The Most Valuable NFL Teams," *Forbes*, August 14, 2013, http://www.forbes.com/sites/mikeozanian/2013/08/14/the-most-valuable-nfl-teams/.

5. Bryan Rose, "NFLPA May Block Playoff Expansion over Injury Concerns, Workers Comp Dispute," *Sports Illustrated*, May 20, 2014, http://nfl.si.com/2014/05/20/nflpa-block-playoff-expansion-workers-compensation/; Jim Cor-

bett, "NFL Owners Table Playoff Expansion for 2014," *USA Today*, May 20, 2014, http://www.usatoday.com/story/sports/nfl/2014/05/20/playoff-expansion-tabled-owners/9324403/.

6. Marcus Thompson, "Warriors Had the Blueprint for a Dramatic Boycott Ready to Go," *Mercury News*, April 29, 2014, http://blogs.mercury news.com/thompson/2014/04/29/warriors-had-the-blueprint-for-a-dramatic-boy-cott-ready-to-go/.

7. Zirin, "CSI: Hockey—How Owners Destroyed the NHL."

Bibliography

"50-Game Season or Bust? Bettman." *Chicago Tribune*, November 16, 1994.

Abrams, Roger I. "The Public Regulation of Baseball Labor Relations and the Public Interest." *Journal of Sports Economics* 4, no. 4 (2003): 292–301.

"Accord Reached in NBA." *The Washington Post and Times Herald*, March 6, 1973.

"Agreement Is Reached on a New NHL Pact." *Newsday*, August 18, 1982.

Aldridge, David. "Talks Stall between NBA, Players Union." *Knight Ridder Tribune News Service*, May 18, 2005.

Allen, Kevin. "Winners and Losers of the NHL Lockout." *USA Today*, January 6, 2013. http://www.usatoday.com/story/sports/nhl/2013/01/06/nhl-lockout-winners-losers/1812017/.

Armour, Terry. "New NBA Deal Means Little NBA Players Still At Odds." *Chicago Tribune*, August 9, 1995.

———. "Players: No Settlement in Sight." *Chicago Tribune*, October 15, 1988.

———. "Stern Says No Agreement, No Season." *Chicago Tribune*, August 16, 1995.

Asher, Mark. "Jordan, Ewing Join Class-Action Lawsuit." *The Washington Post*, June 29, 1995.

———. "NBA, Players Agree on Labor Deal." *The Washington Post*, June 29, 1996.

———. "NBA, Union Reach Six-Year Agreement." *The Washington Post*, June 22, 1995.

———. "NHL Players Make Late Offer, but Owners Reject It." *The Washington Post*, September 30, 1994.

"Average N.F.L. Salary Is $90,102, Survey Says." *The New York Times*, January 29, 1982. http://www.nytimes.com/1982/01/29/sports/average-nfl-salary-is-90102-survey-says.html.

Backman, Scott E. "NFL Players Fight for Their Freedom: The History of Free Agency in the NFL." *Sports Lawyers Journal* 9, no. 2 (2002): 1–56.

Badenhausen, Kurt. "As Stern Says Goodbye, Knicks, Lakers Set Records as NBA's Most Valuable Teams." *Forbes*, January 22, 2014. http://www.forbes.

com/sites/kurtbadenhausen/2014/01/22/as-stern-says-goodbye-knicks-lakers-set-records-as-nbas-most-valuable-teams/.

———. "Billion-Dollar Knicks and Lakers Top List of NBA's Most Valuable Teams." *Forbes*, January 23, 2013. http://www.forbes.com/sites/kurt badenhausen/2013/01/23/billion-dollar-knicks-and-lakers-top-list-of-nbas-most-valuable-teams/.

Baillie, Jim. *An Investigation into the Collective Bargaining Relationship between the NHL and the NHLPA, 1994–2005*, Industrial Relations Centre, Queen's University, 2005.

Banner, Stuart. *Baseball Trust*. Oxford and New York: Oxford University Press, 2013.

Barra, Allen. "How Curt Flood Changed Baseball and Killed His Career in the Process." *The Atlantic*, July 12, 2011. http://www.theatlantic.com/entertainment/archive/2011/07/how-curt-flood-changed-baseball-and-killed-his-career-in-the-process/241783/.

Barron, David. "Protest of Race-Related Slights, Brought '65 Game Here." *Houston Chronicle*, January 16, 2005, http://www.chron.com/sports/texans/article/Protest-of-race-related-slights-brought-65-game-1940910.php.

Barry, Jack. "NBA Players May Sign, With AFL-CIO." *Boston Globe*, January 12, 1957.

Bartlett, Charles. "Lindsay, Two Other Hawks Meet with Hockey Owners." *Chicago Daily Tribune*, January 29, 1958.

"Baseball Announces Expanded Pension Benefits for Players Who Retired between 1947 and 1980." *NBC Sports*, April 21, 2011, http://hardballtalk.nbcsports.com/2011/04/21/baseball-announces-expanded-pension-benefits-for-players-who-retired-between-1947-and-1980/.

"Baseball Players to Strike Today over Pension Issue." *The New York Times*, April 1, 1972.

Beck, Howard. "As Lockout Approaches, N.B.A. Players Wear Unity on Their Shirts." *The New York Times*, June 24, 2011. http://www.nytimes.com/2011/06/25/sports/basketball/as-an-nba-lockout-looms-t-shirts-proclaim-players-solidarity.html.

———. "High-Tension N.B.A. Talks Resume, but They're Between Union Officials." *The New York Times*, November 2, 2011. http://www.nytimes.com/2011/11/03/sports/basketball/nba-talks-resume-between-union-officials.html?_r=0.

———. "In Attempt to Force Talks, N.B.A. Players File Antitrust Suit." *The New York Times*, November 15, 2011. http://www.nytimes.com/2011/11/16/sports/basketball/nba-players-file-antitrust-suit-against-the-league.html.

———. "N.B.A. Reaches a Tentative Deal to Save the Season." *The New York Times*, November 26, 2011. http://www.nytimes.com/2011/11/27/sports/basketball/nba-and-basketball-players-reach-deal-to-end-lockout.html?pagewanted=all&_r=0.

———. "Sides Remain Far Apart in N.B.A. Labor Talks." *The New York Times,* June 21, 2011. http://www.nytimes.com/2011/06/22/sports/basketball/nba-and-players-union-remain-far-apart-in-labor-talks.html?_r=.

Belth, Alex. "Free Agency Turns 30." *Sports Illustrated,* December 23, 2005. http://sportsillustrated.cnn.com/2005/writers/alex_belth/12/23/messer-smith.mcnally/.

Berger, Ken. "NBPA Votes 24–0 to Oust Billy Hunter as Director." *CBS Sports,* February 16, 2013. http://www.cbssports.com/nba/writer/ken-berger/21716401/nbpa-votes-24-0-to-oust-billy-hunter-as-director.

Berri, David J. "Did the Players Give Up Money to Make the NBA Better? Exploring the 2011 Collective Bargaining Agreement in the National Basketball Association." *International Journal of Sport Finance* 7, no. 2 (2012): 158–75.

Berry, Robert C., and William B. Gould, "A Long Deep Drive to Collective Bargaining: Of Players, Owners, Brawls, and Strikes." *Case Western Reserve Law Review* 31, no. 4 (Summer 1981): 685–813.

Blum, Ronald. "Dodgers Top Spender, Ending Yanks' 15–Year Streak." *Yahoo! Sports,* March 26, 2014. http://sports.yahoo.com/news/dodgers-top-spender-ending-yanks-211228074--mlb.html.

Bock, Hal. "Baseball's Emancipation: It Was Twenty Years Ago When Catfish Hunter, Sport's Best Pitcher, Was Declared a Free Agent." *Los Angeles Times,* December 11, 1994. http://articles.latimes.com/1994-12-11/sports/sp-7636_1_catfish-hunter.

Bondy, Flip. "N.H.L. Players Reject 'Final' Offer." *The New York Times,* April 8, 1992.

Bouton, Jim. *Ball Four.* New York: Rosetta Books, 1980.

Bradley, Robert. "Labor Pains Nothing New to the NBA." http://www.apbr.org/labor.html.

———. "Pro Basketball Legal Cases 1946–69." *Robert Bradley's Pro Basketball History Revisited,* 2010. http://apbrbasketball.blogspot.com/2010/12/pro-basketball-legal-cases-1946-69.html.

Brady, Dave. "Players Settled for a Field Goal." *The Washington Post,* August 9, 1970.

"Brain Injuries Haunt Football Players Years Later." *NPR,* January 20, 2011. http://www.npr.org/2011/01/20/133053436/brain-injuries-haunt-football-players-years-later.

Broussard, Chris. "Sources: Michael Jordan Fined $100K." *ESPN,* September 12, 2011. http://espn.go.com/nba/story/_/id/6961508/michael-jordan-charlotte-bobcats-fined-100k-talking-lockout-sources-say.

Brown, David. "Players Get Smaller Slice of MLB Economic Pie in 2014." *Yahoo! Sports,* March 26, 2014. http://sports.yahoo.com/blogs/mlb-big-league-stew/players-get-smaller-slice-of-mlb-economic-pie-in-2014-172418924.html.

Burk, Robert F. *Much More than a Game.* Chapel Hill and London: The University of North Carolina Press, 2001.

Burwell, Bryan. "Fleisher Ready to Bargain as NBA's Deadline Looms." *Newsday*, February 22, 1983.

———. "NBA Threatened with Walkout." *Newsday*, February 18, 1983.

Caldwell, Dave. "N.H.L. and Players Reach Agreement." *The New York Times*, July 14, 2005.

Cameron, Stevie. "Fall of the Eagle." *Maclean's*, March 14, 1994.

Carchidi, Sam. "Fehr Questions NHL's Latest Offer to Players." *McClatchy-Tribune Business News*, October 18, 2012.

Caron, Jeffrey G., Gordon A. Bloom, Karen M. Johnston, and Catherine M. Sabiston. "Effects of Multiple Concussions on Retired National Hockey League Players." *Journal of Sport & Exercise Psychology* 35 (2013): 168–79.

"CBA Principal Deal Points." *NBA.com*, August 4, 2005. http://www.nba.com/news/cba_summary_050804.html.

Chass, Murray "Baseball Owners Delay Spring Training Start." *The New York Times*, February 24, 1976.

———. "Baseball's Labor Dispute Settled with Compromise on Arbitration." *The New York Times*, March 19, 1990.

———. "Baseball Strike Is Settled; Games to Resume Today." *The New York Times*, August 8, 1985. http://www.nytimes.com/1985/08/08/sports/baseball-strike-is-settled-games-to-resume-today.html.

———. "Free-agency Still a Battle." *Chicago Tribune*, December 25, 1985. http://articles.chicagotribune.com/1985-12-25/sports/8503290579_1_dave-mcnally-contract-cabrillo-community-college/2.

———. "Last Minute Deal in Baseball Talks Prevents A Strike." *The New York Times*, August 31, 2002.

———. "NBA Locks Out Its Players as Labor Battle Continues." *Chicago Tribune*, July 1, 1995.

———. "Strike Over; Baseball Resumes Aug.9: 650 Players Affected 7-Week Baseball Strike Ends; All-Stars Will Reopen Season Mediator Not at Meeting." *The New York Times*, August 1, 1981.

———. "Training Slated to Start Today: Kuhn Orders Camps to Open." *The New York Times*, March 18, 1976.

"Chronology of the Baseball Strike." *The New York Times*, August 1, 1981.

Clary, Jack. "Why NFL Players' Strike Failed: 42-Day Holdout Not Only Didn't Achieve Aims, It Left Players' Union in a Weakened Position." *The Christian Science Monitor*, August 26, 1974.

Clayton, John. "Owners Finally Come to Resolution on Revenue Sharing." *ESPN*, March 8, 2006. http://sports.espn.go.com/nfl/columns/story?columnist=clayton_john&id=2360296.

Cobb, Ty, and Al Stump. *My Life in Baseball: The True Record*. Nebraska: University of Nebraska Press, 1993.

Conroy, Steve. "Mediation Fails in NHL." *McClatchy-Tribune Business News*, November 29, 2012.

Conway, Russ. *Game Misconduct: Alan Eagleson and the Corruption of Hockey*. Toronto: Macfarlane Walter and Ross, 1995.

Coon, Larry. "Breaking Down Changes in New CBA." *ESPN*, November 28, 2011. http://espn.go.com/nba/story/_/page/CBA-111128/how-new-nba-deal-compares-last-one.

Coon, Larry. *NBA Salary Cap FAQ*. http://www.cbafaq.com/salarycap.htm#Q24.

Corbett, Jim. "NFL Owners Table Playoff Expansion for 2014." *USA Today*, May 20, 2014. http://www.usatoday.com/story/sports/nfl/2014/05/20/playoff-expansion-tabled-owners/9324403/.

Cosell, Howard. *What's Wrong with Sports*. New York: Simon and Schuster, 1991.

Cotton, Anthony. "New Collective Bargaining Pact Leaves Prospects, Questions." *The Washington Post*, May 17, 1988.

————. "No Fast Break on Union Front." *The Washington Post*, February 29, 1988.

————. "Players Aren't Sure About Union Ploy." *The Washington Post*, February 7, 1988.

Craig, Mark. "The 1987 NFL strike: Picking at an old Scab." *Star Tribune*, June 28, 2011. http://www.startribune.com/sports/vikings/124627618.html.

"Curt Flood's letter to Bowie Kuhn." *MLB.com*. http://mlb.mlb.com/news/article.jsp?ymd=20070315&content_id=1844945&vkey=news_mlb&c_id=mlb&fext=.jsp.

Dale, Mary Claire. "NFL Concussion Settlement: League, Players Reach Tentative $765M Deal in Concussion-Related Lawsuits." *Huffington Post*, August 29, 2013. http://www.huffingtonpost.com/2013/08/29/nfl-concussion-settlement-lawsuits_n_3837474.html.

Dater, Adrian. "NHL Lockout 2012 Compared to 2004–05." *Sports Illustrated*, February 14, 2013. http://m.si.com/1559999/nhl-lockout-timeline-comparing-2004-05-to-2012-13-2/.

Davis, Nate. "Official Statement from NFL Following Union Decertification." *USA Today*, May 11, 2011. http://content.usatoday.com/communities/thehuddle/post/2011/03/official-statement-from-nfl-following-union-decertification/1#.Ufhtf22SAno.

Deacon, James. "Settlement on Ice." *Maclean's*, April 20, 1992.

Deubert, Chris, Glenn M. Wong, and John Howe. "All Four Quarters: A Retrospective and Analysis of the 2011 Collective Bargaining Process and Agreement in the National Football League." *UCLA Entertainment Law Review* 19, no. 1 (2012): 1–78.

Devine, James R. "Baseball's Labor Wars in Historical Context: The 1919 Chicago White Sox as a Case-Study in Owner-Player Relations." *Marquette Sports Law Journal* 5, no. 1 (1994): 1–83. http://scholarship.law.marquette.edu/sportslaw/vol5/iss1/3.

DiComo, Anthony. "Key Points of Collective Bargaining Agreement." *MLB.com*, 2011. http://mlb.mlb.com/news/article.jsp?ymd=20111122&content_id=26026776.

Dine, Philip. *State of the Unions*. New York: McGraw-Hill, 2008.

Donaldson, Laura, Mark Asbridge, and Michael D. Cusimano. "Bodychecking Rules and Concussion in Elite Hockey." *PLS One*, 2013. http://www.plosone.org/article/info:doi/10.1371/journal.pone.0069122.

Dosh, Kristi "Want to Repair the NBA? Start With Revenue Sharing." *Forbes*, August 9, 2011. http://www.forbes.com/sites/sportsmoney/2011/08/09/want-to-repair-the-nba-start-with-revenue-sharing/.

Dowbiggin, Bruce. *Money Players: How Hockey's Greatest Stars Beat the NHL at its Own Game*. Toronto: McClelland and Stewart, 2003.

Dupree, David. "NBA Drops Option Rule, Settles Suit." *The Washington Post*, February 4, 1976.

———. "NBA, Union Agree; Expansion to Dallas Is Voted." *The Washington Post*, February 3, 1980.

———. "Strike Is Averted as NBA, Players Agree in Principle." *The Washington Post*, April 1, 1983.

———. "Strike Date of April 2 Set by NBA Players." *The Washington Post*, February 18, 1983.

Durso, Joseph. "Baseball Strike Is Settled; Season to Open Tomorrow." *The New York Times*, April 14, 1972.

Dwyer, Kelly. "LeBron James and Deron Williams Warn NBA Owners that Cries of Lockout Losses 'Will not Fly with Us This Time.'" Yahoo! Sports, October 6, 2014, http://sports.yahoo.com/blogs/nba-ball-dont-lie/lebron-james-and-deron-williams-warn-nba-owners-that-cries-of-lockout-losses--will-not-fly-with-us-this-time-205656424.html.

Elderkin, Phil. "Bob Cousy Eyes NBA Coaching Career after Playing Days Completed." *The Christian Science Monitor*, February 17, 1959.

———. "Larry O'Brien Trying to Steer NBA toward Black Ink." *The Christian Science Monitor*, November 4, 1982.

———. "NBA Pension: Pro Basketball's Races Are Over but the Playoffs May Not Start." *The Christian Science Monitor*, March 8, 1967.

———. "Strike Threat Bubbles in Pro Court Caldron." *The Christian Science Monitor*, January 28, 1967.

Elkins, Frank. "Rival Basketball Circuits Merge Into One Loop of Eighteen Clubs." *The New York Times*, August 4, 1949.

"Ex-Players Sue NHL over Concussions." *ESPN.com*, November 25, 2013. http://espn.go.com/nhl/story/_/id/10036795/former-players-sue-nhl-.

Fantasia, Rick, and Kim Voss. *Hard Work*. Berkeley and Los Angeles: University of California Press, 2004.

Farmer, Sam. "Bill Radovich, 87; NFL Star Blacklisted After Court Case." *Los Angeles Times*, March 12, 2002. http://articles.latimes.com/2002/mar/12/local/me-radovich12.

Fatsis, Stefan. "NBA Owners Vote to Reopen Labor Pact, Risking Possibility of Strike-Hit Season." *Wall Street Journal*, March 24, 1988.

———. "NBA, Players Reach Accord, Saving Season." *Wall Street Journal*, January 7, 1999.

Felt, Hunter. "Concussions Lawsuit Settlement Lets NFL off the Hook." *The Guardian*, August 30, 2013. http://www.theguardian.com/sport/2013/aug/30/nfl-concussion-lawsuit-settlement-off-the-hook.

Fisk, Dustin. "In Case You Missed It, the NFL/NFLPA Agree on Neuro Benefits." *The Concussion Blog*, December 11, 1012. http://theconcussion blog.com/2012/12/11/in-case-you-missed-it-the-nflnflpa-agree-on-neuro-benefits/.

———. "What Is CTE?" *The Concussion Blog*, n.d. http://theconcussionblog.com/what-is-cte/.

Florio, Mike. "NFLPA Issues Brief Statement on Settlement of Concussion Lawsuits." *NBC Sports*, August 29, 2013. http://profootballtalk.nbcsports.com/2013/08/29/nflpa-issues-brief-statement-on-settlement-of-concussion-lawsuits/.

Foltman, Bob. "NHL's Union Chief Resigns." *Chicago Tribune*, July 29, 2005.

———. "Proposals, No 'I Dos'; NHL, Union Agree to Salary Cap, but not Dollar Amount." *Chicago Tribune*, February 16, 2005.

———. "The Year of No NHL Almost Reaches End; Players Accept Deal; Governors' Turn Next." *Chicago Tribune*, July 22, 2005.

Gage Jack, and Michael K. Ozanian. "Inside The Forbes NBA Valuation List." *Forbes*, December 22, 2005. http://www.forbes.com/2005/12/22/nba-team-valuations_cz_mo_1222nbaintro.html.

Gatehouse, Jonathan. *The Instigator: How Gary Bettman Remade the NHL and Changes the Game Forever*, Chicago: Triumph Books, 2012. Kindle Edition.

Gentille, Sean. "NHL Concussion Lawsuit: What Are the Players Claiming?" *Sporting News*, November 25, 2013. http://www.sportingnews.com/nhl/story/2013-11-25/nhl-concussion-lawsuit-what-are-the-players-claiming.

Gills, Charlie. "Game Over?" *Maclean's*, November 3, 2003.

Goldaper, Sam. "N.B.A. and Players Schedule New Talks." *The New York Times*, February 25, 1983.

———. "N.B.A. Obtains Labor Peace And Plans Talks With A.B.A." *The New York Times*, April 13, 1976.

———. "N.B.A. Owners Will Be Briefed on Talks." *The New York Times*, October 20, 1982.

———. "N.B.A. Players Spurn Offer by Owners as Senate Hearings on Merger Near." *The New York Times*, September 19, 1971.

———. "N.B.A. Target of Players' Antitrust Suit." *The New York Times*, October 2, 1987.

———. "Revenue Sharing Instituted: N.B.A. Strike Averted With 4-Year Pact." *The New York Times*, April 1, 1983.

Goldberg, Daniel S. "Concussions, Professional Sports, and Conflicts of Interest: Why the National Football League's Current Policies are Bad for Its (Players') Health" *HEC Forum* 20, no. 4 (2009): 337–55.

Goldstein, Richard. "Danny Gardella, 85, Dies; Challenged Reserve Clause." *The New York Times*, March 13, 2005. http://www.nytimes.com/2005/03/13/sports/baseball/13gardella.html?ex=1268370000&en=7ae29a51bacee15e&ei=5090&partner=rssuserland.

———. "John Mackey Dies at 69." *The New York Times*, July 7, 2011. http://www.nytimes.com/2011/07/08/sports/football/john-mackey-dies-at-69-helped-revolutionize-nfl.html?_r=0.

Goold, Derrick. "On Jackie and the Cardinals." *St Louis Post-Dispatch*, April 16, 2013. http://www.stltoday.com/sports/baseball/professional/birdland/goold-on-jackie-and-the-cardinals/article_0aecf971-2e97-569f-bc23-1f41a63ae27a.html.

Goplerud, Peter C. III "Collective Bargaining in the National Football League: A Historical and Comparative Analysis." *Jeffrey S. Moorad Sports Law Journal* 4, no. 1, Article 2, http://digitalcommons.law.villanova.edu/mslj/vol4/iss1/2.

Gould, William B. IV. *Bargaining with Baseball*. Jefferson and London: McFarland, 2011.

———. "Labor Issues in Professional Sports: Reflections on Baseball, Labor, and Antitrust Law" *Stanford Law and Policy Review* 15, no. 1 (2004): 61–97.

———. "The 2011 Basketball Lockout: The Union Lives to Fight Another Day—Barely." *Stanford Law Review Online* 64, no. 51 (2012): 51–56.

Green, G. Michael, and Roger D. Launius, *Charlie Finley: The Outrageous Story of Baseball's Super Showman*. New York: Walker, 2010.

Griffiths, Martin, and Michael Schiavone, "Anti-Americanism and Anti-Globalisation" In *The History of Anti-Americanism*, edited by Brendon O'Connor, 19–36. Oxford: Greenwood, 2007.

Gross, Jane. "NBA Absorbs Four ABA Teams for $3.2 Million Each." *Newsday*, June 18, 1976.

———. "NHL's Players Accept A 'Rozelle Rule' Contract." *Newsday*, October 7, 1975.

———. "Strike Losses Heavy and Widespread." *The New York Times*, August 1, 1981.

Gustafson, Elizabeth. "The Luxury Tax in Professional Sports." In *Handbook on the Economics of Sport*, edited by Wladamir Andreff and Stefan Szymansk, 652–60. Massachusetts: Edward Elgar, 2009.

Hackel, Stu. "Study Shows Where NHL Can Improve Concussion Prevention." *Sports Illustrated*, July 19, 2013. http://sportsillustrated.cnn.com/nhl/news/20130719/nhl-concussions-hits-to-head-study/#all.

Hafner, Dan. "East Wins All-Star Classic Delayed by Player Revolt." *The Los Angeles Times*, January 15, 1964.

Handle, Judy. "NHL Players Assn. to Seek $12 Million in WHA Merger." *Boston Globe*, March 16, 1979.

Hart, Alexander C. "NFL Head Injuries a Hot Topic in Congress." *Los Angeles Times*, October 29, 2009. http://articles.latimes.com/2009/oct/29/sports/sp-football-congress29.

Harvin, Al. "A.B.A. Owners Agree to Pay $11-Million Merger Indemnity." *The New York Times*, April 15, 1970.

"Harvey Calls N.H.L. Suit Regrettable." *New York Herald Tribune*, October 12, 1957.

Helyar, John. "Civil War Pits NBA's Players against Players." *Wall Street Journal*, June 23, 1995.

———. "NBA Players Reject Bid to Scrap Union as Faction Led by Jordan Is Defeated." *The Wall Street Journal*, September 13, 1995.

"Heinsohn, Boss in Pension Feud." *Newsday*, January 18, 1964.

Hershey, Steve. "NBA Owners Meet Today On Union Negotiations." *The Washington Post*, October 20, 1982.

Hill, James Richard, and Jason E. Taylor. "Do Professional Sports Unions Fit the Standard Model of Traditional Unionism?" *Journal of Labor Research* 29 (2008): 56–67.

Hill, J. Richard, and Peter. A. Groothuis. "The New NBA Collective Bargaining Agreement, the Median Voter Model, and a Robin-Hood Rent Redistribution." *Journal of Sports Economics*, 2, no. 2 (May 2001): 131–44.

Hochberg, Len. "Last-Minute Deal Saves NHL Season." *The Washington Post*, January 12, 1995.

———. "NHL Players Union Ratifies Labor Deal." *The Washington Post*, January 14, 1995.

———. "Players, NHL Begin Bargaining." *The Washington Post*, August 19, 1994.

———. "Players Offer to Cap Rookies' Salaries, But League Says No." *The Washington Post*, November 11, 1994.

"Hockey Clubs Hit in Antitrust Suit." *The New York Times*, October 11, 1957.

"Hockey Group Survives." *The New York Times*, February 7, 1958.

"Hockey Players Form Association." *Chicago Daily Tribune*, February 12, 1957.

"Hockey Players Organize, Too." *Newsday*, June 8, 1967.

"Hockey Players Plan Peace Moves." *The New York Times*, February 1, 1958.

"Hockey Union Offer Ratification by NHL's 700 Players Would Salvage 48-Game Season." *Chicago Tribune*, January 11, 1995.

"Inside the NHL S-Z." *Hockey Central*, n.d. http://www.hockeycentral.co.uk/nhl/insidenhl/Inside-the-NHL-S-Z.php.

Jackson, Derrick. "Fleisher Anticipates Strike." *Newsday*, March 25, 1983.

Jenish, D'Arcy. *The NHL: 100 Years of On-Ice Action and Boardroom Battles.* Canada: Doubleday, 2013. Kindle Edition.

"Judge Rules against Players in Antitrust Charge on Owners." *The Sun*, December 18, 1987.

"Judge Rules Barry Stays." *The Spokesman-Review*, August 9, 1967.

Justice, Richard. "Bargaining Secrecy Raises Agents' Ire." *The Washington Post*, June 19, 1995.

———. "Judge: NBA Draft, Salary Cap Are Legal." *The Washington Post*, July 19, 1994.

———Justice, Richard. "NBA Players Retain Union." *The Washington Post*, September 13, 1995.

———. "NBA Union Chief Resigns," *The Washington Post*, April 15, 1995.

———. "Stern, Players Tell Court What They're Made Of." *The Washington Post*, July 13, 1994.

————, and Marc Asher. "Owners Approve Agreement." *The Washington Post*, September 16, 1995.

Kaese, Harold. "Hockey Players Seeking Better Pension." *Daily Boston Globe*, February 13, 1957.

Kahane, Leo H. "The Economics of the National Hockey League: The 2004–05 Lockout and the Beginning of a New Era." In *Sports Economics After Fifty Years: Essays in Honour of Simon Rottenberg*, edited by Placido Rodriguez, Stefan Kesenne, and Jaume Garcia, 107–24. Oviedo: University of Oviedo Press, 2006.

Keese, Parton. "Compensation Rule Key to N.H.L. Pact Free-Agent Clause Key to N.H.L. Pact." *The New York Times*, October 7, 1975.

Kendle, Jon. "Players Boycott AFL All-Star Game." *Pro Football Hall of Fame*, February 18, 2010. http://www.profootballhof.com/history/2010/2/18/players-boycott-afl-all-star-game/.

Keown, Tim. "After the NFL." *ESPN Magazine*, June 26, 2013. http://espn.go.com/nfl/story/_/id/9417902/steve-hendrickson-nfl-concussions-taking-their-toll-espn-magazine.

Kiley, Mike. "Hawks Testing the Ice as Strike Replacements." *Chicago Tribune*, March 14, 1992.

————. "Money's the Key Issue in NHL-Union Dispute." *Chicago Tribune*, August 25, 1981.

————. "NHL Strike One Huge Power Play," *Chicago Tribune*, April 2, 1992.

Kobritz, Jordan I., and Jeffrey F. Levine, "Don Fehr Leads the NHLPA: Does the NHL Have Anything to Fear?" *Virginia Sports & Entertainment Law Journal* (Fall 2011): 1–52.

————. "Trying His Luck at Puck: Examining the MLBPA's History to Determine Don Fehr's Motivation for Agreeing to Lead the NHLPA and Predicting How He Will Fare." *University of Denver Sports and Entertainment Law Journal* 12 (2011): 3–70.

Korr, Charles B. "Marvin Miller and the New Unionism in Baseball" In *The Business of Professional Sports*, edited by Paul D. Staudohar and James A. Mangan, 115–34. Urbana and Chicago: University of Illinois Press, 1991.

————. *The End of Baseball as We Knew It*. Urbana and Chicago: University of Illinois Press, 2005.

Kuc, Chris. "50-50: League Offers to Split Hockey Revenue in Bid to Save Full Season." *Chicago Tribune*, October 17, 2012.

Lapointe, Joe. "Hockey Negotiators Stop Talks, For Now." *The New York Times*, December 3, 1994.

————. "Lockout Is First Shot in Hockey's Labor War." *The New York Times*, September 16, 2004.

————. "N.H.L. Owners Drop the Gloves," *The New York Times*, March 27, 1992.

————. "N.H.L. Warning: No Deal, No Season." *The New York Times*, September 23, 1994.

———. "Owners Offer Players a Deal That Will Exclude a Payroll Tax." *The New York Times*, December 21, 1994.

———. "Pact Reached for Salvaging Hockey Season." *The New York Times*, January 12, 1995.

———. "Play Hockey! Settlement Ends 10-Day Strike." *The New York Times*, April 11, 1992.

———. "Players Offer 24% Solution To the N.H.L." *The New York Times*, December 10, 2004.

———. "Playing the Numbers Game, Ownership Style." *The New York Times*, November 17, 1994.

Lava, Michela "The Battle of Superstars: Player Restraints in Professional Teams Sports." *University of Florida Law Review* 32, no. 4 (Spring 1980): 669–700.

Leahy, Sean. "Rams Agree with No. 1 Overall Pick Sam Bradford on Record Contract with $50 Million Guaranteed." *USA Today*, July 30, 2010. http://content.usatoday.com/communities/thehuddle/post/2010/07/rams-agree-with-no-1-overall-pick-sam-bradford-on-record-contract-with-50-million-guaranteed/1#.UfioXW2SAno.

Leone, Jack. "Labor Relations in a Locker Room." *Newsday*, January 15, 1964.

Levine, Jeffrey F., and Bram A. Maravent. "Fumbling Away the Season: Will the Expiration of the NFL-NFLPA CBA Result in the Loss of the 2011 Season?" *Fordham Intellectual Property, Media & Entertainment Law Journal* 1419, no. 4 (2010): 1419–1500.

Lloyd, Jason. "Cavs' Samuels Would Have Accepted Deal but NBA Players Union Rejects Owners' Offer; Season in Jeopardy." *Ohio.com*, November 14, 2011. http://www.ohio.com/sports/cavs-samuels-would-have-accepted-deal-but-nba-players-union-rejects-owners-offer-season-in-jeopardy-1.245552.

Logan, Bob. "NBA Approves Pact with Players, Expansion to Dallas." *Chicago Tribune*, February 3, 1980.

———. "NBA Players Ready to Strike over Pay Limits." *Chicago Tribune*, February 2, 1980.

———. "Owners, Players Make Peace in NBA." *Chicago Tribune*, February 4, 1976.

Lomax, Michael E. "Conflict and Compromise: The Evolution of American Professional Football's Labour Relations 1957–1966." *Football Studies* 4, no. 1 (2001): 5–39.

Lombardo, John. "Inside NBA's Revenue Sharing." *Sports Business Journal*, January 23, 2012. http://www.sportsbusinessdaily.com/Journal/Issues/2012/01/23/Leagues-and-Governing-Bodies/NBA-revenue.aspx.

"Lord Stanley," *Hockey Hall of Fame*, n.d. http://www.legendsofhockey.net/LegendsOfHockey/jsp/LegendsMember.jsp?mem=b194502&type=Builder&page=bio&list=ByName.

Lowenfish, Lee. *The Imperfect Diamond*. Lincoln and London: University of Nebraska Press, 2010.

Maher, Charles. "Pro Basketball: Suit Threatens Life of NBA." *Los Angeles Times*, October 30, 1975.

Mahoney, Brian. "Flex Cap A Small Mark of Progress Still Far From Deal As Deadline Nears." *Pittsburgh Post-Gazette*, June 22, 2011.

Mannix, Chris. "Money Ball." *Sports Illustrated*, December 20, 2010. http://sportsillustrated.cnn.com/vault/article/magazine/MAG1179930/index.htm.

Mawae, Kevin. "Cost of the Concussion Settlement." *Sportsblog*, August 30, 2013. http://kevinmawae.sportsblog.com/post/190840/cost_of_the_concussion_settlement.html.

May, Peter. "NBA and Union Reach Agreement on 6-Year Contract." *Boston Globe*, June 22, 2005.

McClellan, Michael D. "Captain Fantastic: The Bob Cousy Interview." *Celtic Nation*, February 9, 2004. http://www.celtic-nation.com/interviews/bob_cousy/bob_cousy_page7.htm.

McCormick, Robert A. "Interference on Both Sides: The Case against the NFL-NFLPA Contract." *Washington & Lee Law Revue* 397 (1996): 397–428.

McGowen, Deane. "N.B.A. Players Threaten to Strike Playoffs If Pension Demands Are Not Met." *The New York Times*, March 1, 1967.

Meggyesy, David, and Dave Zirin. "How Players Won the NFL Lockout." *The Nation*, July 27, 2011. http://www.thenation.com/article/162397/how-players-won-nfl-lockout?page=ful.

Messeloff, Dan. "The NBA's Deal with the Devil: The Antitrust Implications of the 1999 NBA-NBPA Collective Bargaining Agreement." *Fordham Intellectual Property, Media & Entertainment Law Journal* (2000): 521–69.

"Michael Jordan Convinced . . . Players Association Should Go." *New York Beacon*, August 9, 1995.

Mihoces, Gary. "Judge Orders Mediation on NFL Concussion Suits." *USA Today*, July 11, 2013. http://www.usatoday.com/story/sports/nfl/2013/07/11/nfl-players-concussions-lawsuits/2510275/.

Miller, James Andrew. "N.F.L. Pressure Said to Lead ESPN to Quit Film Project." *The New York Times*, August 23, 2013. http://www.nytimes.com/2013/08/24/sports/football/nfl-pressure-said-to-prompt-espn-to-quit-film-project.html?hp&_r=1&.

Miller, Marvin. *A Whole Different Ballgame*. Chicago: Ivan R. Dee, 2004. Kindle edition.

Mitchell, Fred. "For NBA Teammates, Split Decisions." *Chicago Tribune*, September 14, 1995.

———. "Pro Basketball: Owners Seek New Salary Plan." *Chicago Tribune*, October 21, 1982.

"MLB and Union Agree to Pay Pre-1980 Players' Pensions." *Reuters*, April 21, 2011. http://www.reuters.com/article/2011/04/21/us-baseball-pensions-idUSTRE73K7Q920110421.

"MLB Salaries." *CBS Sports*, 2013. http://www.cbssports.com/mlb/salaries/avgsalaries.

"MLB, Union Announce New Labor Deal." *MLB.com*, 2002. http://mlb.mlb. com/news/article.jsp?ymd=20061024&content_id=1722211&vkey=news_mlb&fext=.jsp&c_id=mlb.

"MLB Players, Owners Announce Five-Year Labor Deal." 2002. http://sports. espn.go.com/mlb/news/story?id=2637615.

Moore, David. "NBA Avoids Potential Work Stoppage with Fresh Labor Deal." *Knight Ridder Tribune News Service*, June 21, 2005.

Morganti, Al. "In the NHL, 'Free' Agents Don't Exist." *Philly.com*, August 22, 1986. http://articles.philly.com/1986-08-22/sports/26063167_1_free-agent-first-refusal-premier.

Moriarty, Tim. "NHL Players Surveying Strike Insurance." *Newsday*, October 23, 1981.

Mortensen, Chris. "NFLPA Sends Email to 2,000 Players." *ESPN*, September 10, 2013. http://espn.go.com/nfl/story/_/id/9650364/nflpa-reminds-players-concussion-rules.

Murphy, Mark. "Big Baby: Everyone Has to Stop 'Sticking Their Chests Out.'" *Boston Herald*, November 14, 2011. http://bostonherald.com/sports/celtics_nba/celtics_insider/2011/11/big_baby_everyone_has_stop_sticking_their_chests_out.

NBA. "NBA Player Dress Code." *NBA.com*, 2005. http://www.nba.com/news/player_dress_code_051017.html.

"N.B.A. and Players Sign a Basic Pact." *The New York Times*, March 6, 1973.

"NBA Approves Players' Association, Arbitration." *The Washington Post and Times Herald*, April 19, 1957.

"NBA Averts Strike with Salary Cap." *Los Angeles Times*, April 1, 1983.

"NBA Boosts Pay." *Chicago Daily Defender*, August 22, 1968.

"NBA Files Suit to Keep Agreement Intact." *The Washington Post*, June 21, 1994.

"NBA Lockout Looming." *Chicago Tribune*, February 11, 2005.

"NBA Minimum Salaries." *Hoops World*, 2011. http://www.hoopsworld.com/nba-minimum-salaries.

"NBA Minimum Salary." *Inside Hoops*, August 10, 2005> http://www.inside-hoops.com/minimum-nba-salary.shtml.

"NBA Okays Pension Plan." *Boston Globe*, May 27, 1964.

"NBA Okays Player Union." *The Sun*, April 19, 1957.

"NBA Owners and Players Talking." *Newsday*, October 5, 1982.

"NBA, Players Announce Terms." *Atlanta Daily World*, October 22, 1970.

"NBA, Players' Association Agree No New Signings after June 17." *The Sun*, June 10, 1987.

"NBA Players Threaten Pension Plan Strike." *Chicago Daily Defender*, March 6, 1967.

"NBA Players Threaten to Strike in Playoffs." *Los Angeles Times*, March 1, 1967.

"NBA Promises Pensions, Players End Strike Threat." *Boston Globe*, March 15, 1967.

"NBA Raises Cage Salary." *Chicago Daily Defender*, October 12, 1970.

"NBA Team Valuations." *Forbes*, December 22, 2005. http://www.forbes.com/lists/2005/32/Rank_1.html.

"NBA Team Values." *Forbes*, January 23, 2013. http://www.forbes.com/nba-valuations/list/.

"NBA to Increase Rookies Salaries." *The New York Times*, August 21, 1968.

"NBA Union, Management Both Loose." *The Washington Post*, December 18, 1987.

NBPA. "About the NBPA." *NBPA website*. http://www.nbpa.com/about-nbpa.

"New NHL Agreement Includes Best-of-7 Series in All Playoffs." *The Sun*, July 26, 1986.

"New 'Union' Formed By Hockey Players, Boss Wonders Why." *Newsday*, February 12, 1957.

"NFL Negotiators Attain Settlement." *The Washington Post*, July 15, 1968.

"NFL Negotiators $1 Million Apart." *The Washington Post*, August 2, 1970.

"NFL Opens up Camps to Veterans." *The Washington Post*, July 30, 1970.

"NFL Owners Approve Six-Year CBA Extension." *ESPN*, March 9, 2006. http://sports.espn.go.com/nfl/news/story?id=2360258.

"NFL Picket Crossing Due to Begin Today." *The Washington Post*, July 3, 1974.

"NFL Players not Fully behind Strike." *Boston Globe*, July 14, 1974.

"NFL Strike: Fans Will Pay." *Boston Globe*, August 6, 1974.

"NFL Team Valuations." *Forbes*, September 2, 2009. http://www.forbes.com/lists/2009/30/football-values-09_NFL-Team-Valuations_Revenue.html.

NFLPA. "History." *NFLPlayers.com*, n.d. https://www.nflplayers.com/About-us/History/.

"N.H.L. Makes Proposals." *The New York Times*, August 5, 2004.

"N.H.L. Players' Group Consents to Merger." *The New York Times*, June 7, 1979.

"NHL Players Lose Bid, but Make Gains." *Chicago Daily Tribune*, February 5, 1958.

"NHL, Players Make Peace: Framework in Place for 10-Year Deal after 16-Hour Bargaining Session Ends Lockout." *Chicago Tribune*, January 7, 2013.

"NHL Players Prepare for Lockout." *Chicago Tribune*, August 26, 1994.

"NHL's Silent Treatment League Toils Quietly on New Player's Deal." *Chicago Tribune*, September 5, 1993.

Nidetz, Stephen. "NBA Union Won't Budge on 'Soft Cap.'" *Chicago Tribune*, August 15, 1988.

"Noon Today Is Deadline in NBA Row." *The Washington Post and Times Herald*, March 14, 1967.

Oates, Bob. "It's Official: NFL Players on Strike." *Los Angeles Times*, July 31, 1970.

———. "Rozelle Counters NFL Strike Threat by Delaying Camps." *Los Angeles Times*, July 8, 1970.

O'Hara, Jane. "In the Name of Greed: As Many Former Players Cheer, Alan Eagleson Goes to Jail." *Maclean's*, January 19, 1988.

O'Keeffe, Michael. "Stern: Lockout Is Coming." *New York Daily News*, May 20, 2005.

"Oscar Robertson Headed NBA Players' Pension Fund Fight." *Philadelphia Tribune*, June 13, 1967.

"Over 900 Players to Receive Money under MLB Pension Deal." *CBC Sports*, April 21, 2011. http://www.cbc.ca/sports/baseball/story/2011/04/21/sp-mlb-pension.html.

"Owners to Assume Full Pension Costs Of N.H.L. Players." *The New York Times*, August 23, 1969.

Ozanian, Mike. "Baseball Team Valuations 2013: Yankees on Top at $2.3 Billion." *Forbes*, March 27, 2013. http://www.forbes.com/sites/mikeozanian/2013/03/27/baseball-team-valuations-2013-yankees-on-top-at-2-3-billion/.

———. "Baseball Team Values 2014 Led by New York Yankees at $2.5 Billion," *Forbes*, March 26, 2014. http://www.forbes.com/sites/mikeozanian/2014/03/26/baseball-team-values-2014-led-by-new-york-yankees-at-2-5-billion/.

———. "Dallas Cowboys Lead NFL with $2.1 Billion Valuation." *Forbes*, September 5, 2012. http://www.forbes.com/sites/mikeozanian/2012/09/05/dallas-cowboys-lead-nfl-with-2-1-billion-valuation/.

———. "NHL Team Values 2012: Toronto Maple Leafs Are First Hockey Team Worth $1 Billion." *Forbes*, November 28, 2012. http://www.forbes.com/sites/mikeozanian/2012/11/28/nhl-team-values-2012-maple-leafs-first-hockey-team-worth-1-billion/.

———. "The Most Valuable NFL Teams." *Forbes*, August 14, 2013. http://www.forbes.com/sites/mikeozanian/2013/08/14/the-most-valuable-nfl-teams/.

———. "The NBA's Most Valuable Teams." *Forbes*, January 26, 2011. http://www.forbes.com/sites/mikeozanian/2011/01/26/the-nbas-most-valuable-teams-2/.

———. "Selective Accounting." *Forbes*, December 14, 1988. http://www.forbes.com/forbes/1998/1214/6213124a.html.

Pelletier, Joe. "Those Were The Days: Salary Cap." *Greatest Hockey Legends*, February 9, 2011. http://www.greatesthockeylegends.com/2011/02/those-were-days-salary-cap.html.

"Pension Plan Approved for Hockey Stars." *The Christian Science Monitor*, September 5, 1947.

"Pension Plan for Hockey Players Gains Momentum: Must Be Voluntary Equal Contribution." *The Christian Science Monitor*, January 17, 1947.

"Pension Plan Started by NBA Players." *The Washington Post*, January 10, 1961.

Peterson, Richard. *Extra Innings: Writings on Baseball*. Illinois: University of Illinois Press, 2001.

"Players Agree to Merger." *The Washington Post*, June 7, 1979.

"Players File Pair of Antitrust Lawsuits against NBA." *NBA.com*, November 16, 2011. http://www.nba.com/2011/news/11/15/tuesday-labor.ap/index.html.

"Players' Group Certifies NHL Option Compensation." *The Washington Post*, October 7, 1975.

"Players Hope Cooler Heads Prevail." *Chicago Tribune*, March 8, 1992.

"Players, NBA Sign New Pact." *The Sun*, April 13, 1976.

"Players, Owners Settle Dispute." *Los Angeles Times*, March 15, 1967.

"Players' Pension, Savings Plan Approved by Hockey Governors." *The New York Times*, September 5, 1947.

"Players Reject NFL Offer, Talks Falter." *Boston Globe*, July 9, 1968.

"Players Reject Offer." *The Washington Post*, December 30, 1987.

"Players Turn down Latest NHL Proposal Friday Deadline Means Season Start Likely to be Delayed." *Chicago Tribune*, September 29, 1994.

Podell, Ira. "NHL Lockout 2012: Mediator Gets League, Union Back Together." *The Washington Times*, January 5, 2013. http://www.washingtontimes.com/news/2013/jan/5/nhl-lockout-2012-mediator-gets-league-union-back-t/?page=all.

Porter, Russell B. "The C.I.O." In *American Labor since the New Deal*, edited by Melvyn Dubofsky, 97–105. Chicago: Quadrangle Books, 1971.

"Pro Football Players End Strike of Clubs." *The Sun*, August 4, 1970.

"Progress Is Reported in Talks on N.H.L. Pact." *The New York Times*, July 10, 1981.

"Progress Made in Salary Talks." *The Sun*, June 24, 1967.

"Pro Hockey Players Organize." *Daily Boston Globe*, February 12, 1957.

Proteau, Adam. "No Room for Alan Eagleson at Summit Series Celebrations." *The Hockey News*, June 9, 2012. http://www.thehockeynews.com/articles/48355-No-room-for-Alan-Eagleson-at-Summit-Series-celebrations.html.

Pugmire, Lance. "Players' Union Head Rejects Contract Offer." *Orlando Sentinel*, May 11, 2011.

Pulver, Ian Craig. "A Face Off Between the National Hockey League and the National Hockey League Players' Association: The Goal a More Competitively Balanced League." *Marquette Sports Law Review* 39 (1991). http://scholarship.law.marquette.edu/sportslaw/vol2/iss1/4.

Quinn, Kevin. G. "Getting to the 2011–2020 National Football League Collective Bargaining Agreement." *International Journal of sports Finance* 7, no. 2 (2012): 141–57.

Quirk, James, and Rodney D. Fort, *Pay Dirt: The Business of Professional Team Sports*. Princeton: Princeton University Press, 1997.

"Raptors' Willis Questions His Union's Stand in NBA Lockout." *Amarillo Globe-News*, December 23, 1998. http://amarillo.com/stories/122398/spo_willis.shtml.

"Red Wings' Squad Quits Association." *The New York Times*, November 13, 1957.

Rhoden, William C. "Sports of The Times; N.F.L.'s Labor Pioneer Remains Unknown." *The New York Times*, October 2, 1994. http://www.nytimes.com/1994/10/02/sports/sports-of-the-times-nfl-s-labor-pioneer-remains-unknown.html?src=pm.

Rieger Carol T., and Charles J. Lloyd. "The Effect of McNeil v. NFL on Contract Negotiation in the NFL—That Was Then, This Is Now." *Marquette Sports*

Law Review 45, 1992. http://scholarship.law.marquette.edu/sportslaw/vol3/iss1/6.

Roberts, Selena. "Key Players' Group Defends Its Negotiating Stance." *The New York Times*, December 30, 1998. http://www.nytimes.com/1998/12/30/sports/basketball-key-players-group-defends-its-negotiating-stance.html.

Robertson v. National Basketball Association, 1975. http://www.leagle.com/decision/19751256389FSupp867_11127.

Rose, Bryan. "NFLPA May Block Playoff Expansion over Injury Concerns, Workers Comp Dispute." *Sports Illustrated*, May 20, 2014. http://nfl.si.com/2014/05/20/nflpa-block-playoff-expansion-workers-compensation/.

Rosenthal, Ken. "Archer's Contract Another Sign of Baseball's Economic Health." *Fox Sports*, April 3, 2014. http://msn.foxsports.com/mlb/story/archer-s-contract-another-sign-of-baseball-s-economic-health-040214?cmpid=tsmtw:fscom:mlbonfox.

Ross, J. Andrew. "Trust and Antitrust: The Failure of the First National Hockey League Players' Association, 1957–1958." *Business and Economic History* 8 (2010): 1–14.

Rothenberg, Fred. "NBA Didn't Surrender to Players—O'Brien." *Boston Globe*, February 22, 1976.

Rovell, Darren. "New Owners' Tax Break Losing Value." *ESPN*, April 15, 2004. http://sports.espn.go.com/espn/sportsbusiness/news/story?id=1782953.

Rutherford, Jeremy. "NHL Owners Reject Players' Counter-Offers Quickly." *McClatchy-Tribune Business News*, October 19, 2012.

Sakamoto, Bob. "NBA Player Reps Vote to Dump Union." *Chicago Tribune*, February 6, 1988.

———. "NBA Union Takes League to Court, but at Least Averts a Strike." *Chicago Tribune*, October 2, 1987.

Sandler, Ariel. "Several NBA Players Are Already Speaking Out Against the Decision to Disband the Union." *Business Insider*, November 15, 2011. http://www.businessinsider.com/nba-lockout-nba-players-against-disbanding-the-union-2011-11.

Sandomir, Richard. "N.H.L. Offers Six Proposals To Cut Costs to the Union." *The New York Times*, July 22, 2004.

———. "The Players Approve Agreement With N.H.L." *The New York Times*, January 14, 1995.

"Sarah Ahmed Quotes." *Goodreads*, n.d. http://www.goodreads.com/author/quotes/11036.Sara_Ahmed.

Schiavone, Michael. "Rank-and-File Militancy and Power: Revisiting the Teamster Struggle with the United Parcel Service Ten Years Later." *WorkingUSA* 10 (June 2007): 175–91.

———. "Social Movement Unionism and the UE." *The Flinders Journal of History and Politics* 23 (2006): 57–82.

————. *Unions in Crisis? The Future of Organized Labor in America*. Westport, CT: Praeger, 2008.

Sell, Dave. "NHL on the Rise, but How High Can It Go?" *The Washington Post*, January 23, 1994.

————. "NHL, Players Association Face Off." *The Washington Post*, March 9, 1992.

————. "NHL Profits and Losses Are Argued Union, Owners Report Little Overall Progress in Bargaining." *The Washington Post*, March 27, 1992.

————. "Vote to Approve Agreement Is 409-61." *The Washington Post*, April 12, 1992.

————. "Ziegler Says Players Not Getting Big Picture." *The Washington Post*, March 22, 1992.

"Setting the Foundation." *Hockey Central*, n.d. http://www.hockeycentral.co.uk/nhl/history/nhl-setfound.php.

Shapiro, Jonathan S. "Warming the Bench: The Nonstatutory Labor Exemption in the National Football League." *Fordham Law Revue* 61 (1993). http://ir.lawnet.fordham.edu/flr/vol61/iss5/9.

Sheridan, Chris. "NBA Union Gets Money, Files Grievance." *New Pittsburgh Courier*, July 18, 1988.

Shrake, Bud. "Let's Get Back to Playing Football." *Sports Illustrated*, July 22, 1968. http://sportsillustrated.cnn.com/vault/article/magazine/MAG1081412/1/index.htm.

Sielski, Mike. "NHL Races Back to Business." *Wall Street Journal*, January 7, 2013.

Singman, Bruce H. "Free Agency and the National Football League." *Loyola L.A. Entertainment Law Revue* 259 (1988). http://digitalcommons.lmu.edu/elr/vol8/iss2/2.

Smith, Sam. "NBA Commissioner, Union Leader Promise Contract Accord." *Knight Ridder Tribune News Service*, February 19, 2005.

————. "NBA Keeps Eye on the Ball, Avoids Strike 3 Players, Owners Announce They'll Play Full Season." *Chicago Tribune*, October 28, 1994.

————. "NBA Owner's Actions Could Lead to Lockout." *Chicago Tribune*, March 28, 1998.

————. "NBA Plan: Exploit Union Cracks for Deal or Call Lockout." *Chicago Tribune*, September 23, 1994.

————. "NBA, Players Reach Deal on Collective Bargaining Agreement." *Knight Ridder Tribune News Service*, June 21, 2005.

————. "Stern Bypasses the Union Commissioner's Letter to Players is Rebutted." *Chicago Tribune*, December 18, 1988.

————. "Stern Now Blames Agents for Lack of Labor Deal." *Chicago Tribune*, November 5, 1988.

————. "Top NBA Players Hope to Decertify Their Union." Chicago Tribune, June 20, 1995.

————. "What Lockout? Free-Agent Clock is Reset." *Chicago Tribune*, July 10, 1996.

————, and Bob Sakamoto. "NBA Players, Owners Settle on 6-Year Deal." *Chicago Tribune*, April 27, 1988.

Smith, Seymour. "Fleisher Big Figure in NBA Labor Moves." *The Sun*, March 7, 1973.

————. "NBA Owners to Drop the Reserve Clause." *The Sun*, September 22, 1971.

Smith, Stephen A. "Group of NBA Players Asks Former Star's Help the Players Want Isiah Thomas to Intervene for Them with the Union." *Philly.com*, January 2, 1999. http://articles.philly.com/1999-01-02/sports/25491332_1_voting-system-thomas-and-two-nbpa.

Snyder, Brad. A *Well-Paid Slave*, London: Plume, 2007.

Stark, Jayson. "How the New CBA Changes Baseball." ESPN, November 22, 2011. http://espn.go.com/mlb/story/_/id/7270203/baseball-new-labor-deal-truly-historic-one.

Staudohar, Paul D. "Baseball Labor Relations: The Lockout of 1990." *Monthly Labor Review* (October 1990): 32–36.

————. "Baseball Negotiations: A New Agreement." *Monthly Labor Review* (December 2002): 15–22.

————. "Labor Relations in Basketball: The Lockout of 1998–99." *Monthly Labor Review* (April 1999): 3–9.

————. *Playing for Dollars*. Ithaca and London: Cornell University Press, 1996.

————. "The Baseball Strike of 1994–1995." *Monthly Labor Review* (March 1997): 21–27.

————. "The Basketball Lockout of 2011." *Monthly Labor Review* (December 2012): 28–33.

————. "The Football Lockout of 2011." *Monthly Labor Review* (August 2012): 29–34.

————. "The Football Strike of 1987: The Question of Free Agency." *Monthly Labor Review* (August 1988): 26–31.

————. "The Hockey Lockout of 2004–2005." *Monthly Labor Review* (December 2005): 23–29.

————. "The Hockey Lockout of 2012–2013." *Monthly Labor Review* (July 2013). http://www.bls.gov/opub/mlr/2013/article/the-hockey-lockout-of-2012.htm.

Sullivan, Dean A. ed., *Late Innings: A Documentary History of Baseball, 1945–1972*. Lincoln and London: Bison Books, 2002.

Surdam, David George. *The Rise of the National Basketball Association*. Urbana and Chicago: University of Illinois Press.

Taubin, Lance. "Welcome to the Real 2011 NBA Lockout: Where Owner-Friendly Tax Provisions and Non-Monetized Benefits Color the Lockout Landscape." *Cardozo Public Law Policy & Ethics* Journal 139 (2012): 139–72.

Taylor, Phil. "The NBA." *Sports Illustrated*, April 24, 1995. http://sportsillustrated.cnn.com/vault/article/magazine/MAG1006502/index.htm.

————. "Wanna Be Like Mike . . ." *Sports Illustrated*, September 4, 1995. http://sportsillustrated.cnn.com/vault/article/magazine/MAG1007044/1/index.htm.

"Teamsters Union Plans to Organize Pro Athletes." *The Sun*, February 5, 1966.

"The Business of Baseball." *Forbes*, 2013. http://www.forbes.com/mlb-valuations/list/.

"The NBA and Players' Union Reach Agreement on a 6-Year Contract." *Los Angeles Times*, April 27, 1988.

"The New Deal." *Chicago Tribune*, August 23, 1982.

Thomas Jr., Robert McG. "Shades of Baseball: N.H.L. Labor Impasse." *The New York Times*, August 9, 1994.

Marcus Thompson, "Warriors Had the Blueprint for a Dramatic Boycott Ready to Go," *Mercury News*, April 29, 2014. http://blogs.mercurynews.com/thompson/2014/04/29/warriors-had-the-blueprint-for-a-dramatic-boycott-ready-to-go/.

Tierney, Mike. "THE FIFTH DOWN; Study Finds Risk of Brain Disease for N.F.L. Players." *The New York Times*, September 6, 2012. http://query.nytimes.com/gst/fullpage.html?res=9C02E3DB143FF935A3575AC0A9649D8B63.

Tommason, Chris. "Hall of Famers Split, Agree Lockout Hurts NBA." *Fox Sports Florida*, October 11, 2011. http://www.foxsportsflorida.com/pages/landing?blockID=580008&tagID=124597.

Trotter, Jim. "Players' Secret Lockout Insurance Could Have Sparked Talks." *Sports Illustrated*, July 15, 2011. http://sportsillustrated.cnn.com/2011/writers/jim_trotter/07/15/secret-lockout-fund/index.html#ixzz2hDALHKJ8.

Velasco, Schuyler. "NHL Lockout: CBA Gives Players Defined Pension Plans. How Rare Is That?" *The Christian Science Monitor*, January 14, 2013. http://www.csmonitor.com/Business/2013/0114/NHL-lockout-CBA-gives-players-defined-pension-plans.-How-rare-is-that.

Voigt, David Q. "Serfs versus Magnates: A Century of Labor Strife in Major League Baseball." In *The Business of Professional Sports*, edited by Paul D. Staudohar and James A. Mangan, 95–114, Urbana and Chicago: University of Illinois Press, 1991.

Vrooman, John. "The Economic Structure of the NFL." *Sports Economics, Management and Policy* 2 (2012): 7–31.

Wallace, William N. "Sports of The Times; The Players Won." *The New York Times*, July 17, 1968.

Washburn, Gary. "NBA Owners Now Offering Players 'Flex Cap.'" *Boston Globe*, June 22, 2011.

Wawrow, John. "Players Wonder What Took so Long for NHLPA to Accept Cap." *USA Today*, February 15, 2005. http://usatoday30.usatoday.com/sports/hockey/nhl/2005-02-15-lockout-players_x.htm.

Weintraub, Robert. "Failed Baseball Union Helped Pave Way for Success." *The New York Times*, December 1, 2012. http://www.nytimes.com/2012/12/02/sports/baseball/failed-baseball-union-helped-pave-way-for-success.html?_r=0.

Weisman, Larry. "NFL Reflects on Changes at Anniversary of Strikes." *USA Today*, October 11, 2007. http://usatoday30.usatoday.com/sports/football/nfl/2007-10-06-sw-labor-anniversary_N.htm.

Wells, Kevin W. "Labor Relations in the National Football League: A Historical and Legal Perspective." *Sports lawyers Journal* 18 (2011): 93–120.

Wertheim, Jon. "Marvin Miller Changed Players' Union—and Baseball—Forever." *Sports Illustrated*, November 27, 2012. http://sportsillustrated.cnn.com/2012/writers/jon_wertheim/11/27/marvin-miller-obituary/index.html.

———. "Marvin Miller on Barry Bonds, Drug Testing, and the NFL Labor Situation." *Sports Illustrated*, April 12, 2011. http://sportsillustrated.cnn.com/2011/writers/jon_wertheim/04/12/marvin.miller/index.html#ixzz2bAQHj851.

Westhead, Rick. "Ice in July Sounds Good to N.H.L. Players." *The New York Times*, July 21, 2005.

White, Paul. "Done Deal: What's New in Baseball's Labor Agreement?" *USA Today*, November 23, 2011. http://usatoday30.usatoday.com/sports/baseball/story/2011-11-22/mlb-collective-bargaining-agreement/51359552/1.

Whitlock, Jason. "Is Fisher in Stern's Back Pocket?" *Fox Sports*, October 29, 2011. http://msn.foxsports.com/nba/story/Whitlock-NBA-lockout-David-Stern-has-Derek-Fisher-in-back-pocket-Billy-Hunter-players-union-not-pleased-102811.

Wilbon, Michael. "NBA, Players Set Signing Moratorium." *The Washington Post*, June 10, 1987.

"Will the NHL Be Next? Players Union President Calls Proposal 'Warfare.'" *Chicago Tribune*, August 9, 1994.

Willis, Jonathan. "NHL Lockout: Donald Fehr Has Avoided the Mistakes of Former NHLPA Head Bob Goodenow." *Edmonton Journal*, November 24, 2012. http://blogs.edmontonjournal.com/2012/11/24/nhl-lockout-donald-fehr-has-avoided-the-mistakes-of-former-nhlpa-head-bob-goodenow/.

Wilson, Michael R. "Why So Stern? The Growing Power of the NBA Commissioner." *DePaul Journal Sports Labor & Contemporary Problems* 45 (2010): 45–62.

Windhorst, Brian. "NBA Fines Heat Owner Micky Arison." *ESPN*, November 2, 2011. http://espn.go.com/nba/truehoop/miamiheat/story/_/id/7175679/nba-lockout-miami-heat-owner-micky-arison-fined-500000-twitter-comments-labor-talks-sources-say.

Wise, Mike. "Is Falk Calling the Shots For Players in N.B.A. Talks?" *The New York Times*, December 28, 1998. http://www.nytimes.com/1998/12/28/sports/pro-basketball-is-falk-calling-the-shots-for-players-in-nba-talks.html.

"Wizards Owner's Words Draw Fine." *Philadelphia Daily News*, September 30, 2010.

Wojciechowski, Gene. "NFL STRIKE: 1982: A History Lesson Not Learned." *Los Angeles Times*, September 23, 1987. http://articles.latimes.com/1987-09-23/sports/sp-6303_1_nfl-strike.

Wojnarowski, Adrian. "Hunter's Actions in NBA Labor Talks Weaken Union." *Yahoo! Sports*, November 1, 2011. http://sports.yahoo.com/nba/news;_

ylt=AtACK8MQYNrL8lI41qbg4SY5nYcB?slug=aw-wojnarowski_nba_
lockout_billy_hunter_110111.

Wyshynski, Greg. "Winners and Losers of the NHL Lockout." *Yahoo! Sports*,
January 7, 2013. http://sports.yahoo.com/blogs/nhl-puck-daddy/winners-
losers-nhl-lockout-233434771--nhl.html.

Yannis, Alex. "Free Agency Is Hockey Topic." *The New York Times*, February
10, 1981.

Zimbalist, Andrew S. "Economic Issues in the 1998–1999 NBA Lockout and the
Problem of Competitive Balance in Professional Sports." In *The Economics
of Sports*, edited by William S. Kern. Kalamazoo: W. E. Upjohn Institute
for Employment Research, 2000.

———. *In the Best Interests of Baseball?* Lincoln and London: University of
Nebraska Press, 2013.

———. "Labor Relations in Major League Baseball." *Journal of Sports Economics*
4, no. 4 (2003): 332–55.

———. *May the Best Team Win.* Washington, DC: Brookings Institution Press,
2004.

Zirin, Dave. "CSI: Hockey—How Owners Destroyed the NHL." *Edge of Sports*,
February 24, 2005. http://www.edgeofsports.com/2005-02-24-118/.